BEYOND SALSA FOR BEGINNERS
THE CUBAN TIMBA REVOLUTION

AN INTRODUCTION TO LATIN MUSIC
FOR DANCERS AND LISTENERS

KEVIN MOORE

downloadable audio file product and free download available at: www.timba.com/audio

ISBN-10: 1480160938
ISBN-13/EAN-13: 978-1480160934

www.timba.com/audio
www.timba.com/percussion
www.timba.com/clave
www.timba.com/bass
www.timba.com/encyclopedia_pages/beginners
www.timba.com/piano
www.timba.com/users/7
kevin@timba.com

Table of Contents

Introduction

Beyond Salsa for Beginners is for dancers and listeners who enjoy attending Latin music concerts and dances and simply want to learn more about the history, discography and basic rhythms for their own personal enjoyment. The goals of the book are as follows:

- to give you a working knowledge of the full history of this music

- to increase your appreciation with some basic clapping, singing and dancing exercises to help you understand how it all fits together

- to provide a little inside information for those taking dance classes, attending concerts and traveling to Cuba

Listening Tours

The course is built around "listening tours", with the idea of making an emotional connection with specific classic recordings before going into "study mode". The listening tours go through the history of Latin music, genre by genre. Each section consists of:

- a recommended listening track – analyzed section by section

- a brief history of the genre

- a list of "further listening" tracks

The game plan for the Listening Tours is to make a playlist, or burn an audio CD, consisting of the recommended track for each section (or if you prefer, an alternate track from the longer list), and to listen to the playlist over and over until you can sing along and have started to develop a passion for the music. The idea is to become a fan of the genre *before* you go into "student" mode to study the genre's history and learn to clap and sing its rhythms.

Cuban musicians tend to have a great awareness of, and respect for, the history of their country's music – perhaps more so than in many other countries. You'd be unlikely to hear a rock and roller or a hip-hop musician quoting Frank Sinatra unless for comic effect, and few would even know the names of such mid-century giants as Lester Young, Bud Powell, Jerome Kern and most others who haven't had a recent Hollywood movie made about them. In contrast, every young Cuban musician knows and loves Beny Moré, Lilí Martínez, Abelardo Barroso and the full range of *rumba, changüí* and Afro-Cuban folkloric music. It's part of their national identity – their sense of "being Cuban". They consciously and subconsciously quote and refer to aspects of this communal musical legacy in every performance and arrangement. This is of course a broad cultural generalization and there are many exceptions. For example, English-language pop artists have begun in recent decades to build their tracks over sampled snippets of James Brown grooves, but the continuity between generations in Cuba is more organic and has been going on uninterrupted for over a century.

As a listener, dancer or music student who hasn't grown up in Cuba or Puerto Rico, your appreciation of your favorite songs will grow geometrically as you start to hear them in their broader historical context and enjoy their dozens of references to the past. I myself studied this music in *reverse* chronological order, falling in love with timba and salsa before working my way back to the turn of the 20th Century. As I did so, I found myself in a state of continual amazement, thinking to myself: *"Aha! So **that's** where that came from!"*, only to later learn that it actually came from even *farther* back. In many cases, the musical hook I was so enamored of dated back to rumba, changüí or Afro-Cuban folkloric music.

A chronological survey of Latin music, then, would begin with Afro-Cuban folkloric music and branch out to secular folkloric genres like *rumba* and *changüí* before arriving at the first recordings of *danzón* made around 1900. *Son,* also originally a folkloric genre, was first recorded commercially around 1918 and became wildly popular in the late 1920s. *Son montuno* and *danzón-mambo* arrived in the 1940s, followed by *mambo* and *chachachá* in the 1950s. After the Cuban Revolution of 1958, *salsa* developed in New York and Puerto Rico while the Cubans moved on to *mozambique, pilón, upa-upa, simalé, dengue,* and *changüí-68* in the 1960s; the *songo* of Los Van Van, the jazz-classical-Afro-Cuban fusions of Irakere, and the modernized charanga of Ritmo Oriental in the 1970s; and the modernized son of Rumbavana, Son 14 and Adalberto Álvarez and the *charangón* of Revé in the 80s. The timba era, beginning around 1989, draws heavily on all of these genres.

Because of the "listen before studying" philosophy of this course, I had to modify the historical chronology slightly. Years of observation have made it clear that music students and new listeners have a strong tendency to hear Afro-Cuban folkloric music, changüí and rumba incorrectly. If you immerse yourself in listening to these rhythms before you're absolutely certain where the correct beat is, you can easily wind up doing yourself more harm than good. The vocals and tres of changüí, for example, are almost entirely syncopated and there's no bass or chordal instrument to make it clear where the real beat is. The result is that many new listeners hear the omnipresent *offbeats* of changüí as *onbeats*. As we'll discuss later on, the human brain can't be stopped from guessing where "1" is when it hears a new piece of music. And once it makes its first guess, it commits itself strongly, and before you know what hit you, you've learned the song incorrectly and have to go through a long and painful process of "unlearning" it.

Thus, although Afro-Cuban music, rumba and changüí are the first genres historically, we'll save them for the final listening tour, after we've mastered the rhythmic tools we'll need to learn them correctly.

Rhythmic Exercises

A secondary goal of this book is to provide a preparatory "head start" course for people considering taking lessons on an instrument but who haven't yet taken the plunge, or for people who simply like to know more about the rhythms they're hearing. The other 20 volumes (as of 2012) of the *Beyond*

Salsa series assume that you already have at least a little facility on your instrument of choice, but for this book, it's actually an advantage if you've never even held a pair of drumsticks in your hands. Our strategy is to learn to sing and tap all the basic rhythms *before* taking your first lesson and there's a very important reason for doing it this way.

As with golf or tennis lessons, learning to play a musical instrument is about physical movements, dexterity, timing, coordination and body language – the types of things that are easier to demonstrate than to explain and are easier to master when your brain stays calmly out of the way as your body goes through the learning process. If your brain is struggling to learn *what* to play, it interferes with your body's natural ability to learn *how* to play. To put it another way, if you're concentrating on mastering the sound and mechanics of a new rhythm, you won't be able to give 100% of your effort to tone production, posture, hand position, and feeling the groove, and you're likely to develop "bad habits" that are hard to unlearn later. But if you've already learned to sing, clap and tap the rhythms *before* you take your first lesson on and instrument, you'll be much more likely to succeed, and – just as important – you'll be much more likely to enjoy the process.

In summary, here's our roadmap:

Listening Tour 1	Pre-Revolution: Popular Music up to 1959
Rhythm Exercises 1	Introduction to Latin Rhythms
Listening Tour 2	Post-Revolution: Salsa and Cuban Popular Music from 1959-1989
Rhythm Exercises 2	Basic Rhythms (2-beat cells)
Listening Tour 3	Timba: 1989 to the present
Rhythm Exercises 3	Basic Rhythms (4-beat cells, including dance and clave)
Rhythm Exercises 4	Rhythmic Perception Exercises to Prepare for Listening Tour 4
Listening Tour 4	Afro-Cuban Folkloric Music, Changüí, Comparsa and Rumba

About the Free Downloadable Audio Files

Each of the Rhythm Exercise chapters has a wide range of clapping, singing and dancing exercises. We provide free, downloadable audio files for many of them, available at timba.com/audio. If you enjoy the free files, a more extensive collection is available for purchase, also at timba.com/audio.

For most exercises there are four audio files provided:

> a) the exercise at full speed
>
> b) the exercise in slow motion
>
> c) a special "build-the-rhythm" method at full speed
>
> d) a special "build-the-rhythm" method in slow motion

Other files are included to demonstrate specific points and only have one or two versions.

Collecting Music in 2012

As of 2012, the music industry is in a such a state of upheaval – in terms of both the production and marketing – that the advice in this section may have a very short shelf life. Before the advent of downloadable MP3s, when the only way to collect music was on physical CDs and tapes, there were many problems for collectors. The same tracks were issued and reissued in various ways by various labels, often going in and out of print. With the advent of digital downloads, the confusion has increased geometrically. The good news is that a Google search will usually turn up new and used CDs, downloadable albums and single tracks, and even YouTube videos that play the whole track while displaying still photos. Another factor is the 50-year rule. As it's been explained to me, in Europe, the copyright on a sound recording expires after 50 years, so all of the Cuban music released before 1962 (as of this writing) can be reissued on CDs in Europe and exported to other countries. This results in another geometric increase in the number of reissues, but also creates a market for labels run by real music connoisseurs to sell well-organized and well-documented CDs of important artists. The leader in this field, with regard to Cuban music, is Tumbao Cuban Classics.

Kevin's Music Collecting Advice

- Use the **Díaz-Ayala database** at latinpop.fiu.edu/discography.html. This incredible online database, which can be downloaded in PDF format, is by far the most complete listing of pre-Revolution Cuban music and has a long and interesting history of each artist.

- Avoid programs like iTunes that try to "help you" organize your music. These programs look at the "ID tag" of each file and try to cleverly store the music in some unspecified part of your hard drive and display it for you in some useful way. *It's infinitely better to make and name your own folders.* You'll learn and memorize huge amounts of information by going through this process, and then using your filing system to listen, burn CDs, and create playlists. Every time you file or play a track, you'll be reviewing and solidifying your knowledge of its place in the overall history of music. And if you do the same thing with jazz and other pop genres, the parallels can be endlessly fascinating.

- If you like computers, you can also get inexpensive programs like **dBPowerAmp** and/or **MP3 Tag** that will let you fill in all the information and artwork in each track's ID tag to fit your own filing system.

- *Be absolutely certain to back up regularly to a **different physical hard drive**.* Hard drives are like pet hamsters. No matter how well you care for them, they die after a few years. It's not a question of "if" – it's a question of "when". So back up regularly. One of my favorite programs is called **AllWays**. It can be programmed to automatically find changes and additions and update your backup every time your computer is idle. It's free, but if you like it, send the guy a few bucks!

- Use 320k/sec constant bit rate (CBR) for your MP3 files. My favorite encoder is **dBPowerAmp**, another "shareware" program. MP3s shrink audio tracks drastically by throwing out information. The greater the shrinkage, the more possible it is to hear degradation. At 320k/sec, I myself can't hear any degradation. At 128k/sec, I can. Now, I have purist friends who claim that they can hear some difference between an audio CD and a 320k/sec MP3. I don't believe them, but if you do, then you can either use .WAV, .AIFF, or .FLAC. They're huge, but guaranteed to sound exactly like the original CD.

Listening Tour 1: Pre-Revolution (1900-1959)

Category	Highlighted Track	Source
son	*Tres lindas cubanas*	Sexteto Habanero: *Las raíces del son* – Tumbao Cuban Classics
danzón	*Mi gran pasión*	Gonzalo Rubalcaba: *Mi gran pasión* – Pimienta Records
son montuno	*Tintorera ya llegó*	Arsenio Rodríguez: *Legendary Sessions* – Tumbao Cuban Classics
danzón-mambo	*Arcaño y su nuevo ritmo*	Arcaño y su Maravilla: *Danzón-mambo* – Tumbao Cuban Classics
"jazzbands"	*Qué bueno baila usted*	Beny Moré: *The Great Beny Moré, Vol. 3* – Black Round Records
1950s charangas	*Fajardo te pone a gozar*	José Fajardo: *Chachachá in Havana* – Panart
1950s descargas	*Descarga cubana*	Cachao y su Ritmo Caliente: *Cuban Jam Sessions* – Balboa

How to Use the Listening Tours

- Find the seven highlighted tracks listed above, or pick an alternate track from each category using the "Further Suggested Listening" lists at the end of each sub-section below. Many can be found on YouTube or inexpensively downloaded as single tracks at online retail sites. The titles and labels of the source CDs are listed for each track. You can also check online yahoo newsgroups like timba_geeks and latinperc to get tips from other collectors.

- If you listen to music on a computer or an MP3 player, make a playlist, or if you prefer CDs, burn yourself a special CD with these seven tracks.

- Listen, listen, listen! Your goal is to become a fan of each of these genres of music. The suggested tracks are carefully selected after years of listening and multiple interviews with people who have been passionate fans of each genre for years, so you can rest assured that each song you're listening to is *the* all-time favorite desert island classic for many connoisseurs of that genre. If one of the highlighted tracks doesn't do it for you, try substituting one of the alternates. And if you find one that really knocks you out, try making a playlist of just that genre's Further Listening tracks.

- After this listening process, you'll have made an emotional connection. These tracks will have become "your music" rather than a list you're supposed to study because some book suggested it. You'll be out of the schoolroom and into the dancehall, and ready to continue reading, to follow along with the analysis of the highlighted track, learning the histories of the artists, and learning to sing and clap the rhythms that form the foundation of the music.

Listening Tour 1 covers Cuban popular music from the beginning of the recording industry to the Cuban Revolution.

Son

highlighted track: *Tres lindas cubanas* – **Sexteto Habanero:** *Las raíces del son* – **Tumbao Cuban Classics**

time	tempo	comments
0:00	69	**intro:** Tres and guitar enter first, then marímbula, clave, maracas, and bongó.
0:14		**cuerpo:** Listen to the bongosero, Agustín Gutiérrez, a master of *rumba* and *abakuá* as well as son. Instead of a static *martillo* accompaniment, he improvises constantly, commenting on and responding to the vocalists.
0:34		Listen for scooping bongó sounds *(glissade)*, borrowed from abakuá-drumming.
1:09	74-87	**montuno section:** Listen to the sublime modulation while the marímbula (bass) part remains unchanged. In general, listen for the unique contrast between the marímbula, which is in the original key but doesn't respond to the chord changes, the basic guitar and tres harmonies, and the wonderfully nuanced and sophisticated vocal harmonies. Somehow, perhaps due to the timbres, it all fits together magically.

The son sexteto inherited four critical instruments from the five-instrument changüí ensemble: bongó, maracas, tres and marímbula, with the marímbula being largely replaced by the upright bass by the end of the 1920s. A guitar was added and the guayo was replaced by claves, an extremely important difference in that changüí doesn't use the instrument *or the concept* of clave. By the end of the 1920s, many sextetos became *septetos* with the addition of a trumpet. It was still illegal to play hand drums in public but Cuba's otherwise heinous dictator, Gerardo Machado, had a serious weakness for son and legalized the bongó – at first only for his favorite band, Sexteto Habanero. (See Listening Tour 4 for more on changüí.)

Having started out as folk music, like changüí and rumba, son exploded commercially in the 1920s when Sexteto Habanero and others recorded a large treasure of historic 78s, including our highlighted track above, *Tres lindas cubanas,* from 1926. A few years later, the Great Depression put a damper on both the recording and tourism industries, but the impact of son on Cuban and global music was permanent, forming the foundation for most of the other genres we'll be studying here.

Son is slower, less syncopated, and has richer, more clearly stated harmonies than changüí, so it's easier to follow for first time listeners. This is why we're starting our listening tour with son and saving its direct predecessor, changüí, for later. Son also features a much larger repertoire and features more emphasis on songwriting and nuanced vocal harmonies, especially in the case of the extraordinary Sexteto Habanero.

The most stunning revelation of the early son recordings is the bongó. The steady *martillo* pattern used today had not yet developed and the bongosero, who was very often the best musician in the sexteto, was free to play extremely polyrhythmic and soloistic parts continuously throughout each track. In fact, early son bongoseros like Agustín Gutiérrez played even more freely than *quinto* players in *guaguancó*, whose parts are expected to lock with the other two drums in more predictable ways. (See Listening Tour 4 for more on guaguancó.)

(**Photo:** Sexteto Habanero from the booklet of the Tumbao Cuban Classics box set. The musician at the lower left is holding a *botija* or *botijuela,* sometimes used instead of marímbula for the group's bass instrument. The phantom seventh man at the lower right is a big mystery.)

These early son recordings are also the first to make extensive use the actual clave instrument, heard clearly throughout most son tracks. At this point, the conscious philosophy of maintaining a strict alternation between the 3-side and the 2-side of clave had not fully evolved. The claves were played by singers and you can hear them switch direction, and sometimes play other rhythms briefly. The clave pattern they play is of course *son clave* (Exercise 3-7). It's very interesting to listen on these early recordings for the way different coros are sung against the clave. It's like being a fly on the wall witnessing the birth and maturation of the clave conventions that govern later genres.

Further Listening Recommendations for Son

Year	Song	Source
1918	*Mujer bandolera*	Sexteto Habanero: *Early Music of the North Caribbean* – Harlequin
1925	*La loma de Belén*	Sexteto Habanero: *Las raíces del son* – Tumbao Cuban Classics
1926	*Échale candela*	Sexteto Boloña: *Sextetos Cubanos* – Arhoolie
1926	*Quiéreme Camagüeyana*	Sexteto Boloña: *Sextetos Cubanos* – Arhoolie
1927	*Ésas no son cubanas*	Sexteto Nacional: *Cubaneo* – Tumbao Cuban Classics
1927	*Aquella boca*	Sexteto Habanero: *Las raíces del son*– Tumbao Cuban Classics
1928	*Engancha carretero*	Sexteto Matancero: *Sextetos Cubanos* – Arhoolie
1930	*Me voy a Baracoa*	Sexteto Machín: *Sextetos Cubanos* – Arhoolie
1930	*El camisón de Pepa*	Sexteto Machín: *Sextetos Cubanos* – Arhoolie

Danzón

highlighted track: *Mi gran pasión* – Gonzalo Rubalcaba: *Mi gran pasión* – Pimienta Records

time	tempo	comments
0:00	69	A1: Each A-section is repeated; flute and piano alternate phrases; dancers flirt and fan themselves rather than dancing, then begin to dance in tandem at the B section.
0:33		B: (flute) – dancers start together
1:03		A2: dancers stop, as they do for every A section
1:31		C: based on the jazz standard *Smoke Gets In Your Eyes*, with its own internal form of AABA (piano-trumpet-flute-trumpet) – ends with a *bloque* (rhythmic break)
2:33		A3
3:02		montuno section: with various solos and bloques – uses danzón bell pattern (see below)
6:17		coro: (The coro and the hand bell are modern additions not used in traditional danzón.)
7:27		coda: brief return to the *baqueteo* rhythm (Exercise 3-25)

Sublette makes the fascinating point that the first danzón, Miguel Failde's *Las alturas de Simpson*, was written in Matanzas in the late 1870s around the time that *guaguancó* was developing in the same city. The two genres could scarcely sound more different. Guaguancó uses only voices and percussion and has deeply-syncopated, overtly sexual dancing. Danzón was played on orchestral instruments, from written music, for stately, European-style dancers. The African influence in danzón was the addition of mildly-syncopated, clave-based rhythms, primarily the *baqueteo* pattern we'll learn in Exercise 3-25. While it's admittedly a broad generalization, one could say that *rumba* and *changüí* are best thought of as essentially Afro-Cuban music with European influences on their instrumentation, melodies and lyrics, while *danzón* would be better described as European music with African influences on its percussion parts.

A fascinating, forward-looking aspect of danzón was the coordination of specific dance moves to the arrangement. Danzón dancers knew they could expect a recurring A-section with a very specific length and rhythmic accompaniment, ending with a rhythmic break. This section was used for ritualized "flirting". Instead of dancing, the couple would engage in polite social conversation while the woman would fan herself with a decorative fan (called an *abanico*). Everyone knew when the break was coming, and would use that time to get into dancing position. As the women placed their arms around their partners, they would collapse the fans in tandem. It's an urban legend that the synchronized closing of so many fans created a clearly audible rhythmic effect, and that this is the genesis of the use of the term *abanico* to describe the rhythmic figure timbaleros play to lead in a new section. From a more practical point of view, the fanning breaks for the A-sections served the purpose allowing the formally-attired dancers to cool off at regular intervals. In any case, the dancers would return to their normal steps at the onset of the B-section, anticipate the next A-section, and stop dancing again when it arrived.

Suggested Viewing: *Un trío inseparable* (dance instruction) – Roberto Borrell – Boogalú Video

This excellent instructional video from master Cuban dancer/drummer Roberto Borrell demonstrates the danzón routine described above and also covers *son* and *chachachá* dancing, hence the title, *Un trío inseparable.*

Another interesting feature of danzón is its fairly intricate form, which begins much like a classical *rondo* (ABACA). As time went on, the form was further extended, adding *estribillo* and *montuno* sections in response to developments in the other most important genre of the era, *son.*

As we'll learn in Listening Tour 4, it can take a while to acquire a taste for changüí and rumba because they're so difficult. Without the expected bass and piano parts, even today's sophisticated non-Cuban listeners become easily lost in the syncopations, and the often blistering tempos make the wild ride that much wilder. Danzón also requires an acculturation period, but for the opposite reason. The rhythms – which at the time were such a breakthrough – sound very quaint and old-fashioned to ears raised on rock, jazz and hip-hop, to say nothing of salsa and timba. Danzón was also a big deal in 1900 because of what were then complex harmonies for popular music. Many danzón arrangements included paraphrases of classical music and opera arias. But again, these harmonies sound tame and old-fashioned to modern ears used to The Beatles, Stevie Wonder and Radiohead. Having said all of this, the fact is that Cubans are fiercely proud of their danzón heritage, and short of a hardcore timba concert, most Cuban musical events include some sort of danzón reference, even if only in an introductory section.

To appreciate the subtleties of danzón – and there are many beautiful subtleties – you'll need to slow yourself down, imagine yourself in an earlier age, and surrender yourself to the sounds of the timbales. This "acquiring the taste" period can be significantly shortened by attending a live performance of a master danzonero like Orestes Vilató or Calixto Oviedo. *Beyond Salsa Percussion, Volume 2* has a long Rhythm Exercises on danzón in which Calixto demonstrates many nuances of the style.

For these listening tours, I've generally tried to choose examples from the period when the genre under study was current, but in this one case, I've made an exception and chosen a 1986 Gonzalo Rubalcaba track. Unlike most "jazz danzón" pieces, which attach a bit of *baqueteo* to the beginning of a *chachachá*, Rubalcaba really took the genre seriously and created a full album of danzones combining his virtuosic and ultra-sophisticated jazz chops with all of the arrangement subtleties of authentic danzón.

The danzón bell pattern used in the montuno section is played on the small cha bell. The larger bell at the end of *Mi gran pasión* is a modern addition. (This graphic notation system is explained is the first Rhythm Exercises section.)

After using the Rubalcaba track to warm up to the genre, I'd suggest exploring the recordings of the mini-revival of danzón that occurred in the late-1950s, producing two exquisite albums by José Fajardo *(Danzones para bailar)* and two by Orquesta Aragón *(Danzones de ayer y hoy)*. Aragón and Fajardo were primarily playing chachachá and other modern rhythms by this point, but made these albums as a special and faithfully authentic tribute to the danzón era, so you get the advantage of 1950s recording technology and musicianship. After learning to appreciate these heritage albums, you'll be ready to hear the beauty and innovation of the scratchy vintage recordings that caused so much excitement in the early 20th Century. From 1900 to about 1920 danzón was played by *orquestas típicas,* (with horns as well as strings) before being replaced by the *charanga francesa* format (with strings and flute), the forerunner of the modern charanga.

Further Listening Recommendations for Danzón

Year	Song	Source
1918	*Mi testamento* (charanga típica)	Orquesta Félix González: *Early Cuban Danzón Orchestras* – Harlequin
1919	*Gasolina pa' mi máquina*	Orquesta Francesca Reverón: *Early Cuban Danzón Orchestras* – Harlequin
1928	*Bururú barará*	Orquesta Romeu: *Hot Music from Cuba 1907-1036* – Harlequin
1959	*Almendra*	Orquesta Aragón: *Danzones de ayer y hoy* – Reyes
1960	*Una rosa de Francia*	Fajardo y sus Estrellas: *Danzones completos para bailar* – Antilla
1960	*La gioconda*	Fajardo y sus Estrellas: *Danzones completos para bailar* – Antilla

The Master of the Danzón: Orestes Vilató with John Santos – 2012 – photo by Tom Ehrlich

Son Montuno

highlighted track: *Tintorera ya llegó* – Arsenio Rodríguez: *Legendary Sessions* – Tumbao Cuban Classics

time	tempo	comments
0:00	62	introduction
0:15		coro with trumpet solo
0:54		verse, coro, verse, coro: The title coro literally means *"the female shark has arrived – little fish to the shore!"*, but the double meaning was an inside joke to warn the trumpet player to hide his mistresses because his wife had arrived.
1:54		piano solo: by Lilí Martínez, Arsenio musical soulmate, and probably the best pianist and arranger of the era
2:24		trademark figure used for the transitions from solos to bloques
2:26		fascinating bloque with polyrhythms and whole tone scale harmonies
2:30		*diablo* section: This is a classic example of the innovation upon which the modern idea of the horn mambo is based. This one continues the incredibly complex and dissonant harmonies introduced by the bloque – the whole section is amazing in every way.

I'd start by saying something like *"Arsenio Rodríguez is arguably the most important figure in the history of Cuban music",* but, frankly, there's not much argument about it, although it's important to also give credit to the Lennon & McCartney-esque chemistry Arsenio shared with pianist, arranger and composer Lilí Martínez. Arsenio produced six glorious hours of 78 RPM recordings before his departure from Cuba in the early 1950s. Among them you'll find the foundations of modern arranging, lyric-writing, bass tumbaos, efectos, horn-writing, conga-playing and many of the intangible emotional and artistic qualities of Cuban music that we now take for granted. From there it's a very small leap to understand that Arsenio's 1940s innovations were as seminal to the development of rock and R&B as they were to son, salsa and timba.

Further Listening: In addition to the pictured CD, Tumbao Cuban Classics label has released a 6-CD box set containing most of Rodríguez's Cuban recordings, well-documented and in chronological order. Highlights are available on *Montuneando* and *Dundunbanza,* on the same label.

Further Study: Start with chapters 30-34 of Sublette's *Cuba and its Music* to understand Arsenio's role in the overall narrative of 20th Century Cuba. Then move on to David F. García's *Arsenio Rodríguez and the Transnational Flows of Latin Popular Music.* As you read, take to the internet and find the MP3 archives of radio veteran Emiliano Echeverría's many documentaries devoted exclusively to Rodríguez and including interviews with the authors mentioned above. Arsenio and those who influenced him also figure prominently in Juliet E. Hill's doctoral thesis, *The Conjunto Piano in 1940s Cuba: An Analysis of the Emergence of a Distinctive Piano Role and Style* and Orlando Fiol's *Transforming the Bass: Phenomenology, Aesthetics and Cultural Identity in Cuban Popular Music.* Finally, I've written several articles on Arsenio: *Roots of Timba* (online, with audio examples), and instrument-specific studies in *Beyond Salsa Piano, Vol. 1* and *Beyond Salsa Bass, Vol. 1*.

When Arsenio moved to New York in the early 1950s, members of his band who stayed in Cuba formed two other important conjuntos – Chappottín y sus Estrellas and Conjunto Modelo. Other important conjuntos of the 1950s were René Álvarez y Los Astros, Conjunto Roberto Faz, Cheo Marquetti, and Sonora Matancera with Celia Cruz.

Further Listening Recommendations for Son Montuno

Year	Song	Source
1944	*Mi china ayer me botó*	Arsenio Rodríguez: (Box Set) – Tumbao Cuban Classics (TCC)
1945	*Deuda*	Arsenio Rodríguez: (Box Set) – Tumbao Cuban Classics (TCC)
1946	*Juventud amaliana*	Arsenio Rodríguez: (Box Set) – Tumbao Cuban Classics
1948	*No toque el guao*	Arsenio Rodríguez: (Box Set) – Tumbao Cuban Classics
1948	*Yo no engaño a las nenas*	Arsenio Rodríguez: (Box Set) – Tumbao Cuban Classics
1948	*Déjame tranquilo*	René Álvarez y su Conjunto los Astros: *Yumbalé* – TCC
1949	*No me llores más*	Arsenio Rodríguez: (Box Set) – Tumbao Cuban Classics
1950	*Kila, Quique y Chocolate*	Arsenio Rodríguez: (Box Set) – Tumbao Cuban Classics
1951	*Guaragüí*	Arsenio Rodríguez: (Box Set) – Tumbao Cuban Classics
1952	*No quiero*	Arsenio Rodríguez: *Clásicas de un sonero* – Seeco
1950s	*No tiene teleraña*	Chappottín y sus Estrellas: *Sabor tropical* – Antilla
1951	*Yembe laroco*	Celia Cruz with Sonora Matancera: *Homenaje a los santos, V.2* – Fania
1953	*Nuevo ritmo omelenkó*	Celia Cruz with Sonora Matancera: *Canta Celia Cruz* – Fania
1954	*La maruga*	Conjunto Modelo: *Guaguancó en La Habana* – TCC

Statues at Casa del Changüí in Guantánamo: Elio Revé, Lilí Martínez, Chito Latamblet
photo by Michelle White – 2007 – Casa del Changüí, Guantánamo

Danzón-Mambo

highlighted track: *Arcaño y su nuevo ritmo* – Arcaño y sus Maravillas: *Danzón-Mambo* – Tumbao Cuban Classics

time	tempo	comments
0:00	63	danzón A1 (no repeat)
0:17		danzón B
0:47		danzón A2
1:02	68	mambo 1
1:23		mambo 2: flute solo with pizzicato violin guajeos
1:51		(flute plays extended paraphrase of melody of Arsenio's *Mi china ayer me botó*)
2:57	72	bloque and coda

Arcaño's charanga and Arsenio's conjunto were tied together in many ways: they regularly played at the same venues on the same bill; each was the most popular group of the 1940s in its genre; each redefined its genre; each had an early evening radio show on the all-important *Mil Diez* radio station; each played a critical role in the development of *mambo;* and each employed many of the most important musicians of the 1950s.

Among Arcaño's musicians were flautist José Fajardo (the leader of one of the best charangas of the 1950s), violinist/composer Enrique Jorrín (credited with introducing the chachachá), Félix Reina (composer of *Angoa),* Jesús López (one of the most important and influential figures in the development of the piano tumbao), and – most importantly – the López brothers, Orestes and Israel, the latter better known by his nickname, "Cachao". Orestes and Cachao composed and/or arranged most of the group's material and Cachao was equally important to Cuban music history as a bassist. As a contrabassist with extensive experience in the upper echelons of Cuba's symphonic scene, Cachao brought a previously unheard of level of musicianship to Cuban bass-playing. Prior to Cachao, many Cuban bassists were converted marimbuleros and/or had no formal training. They had great timing but were limited to playing very simple parts. Cachao was able to play intricate parts with perfect intonation, to use the bow virtuosically, and to play bass solos.

Cachao was undoubtedly the most important figure in the development of Cuban bass-playing, but in my opinion, the most important figure in the development of the bass *tumbao* was Arsenio Rodríguez, who is generally agreed to have created most of the game-changing bass tumbaos used

24

in his arrangements. Of course, Arsenio and Cachao played back-to-back (with their illustrious bandmates) on the same stages and radio shows night after night, so in the end, the old truism "it takes a village" may be the best explanation for many the musical miracles of the 1940s.

Mambo in Charangas

In salsa and timba arrangements, the term *mambo* is used for the horn riff sections that alternate with *coro* and *guía* sections. Cachao was the first to use the word for repeating riffs – in this case, the string *guajeos* he added to the montuno sections of Arcaño's danzones as the group strived to compete with the increasing popularity and danceability of the son groups. Around the same time, Arsenio began to conclude his arrangements with similar but much more intense sections that he called *diablos,* pitting repeated horn riffs against coros and often solos. The term *mambo* was later given to the genre that became extraordinarily popular in the 1950s when Pérez Prado and others created jazzband arrangements that dispensed with everything *except* the mambos and added a sax section to increase the layering potential. To really wrap your head around the concept of mambo, simply compare the suggested listening tracks for Arsenio, Arcaño and (coming in a few pages) Beny Moré. Each uses the concept of the syncopated layering of riffs in a different way.

When studying Arcaño, keep in mind that each track *begins* as a danzón, so the same listening tips we discussed in the danzón section apply: listen to the form, the orchestration, the timbales, and in this case, listen especially to the nuances of Cachao's bass lines. But it's in Arcaño's montuno sections – after the danzón cuerpos – that things get really interesting. Listen for the funkier groove (the *nuevo ritmo),* the layering of various guajeos in the bass, piano, strings, and the antiphonal coro sections in the famous *Mambo* arrangement, which Arcaño was playing live as early at 1937, but didn't record until 1951 because he felt the short track lengths afforded by 78s couldn't do justice to a song that stretched to seven minutes or more in concert. What a shame that there were no cell phone video cameras and YouTube channels in 1937.

Further Listening Recommendations for Danzón-Mambo

Year	Song	Source
1937	*El vendedor*	Arcaño – Emiliano Echeverría radio shows online (kpfa.org)
1940	*Canta contrabajo canta*	Arcaño: *Cuban danzoneras* – Harlequin
1940	*Rarezas*	Arcaño: *Cuban danzoneras* – Harlequin
1944	*Arriba la invasión*	Arcaño: *Danzón-Mambo* – Tumbao Cuban Classics
1946	*Jovenes de la defensa*	Arcaño: *Danzón-Mambo* – Tumbao Cuban Classics
1946	*Se pasó*	Orquesta Almendra: *Mi escorpión* – Tumbao Cuban Classics
1948	*Angoa*	Arcaño: *Danzón-Mambo* – Tumbao Cuban Classics
1948	*El mulato en el morro*	Arcaño: *Danzón-Mambo* – Tumbao Cuban Classics
1951	*Mambo*	Arcaño: *Danzón-Mambo* – Tumbao Cuban Classics

Jazzbands

highlighted track: *Qué bueno baila usted – The Great Beny Moré, Vol. 3 –* **Black Round Records**

time	tempo	comments
0:00	84	intro: piano tumbao
0:15		layered saxophone mambo figures
0:35		coro and lead vocals over sax mambo figures
1:16		trombone solo over sax mambo figures
1:48		coro and lead vocals over sax and then sax and brass mambo figures
2:15		vocals drop out
2:25		new brass mambo figure plus trumpet solo
2:51		vocals return, coda

Cuban popular music can be thought of as developing from three traditions, or "bloodlines", as Orlando Fiol calls them. We've already discussed two: *danzón (danzón, danzonete, danzón-mambo, chachachá, pachanga, songo)*; and *son (son, son montuno)*. The third bloodline – big band, or *jazzband* (pronounced *yassbahng* as per Sublette) – is much harder to describe and study. For one thing, its instrumentation is all over the map:

	percussion	non-percussion
danzón	timbales, güiro, (later congas)	bowed strings, flute, bass, piano
son	bongó, clave, maracas, (later congas)	trumpet(s), tres, guitar, marímbula or bass, (later piano)
jazzband	any combination, usually including drumset	two or more types of horn section, bass, piano

Another reason the jazzband category is hard to pin down is that in order to employ larger numbers of players, they had to be responsive to a wider range of commercial demands in their choice of repertoire.

Jazzbands were originally formed to play for tourists who wanted to dance to North American big band material like show tunes and foxtrots. North American popular music was at that time dominated by big bands such as those of Paul Whiteman, Harry James and Glenn Miller, although, in that highly-segregated society, it was the less commercially successful, Afro-American big bands –

Count Basie, Duke Ellington, Chick Webb, Dizzy Gillespie and Fletcher Henderson – whose music has best stood the test of time. When the Great Depression put a damper on the tourist trade, Havana jazzbands began to add Cuban percussion and repertoire in order to appeal to the local population.

The first jazzband to record extensively was Orquesta Casino de la Playa, named after the gambling establishment where it was the house band. Later Cuba-based jazzbands included Orquesta Julio Cueva, Los Hermanos Castro, Los Hermanos Aviles, Havana-Riverside, Chepín-Chovén, Pérez Prado, Bebo Valdés, Ernesto Duarte and Beny Moré's Banda Gigante, but the big band format was just as important in New York's Latin music scene, where Machito and his Afro-Cubans, Tito Puente and Tito Rodríguez reached incredible levels of popularity and were hailed as "the big three".

It was through the jazzband format that the musical connections between Havana and New York were most firmly established. Among the key figures in this phenomenon were trumpeter and arranger Mario Bauzá and his brother-in-law Frank "Machito" Grillo, who came to New York from Havana in the late 1930s to form Machito and his Afro-Cubans. The band often featured the great Cuban singer Miguelito Valdés and played material by Arsenio Rodríguez and Chano Pozo as well as a full range of jazz and commercial North American music required to play their dance circuit gigs.

The Machito group was probably the first to record with what would become the standard salsa rhythm section configuration: bongó, congas and timbales, the timbalero in question being the young Tito Puente. With both a bongosero and timbalero, the practice of using two interlocking bell patterns began to take hold.

Machito and his Afro-Cubans – 1946 – New York – photo from recommended Properbox box set

By the 1930s, the music of the descendants of African slaves had begun to dominate and redefine popular music in both Cuba and the United States, but – as Sublette explains in utterly fascinating detail in his two books on New Orleans – the Afro-Cubans and Afro-Americans were drastically different from each other – with cultural heritage from different parts of Africa that they mixed in different ways with the different strains of European music they found in the New World. Sublette traces blues intonation and jazz "swing" rhythms to the more Islamized North African regions while Cuba inherited the intense polyrhythms and clave-oriented approaches of West Africa. When Cubans like Mario Bauzá and Chano Pozo began to work with North Americans like Chick Webb and Dizzy Gillespie, the two Afro-European fusions began to fuse with each other, forming the essential basis for almost every subsequent North American and Cuban genre, whether it be English-language, Spanish-language or instrumental.

Among the genres stemming from the interactions of Bauzá, Pozo and Gillespie is Latin jazz. Sublette calls Bauzá's *Tanga* (first played by Machito and his Afro-Cubans in 1943) "the first piece we can unequivocally call 'Afro-Cuban jazz'", pointing out that at this point, big band jazz was the popular music and the dance music of its day, rather than the esoteric concert music we now associate with the genre.

In the case of rock and R&B, the idea of the song-specific, syncopated bass, piano or guitar riff can be traced back through Gillespie's collaborations with Pozo on songs like *Manteca* to Pozo's exposure to Arsenio Rodríguez, and traced forward to the rhythm sections of Motown – Detroit jazz musicians who played Latin jazz songs like *Night in Tunisia* at nightclubs when they got through with their day jobs recording with the Supremes and the Four Tops. It's very easy to connect the rest of dots once you get your head around Sublette's revelations that *I Can't Get No Satisfaction* is a chachachá and *Louie Louie's* main hook was first recorded note-for-note by the Cuban pianist René Touzet.

Mambo in Jazzbands

In his classic song, *Elige tú que canto yo*, Beny Moré boasted that he was equally comfortable singing in any genre and the same claim could have been made by the jazzbands, who were equally comfortable playing son montuno, chachachá, guaracha, and bolero, but the one genre that *required* the multiple horn sections of a jazzband was *mambo*. The underlying concept of layered riffs was developed in a son montuno band (Arsenio Rodríguez) and named "mambo" by members of a charanga band (Arcaño), but the mambo *genre* that swept the world in the 1950s was the province of the jazzbands.

At the climaxes of his son montuno arrangements, Arsenio Rodríguez used multiple trumpets to play repeating riffs that interlocked with the coros, often with lead vocals and/or solos thrown into the mix. Arsenio called these innovative and inspired passages *diablos*. Arcaño's band adapted the concept to their charanga instrumentation, calling it *nuevo ritmo,* and later *mambo*, after a song written by Cachao's brother Orestes. These sections were so popular that jazzband arrangers like Pérez Prado started leaving out everything else and writing arrangements that began immediately with mambos. Prado had a whole book of them, with numbers instead of titles – hence, his trademark hit, *Mambo No. 5,* which was in fact the second of its name. If you can find the original 1947 *Mambo No.5,* you'll hear Pérez Prado, before super-stardom, sounding more like Thelonius Monk than Xavier Cugat.

The jazzband instrumentation was perfect for mambo because the saxes could be pitted against the trumpets and/or trombones with each section harmonized. Some 1950s big bands specialized almost exclusively in mambos but almost all included them in their repertoires, including Tito Puente and Beny Moré.

Further Listening Recommendations for Cuban Big Band or "Jazzband"

Year	Song	Source
1937	*Dolor cobarde* (pno solo: Anselmo Sacasas)	Casino de la Playa (w/Miguelito Valdés): *Cuban Originals* – RCA Intl
1937	*Bruca Maniguá* (comp: Arsenio Rodríguez)	Casino de la Playa (w/Miguelito Valdés): *Cuban Originals* – RCA Intl
1937	*Cachita*	Casino de la Playa (w/Miguelito Valdés): *Cuban Originals* – RCA Intl
1938	*Se va el caramelo* (tres solo: A. Rodríguez)	Casino de la Playa (w/Miguelito Valdés): *Cuban Originals* – RCA Intl
1939	*Babalú*	Casino de la Playa (w/Miguelito Valdés): *Cuban Originals* – RCA Intl
1939	*Traqueatéala*	Orquesta Chepín-Chovén: *Merenguito* – Tumbao Cuban Classics
1942	*Sopa de pichón* (timbales: Tito Puente)	*Machito and his Afro-Cubans* – Ritmo Caliente box set – Properbox
1942	*Nagüe nagüe nagüe* (voc. Miguelito)	*Machito and his Afro-Cubans* – Ritmo Caliente box set – Properbox
1944	*Pasito pa'lante*	Julio Cueva y su Orquesta: *Desintegrando* – Indie Europe
1946	*Desintegrando*	Julio Cueva y su Orquesta: *Desintegrando* – Indie Europe
1947	*Mambo No. 5* (original version)	Pérez Prado: *1947-1949* – Tumbao Cuban Classics
1949	*Tanga*	*Machito and his Afro-Cubans* – Ritmo Caliente box set – Properbox
c. 1949	*La atómica*	Beny Moré-Pérez Prado: (out of print but well worth finding)
1949	*Anabacoa*	Beny Moré-Pérez Prado: *The Originals* – YOYO USA
c. 1949	*Timbal y bongó*	Tito Puente: *Cuando suenan los tambores* – Sony US Latin
c. 1949	*Ariñañara*	Tito Puente: *Cuando suenan los tambores* – Sony US Latin
1953	*Mañana por la mañana*	Orq. Havana-Riverside: *One Night in Havana* – Columbia
1955	*Santa Isabel de Las Lajas*	Beny Moré: *The Great Beny Moré, Vol. 2* – Black Round Records
1957	*El agarrao*	Beny Moré: *The Great Beny Moré, Vol. 3* – Black Round Records
1957	*Elige tú que canto yo*	Beny Moré: *The Great Beny Moré, Vol. 3* – Black Round Records
1957	*Francisco Guayabal*	Beny Moré: *The Great Beny Moré, Vol. 3* – Black Round Records
1960	*Amor eterno*	Bebo Valdés: *World Music Cuba* – Digital Natives

1950s Charanga

highlighted track: *Fajardo te pone a gozar* – José Fajardo: *Chachachá in Havana* – Panart

time	tempo	comments
0:00	83	intro: bloque
0:09		coro: This arrangement has no cuerpo and begins in chachachá.
0:47	90	piano solo: Note the efecto at 0:54.
1:13		bloque
1:19		coro (note famous *hierro* bloque at 1:26)
1:41		trumpet moña: (a short mambo) (usually no brass in charangas!)
1:57	92	coro: with flute solo (first with coro, then with percussion efectos)
3:00	93	coda

The 1950s was the "golden era" for groups of the charanga format. They finally found themselves on the leading edge again after 30 years of playing catch-up with the more aggressive, more innovative son sextetos and conjuntos. The Cuban music scene was suddenly inundated with a wave of ultra-popular charangas, led by José Fajardo y sus Estrellas, Orquesta Aragón, and the Orquestas América, América del 55, Sensación, Sublime, Enrique Jorrín, Melodías del 40 and Pancho el Bravo.

There were many reasons for this surge in the popularity of the charanga groups. They switched from a mostly instrumental format to using vocals in every arrangement. Their ranks were graced by a generation of truly extraordinary flautists such as Richard Egües, José Fajardo and Pancho el Bravo. Their timbaleros were equally brilliant and 1950s charanga arrangements are laced with all sorts of intricate *efectos* and *mambitos* combining flute and percussion. They saved their formerly obligatory danzón arrangements for special occasions and began to choose their material freely from the full range of Cuban genres, including *sones, boleros, guarachas* and even an occasional *guaguancó* or *comparsa*. Most importantly, they developed a new genre of their own – *chachachá* – and it took the world by storm.

Arcaño's violinist Enrique Jorrín had moved on to Orquesta América when, in 1951, he wrote *La engañadora,* generally considered to be the first chachachá. To be clear, Jorrín didn't invent the chachachá *dance,* but it was for dancers that he created the chachachá style. In an often quoted and extremely candid interview, Jorrín explained his strategy. Playing in danzón-mambo format groups for many years, he had studied the dancers, many of whom were tourists who got flustered with the more syncopated montuno sections. Jorrín decided that it was the melodies, whether vocal or instrumental, that were throwing them off. In support of his theory, even today many first time listeners hear changüí offbeats (Exercise RP-1) as onbeats because of the fast tempo and the lack of a bass or chordal instrument to use as an anchor. Danzón-mambo was of course much slower, less syncopated and had both bass and piano playing relatively simply parts, but in 1951, even this was too much too handle for rhythmically-challenged white folks from segregated communities, people for whom Fred Astaire and Bing Crosby were the godfathers of soul. Jorrín's epiphany was to compose melodies that could be easily danced to even when sung *a cappella* (without any accompaniment), and as if to test for this, he often included such sections in his arrangements.

Shown with a graphic notation system explained in the next section, here's the rhythmic roadmap for the opening verse of *La engañadora*:

○○○○ ○○○○ ○○○○ **XXXX** *a Pra- do'y Nep-*
XX○○ ○○○○ ○○○○ **XXXX** *tu-no … i-ba'un-a chi-*
XX○○ ○○○○ ○○○○ **XXXX** *qui-ta … que to-dos los*
X○**X**○ ○○**XX** **X**○**X**○ **X**○**X**○ *hom-bres … la te-ní-an que mi-*
X○○○ ○○○○ ○○○○ ○○○○ *-rar*

Jorrín's timbaleros also simplified the bell part:

X○**X**○ **X**○**X**○ **X**○**XX** **XXXX** *danzón bell*
X○**X**○ **X**○**X**○ **X**○**X**○ **X**○**X**○ *chachachá bell*

If beginning dancers provided the inspiration for the chachachá rhythm, it was the advanced dancers who inspired the name. Jorrín said he used to listen to the dancers' feet shuffling on the dance floor as they danced what we now call the chachachá step (Exercise 3-6).

Orquesta Aragón 1969: left to right: Francisco Arboláez, Joseíto Beltrán, Pepe Olmos, Felo Bacallao, José Palma, Orestes Varona, Guido Sarría, Richard Egües, Alejandro Tomás Valdés, Dagoberto González, Rafael Lay, Celso Valdés

Chachachá became perhaps the world's most popular dance in the 1950s, providing the top Cuban charanga bands with recording and touring opportunities, allowing them to maintain steady lineups featuring the best musicians, and giving them the chance to play many other genres, resulting in a huge discography of wonderful recordings. And with a few changes to its language, instrumentation, volume level, and attitude, chachachá also became rock & roll.

My listening advice is to start with the 1950s recordings of either Aragón or Fajardo, depending on your tastes. Aragón is more refined and melodic while Fajardo is funkier and more aggressive. Then focus on the flute, the timbales and the layered *guajeos* (repeating, syncopated riffs in the bass, piano and strings). After you've caught the charanga fever, move on to the other classic groups listed below.

Further Listening Recommendations for 1950s Charanga

Year	Song	Source
1953	*La engañadora*	Orquesta América: *Silver Star* – Tumbao Cuban Classics
1954	*Cero codazos, cero cabezazos*	Orquesta Aragón: *Primeras grabaciones* – Tumbao Cuban Classics
1954	*Los parqueadores*	Fajardo y sus Estrellas: *Chachachá* – Balboa
1955	*El bodeguero*	Orquesta Aragón: *That Cuban Cha-Cha-Chá* – RCA
1955	*Me voy pa' Morón*	Orquesta Melodías del 40: *Montuno favorito* – Tumbao Cuban Classics
1955	*Se va conmigo*	Orquesta Melodías del 40: *Montuno favorito* – Tumbao Cuban Classics
1956	*Calculadora*	Orquesta Aragón: *Cuban Originals* – RCA
1956	*El panquelero*	Orquesta Sensación: *No hay como mi son* – Tumbao Cuban Classics
1956	*Fajardo está de bala*	Fajardo y sus Estrellas: *Volume 2* – Balboa
1956	*Seis perlas cubanas*	Orquesta Sublime: *Charangas de siempre* – EGREM
1957	*Ven morena*	Orquesta Aragón: *The Heart of Havana, Vol. 2* – RCA
1957	*Mira a ver quien es*	Orquesta Aragón: *Latin Grooves – Cha Cha Cha* – RCA
1957	*Macorina*	Orquesta Sensación: *Charangas de siempre* – EGREM
1957	*Las lavanderas de Portugal*	Fajardo y sus Estrellas: *Una noche en Montmartre* – Rodven
1957	*La botija de abuelito*	Fajardo y sus Estrellas: *Volume 3* – Balboa
1958	*Ritmo de pollos*	Fajardo y sus Estrellas: *José Fajardo* – Charly Records
1958	*Ven cosa buena*	Orquesta América del 55: *Charanga!* – Fania
1958	*Tiene sabor*	Orquesta Sensación: *Tiene sabor* – Antilla
1959	*Chao chao*	Fajardo y sus Estrellas: *Volume 6* – Balboa
1959	*La chica que yo soñé*	Orquesta Estrellas Cubanas: *Baila mi gente* – Antilla (iTunes)
1959	*Lola catula (pachanga)*	Orquesta Pancho el Bravo: *Bótate na'ma'* – Caney
1960	*Changüí monte*	Orquesta Sensación: *No hay como mi son* – Tumbao Cuban Classics
1961	*Kilimanjaro*	Orquesta Aragón: *Charangas y pachangas* – Eben Entertainment
1960	*Sabrosa pachanga*	Fajardo y sus Estrellas: *Volume 8* – Balboa

Descargas of the 1950s

highlighted track: *Descarga cubana* – Cachao y su Ritmo Caliente: *Cuban Jam Sessions* – Balboa

Collecting the classic descargas is no picnic. There are many compilations with many mistakes in the documentation and disparity in audio quality among multiple releases of the same tracks. There are even online labels that PhotoShop vinyl covers of the wrong albums – adding to the confusion. The above collection has two pluses and one minus. The minus is that the documentation – what little there is – is confusing and even mixes up some of the track titles. The first plus is that you get three CDs for a very low price. The second plus – the deciding factor – is that the audio quality is drastically better than the better organized and more complete MP3 download products currently available.

time	tempo	comments
0:00	105	**intro:** bass tumbao alone
0:04		Güirero (Gustavo Tamayo) and timbalero (Güillermo Barreto) enter. Barreto gives a master class in cáscara-playing, which at this point was a fairly new technique on timbales.
0:10		**conga solo**: Tata Güines. This is an incredibly influential recording. Many great congueros have reported learning this solo exactly. Tata Güines was among the first to use two drums and much what is now the standard vocabulary for both conga marchas and conga-soloing stems from his playing during this period. He integrates influences from rumba, changüí and abakuá and utilizes many innovative timbral variations. Modern ears, hearing this solo for the first time, will find many of the figures very familiar. This was not the case in 1957! If you have the time and inclination, learn to sing this solo from memory and then see how often you hear phrases from it in later recordings.
0:36		**coro 1:** *como mi ritmo no hay dos* (conga solo continues)
1:15	96	**timbalero's solo:** Many of the comments made above pertain equally well to Güillermo Barreto's solo, which draws heavily on rumba quinto vocabulary. Trivia note: Barreto is the uncle of NG La Banda/Klímax drummer Giraldo Piloto.
1:29		**coro 2:** *suena la paila* (timbales solo continues)
2:04	109	**bass solo:** Cachao's soloing was equally influential. In fact, before Cachao, bass solos were extremely rare in Cuban music.
2:38		efecto
2:40		**coro 3:** *me voy con mi ritmo – ritmo cubano ...* fades out

The popular and extremely influential practice of recording *descargas* (in-studio jam sessions) began in 1952 with groups led by Bebo Valdés, Julio Gutiérrez and Pedro "Peruchín" Justiz. The material was very loose, with simple lyrics on the subjects of music and rhythm. Some tracks were only two minutes long, focusing on just one instrument or rhythm and others ran to 17 minutes, providing extensive solo opportunities for such seminal figures as Tata Güines, Güillermo Barreto, Walfredo de los Reyes, Peruchín, Richard Egües and many more. The most famous and influential of the descargas were Cachao's 1957 productions. These historic recordings paved the way for Latin jazz. Orlando Fiol points out that it was in these sessions that much of the standard vocabulary for soloing on the various instruments of the Latin ensemble was established.

Further Listening Recommendations for 1950s Descargas

Year	Song	Source
1952	*Con poco coco*	Bebo Valdés: *Descarga caliente* – Caney
c. 1952	*Theme on Perfidia*	Julio Gutiérrez and Peruchín: *Cuban Jam Sessions, Vol. 1* – Panart
c. 1952	*Cimarrón*	Julio Gutiérrez and Peruchín: *Cuban Jam Sessions, Vol. 1* – Panart
c. 1952	*Montuno guajiro*	Niño Rivera: *Cuban Jam Sessions, Vol. 3* – Panart
1956	*The Big Four*	Tito Puente (with Mongo Santamaría, Patato Valdés): *In Percussion* – Fonotron
1957	*Cógele el golpe*	Cachao: *The Havana Sessions* – Yemayá Records
1957	*Goza mi trompeta*	Cachao: *The Havana Sessions* – Yemayá Records
1957	*A gozar timbero*	Cachao: *The Havana Sessions* – Yemayá Records
c. 1959	*Pa' coco solo*	José Fajardo y sus Estrellas: *Cuban Jam Sessions, Vol. 3* – Musart
1961	*Estoy buscando a Kako*	Alegre All Stars (New York): *Alegre All Stars* – Fania
c. 1952	*Descarga cubana #2*	*Los mejores músicos de Cuba* – Palladium Latin Jazz
c. 1952	*Batakún*	*Los mejores músicos de Cuba* – Palladium Latin Jazz

Walfredo de los Reyes with Orquesta Julio Gutiérrez – c. 1954 – Havana Channel 4 TV
photo courtesy of Walfredo de los Reyes – photo of photo by Sue Taylor

Rhythm Exercises 1: The Grid

Cuba's answer to Bernard Purdie: With Bamboleo and Los Que Son Son, Duniesky Barreto has laid down the grooves for some of the greatest dance tracks of all time. Photo by Tom Ehrlich – 2010 – Yoshi's San Francisco

Painters and photographers arrange shapes and colors on a fixed canvas. You can look at the canvas from different angles and from different distances, and the same painting can affect you differently each time you look at it, but you can always see the full canvas and all its contents – all at once.

The images above show a blank canvas and the same canvas after the photographer has filled it with shapes and colors.

Close your eyes, then open them for an instant, then close them again. Now stare at the photo for 30 seconds. Now step back a few feet. Now move as close as you can. In each case you're getting a different experience of the artwork in its entirety.

You can't do any of this with music because the complete piece of art is never audible in its entirety. The musical equivalents of shapes and colors pass gradually before you over a period of minutes. If you're a really good listener, you'll be able to use your memory to construct an aural image of a "fully painted musical canvas" when the piece is over.

In Listening Tour 1, we discovered Arsenio Rodríguez's *Tintorera ya llegó,* a blind man's masterpiece painted on the canvas of time. Arsenio's canvas consists of 180 seconds – 47 claves – 47 basic dance steps - 188 taps of your foot – 3 minutes of your life – maybe the best three minutes of your life. Hearing those three minutes as a singular whole is the goal, and the art, of the listener.

Time is the canvas, and the essence of musical talent is the ability to communicate the passage of time – to illuminate the frame for listeners, other musicians, and dance partners – to make those three minutes as solid and as real as a piece of canvas stretched tightly across a wooden frame.

Before we learn any rhythms or dance steps, we need to learn to feel, measure, and notate the passage of time – to feel the grid – the matrix – the groove. We'll do this with audio tracks, and the **optional** help of written notation. Seeing a rhythm on paper helps many people, but look no further than Arsenio *"El Ciego Maravillas"* Rodríguez ("the blind marvel") for proof that it's not necessary.

Demystifying Music Notation

or

Four Ways to Say Nothing

Take a good long look at the following graphic, an example of matrix notation, one of four methods we'll use to show rhythms. How would you describe it to someone who's not looking at the page?

There are 16 squares in all, with heavier black vertical lines dividing them into four groups of four. Let's call each group of four squares a *beat* and each individual square a *subdivision:*

subdivision	subdivision	subdivision	subdivision	subdivision	subdivision	subdivision	subdivision	subdivision	subdivision	subdivision	subdivision	subdivision	subdivision	subdivision	subdivision
Beat 1				Beat 2				Beat 3				Beat 4			

Now let's show the same four beats of silence in **X**&○ notation – another easy and intuitive notation system. In this case, the sounds are shown with red "**X**" symbols, the silent subdivisions are shown with grey "○" symbols, and the beats are shown by leaving a space after each group of four:

○○○○ ○○○○ ○○○○ ○○○○

These graphic methods are easier to learn and much more intuitive than standard music notation, but even if you're already skilled in standard notation, graphic notation is superior for showing how the various parts of a given groove come together at key points. All the parts align vertically, so **X**&o notation allows us to quickly and easily show complex relationships like this one:

2-3 bell *(campaneo)*	XoXo	XoXX	XoXX	XoXX
2-3 rumba clave	ooXo	Xooo	XooX	oooX
2-3 timba kick drum	XooX	oooo	oXoo	XoXo

Don't worry about what these rhythms are or what they mean – just note *when* each stroke occurs. Can you see from the top two lines that the clave only plays when the bell is playing? Now look at the second and third lines. Can you see that the clave never plays when the kick drum is playing?

The clave is a subset of the bell pattern, while the clave and kick drum parts never line up. Again, don't worry about *why* – just scan vertically to see which **X**s line up, i.e., which percussion strokes are played at the same time. This is the key to every rhythm section groove and dance step.

Now let's look at the same relationships in matrix notation. We'll use shading to highlight the five subdivisions where the bell and clave come together.

2-3 bell *(campaneo)*	•		•		•		•	•	•		•	•	•		•	•
2-3 rumba clave			•		•				•			•				•

The next diagram has no shading, because, as pointed out above, the kick drum and clave never coincide – they *converse* with each other rather than *reinforcing* each other. In funk and rock the kick drum is used to "fatten" and reinforce bass and other important parts, while in Cuban music, the kick drum is an independent voice that converses with the bass part.

2-3 rumba clave			•		•				•			•				•
2-3 timba marcha kick 1	•				•					•			•		•	

Now, don't panic. We won't have to study such complex relationships in this book. The point is that these two notation methods *allow* us to talk about this kind of thing in a way that's very easy to see and understand. With these methods, even the most complex grooves can be shown clearly.

On first impression, do you prefer matrix notation or **X**&o notation? Can you think of other logical ways to notate these rhythms? If you can, one of the best exercises you could possibly do to internalize and improve your understanding of these rhythms would be to write them out in a notebook using another system – *any* other system. The more ways you can think of to visualize these patterns, the better you'll grasp them and the more you'll feel like you "own" them.

Of course, there's also a standardized system for writing rhythms (and notes) that's been in use for hundreds of years. Standard notation takes longer to learn and its rules are less intuitive, but it can also express pitches, durations and important nuances far beyond the capabilities of any graphic notation system. You definitely won't need standard notation for anything in this book, but it's included for those who either know it, or have an interest in learning it. If you don't read music you can skip ahead to the next page and save yourself a headache. Otherwise, please read on!

Unfortunately, when it comes to standard notation, the world of Latin music is divided between two styles: 16th note notation in 4/4 versus 8th note notation in 2/2. (I warned you about that headache.)

Writing music in 16th note notation is more common within Cuba, and reveals the deep connections that exist between Latin music and North American genres such as funk, R&B and hip-hop. On the other hand, 8th note notation is used almost universally by professional Latin musicians *outside* of Cuba.

There are many strong arguments for and against each style, so we always show each exercise both ways, one right above the other.

The following standard notation shows exactly the same rhythm we showed above in graphic notation: 16 subdivisions of silence. The top line is in 16th note notation and the bottom line shows the same rhythm (4 beats of silence) in 8th note notation. Note that 8th note notation is often incorrectly written in 4/4 instead of 2/2. Even when is *says* 4/4, it *means* 2/2.

Whatever you do, don't try to feel the tempo twice as fast as it should be. Each line gets four beats – *not eight beats* – regardless of how it's notated. There's no controversy whatsoever about this.

We use the words "claves" or "basic steps" for groups of four main beats instead of the usual terms: *measure* and *bar*. In non-Latin music, "measure" and "bar" work perfectly (think of "the 12-bar blues"), **but** – because of this annoying disagreement about 2/2 and 4/4, measure and bar have conflicting meanings in Latin music. To understand this, look at the following chart:

subdivision	subdivision	subdivision	subdivision	subdivision	subdivision	subdivision	subdivision	subdivision	subdivision	subdivision	subdivision	subdivision	subdivision	subdivision	subdivision
Beat 1				Beat 2				Beat 3				Beat 4			
Bar or Measure – 16th note notation (4/4)															
Bar or Measure – 8th note notation (2/2)								Bar or Measure – 8th note notation (2/2)							

So, unfortunately, we can't say *measure* or *bar* without *also* specifying whether we're thinking in 16th notes (4/4) or 8th notes (2/2). To get around this, when we need to talk about how long a pattern lasts, we substitute the term *clave* (or *basic step* if we're talking about dancing).

In Latin popular music, one *clave,* or one *basic step,* always lasts four beats – 16 subdivisions – four groups of four – regardless of how someone might choose to write it in standard notation or talk about it in measures or bars. So, if you want to tell your singer how long to wait before coming in, it's much safer to say "come in after four claves" than it is to say "come in after four bars".

Four Ways to Say Nothing

In music, silence is just as important as sound. That's why we began this section by showing how the notation looks when the band is playing, but the individual part being studied consists only of silence. We've now learned four ways to show this – i.e., "four different ways to say nothing". And remember, as every old jazz musician will tell you, *"what you don't say is more important than what you do say".*

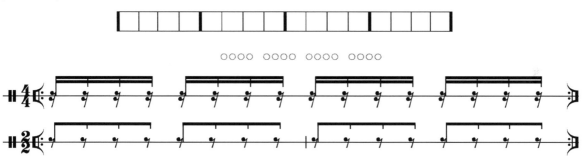

The Holy Grail for Dancers and Beginning Musicians: Feeling the Subdivisions

These diagrams don't represent any sounds being played – just the passage of time – but feeling the passage of time accurately is the single most important ability for dancers and musicians. This is by far the most important concept in this book, so let me repeat it once more for good measure:

Feeling the passage of time accurately is the single most important ability for dancers and musicians.

Now let's use the same four notation methods to show a rhythm consisting of a note or percussive sound on *every* subdivision. Compare the notation above and below until both make perfect sense.

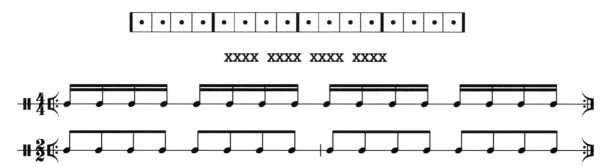

At the risk of being annoyingly redundant, let's hammer away at this all-important concept of subdivisions a little bit more before we learn a single rhythm.

The Yardstick Analogy

Let's say you you're trying to measure how tall someone is with a measuring stick that's exactly one yard long (.9144 meters, 3 feet), but has no markings. You can use your measuring stick to confirm that the person is taller than one yard and shorter than two yards (1.8288 meters, 6 feet), but after that point you have to estimate. If your measuring stick has markings for inches or centimeters, however, you can get a reading that's much more accurate. Depending on the accuracy needed, each inch or centimeter can be marked with successively smaller subdivisions.

Measuring the Passage of Time

With music, you're measuring time. If the smallest subdivision you're feeling is one beat, that's like having a yardstick with only the inches marked. If you measure someone's height as 5'9", that's fine for most purposes, but if you were to use this level of accuracy for a critical part of the space shuttle, you'd be putting people's lives in danger. Playing or dancing with an accuracy level of one beat will not kill your audience, fellow musicians or dance partners, but it may very well make them *wish* they were dead. To play or dance Latin music at a professional level, you have to feel four subdivisions per beat and you have to make sure your audience and dance partners feel them too.

The Meaning of Musical Talent

Many subjective descriptions of musical ability boil down to how well a musician or dancer can feel the subdivisions and how well he or she can convey that feeling to others. When we say a player or dancer has *"great time"*, a *"funky groove"*, *"tremendo swing"*, *"tumbao"*, *"aché"*, or *"sentimiento manana"*, what we're really waxing poetic about is this ability to feel and express subdivisions. The accents, dynamics, durations and body language that go along with these superlatives can be thought of as the *means* by which the person communicates and gives style to the magical, sometimes trance-like flow of subdivisions, but the subdivisions themselves are the message that's being communicated. Whenever a musical performance causes you to feel the subdivisions more strongly, it gives you a rush of euphoric excitement, and one of the main reasons human beings love music so much is that it allows us to chase after that rush, and to feel it ever more intensely.

The obvious mark of a non-professional musician or an awkward dancer is that the person feels the time in beats (but not subdivisions) and has to "guess" when to execute a stroke or step that falls *between* the beats. A professional will not only feel every subdivision but will also often add small additional sounds and movements on unplayed subdivisions that clarify and solidify the groove. Everyone knows how much easier it is to dance with a partner who *shows* you where the groove is, and lesser bands often hire one strong player (the "ringer") who lays down lots of subdivision-reaffirming markers for the weaker musicians to "lean on".

When you dance with a master to a band where *everyone* is feeling all the subdivisions at a deep level, it opens the door for that magical throbbing groove that you probably experienced at that life-altering Cuban music concert, or trip to Cuba, that inspired you to seek out this book.

Alain Pérez – recording the audio and video for *Beyond Salsa Bass* – 2011 – photo by Michael Cába

Exercise 1-1: Feeling the Groove • Audio Tracks 1-1a & 1-1b

Our first exercise is very easy – all you have to do is close your eyes and listen. **Audio Track 1-1a** is an excerpt from *Beyond Salsa Bass, Volume 6*. Alain Pérez, one of the greatest Cuban bass players, is legendary for his rock-solid groove. Listening to his bass part by itself, you can hear the symphony of percussive sounds that he produces (each one lovingly transcribed in the book, I might add!). With the whole band playing, these sounds are nearly inaudible, but they can be heard by other musicians on stage and playing them allows Pérez to place the louder notes of his tumbao with uncanny precision. **Audio Track 1-1b** is the same recording, digitally slowed down. The pianist in the left channel is Melón Lewis, subject of *Beyond Salsa Piano, Volumes 6-9*. To hear the bass more clearly, turn the balance control all the way to the right.

Establishing Your Own Groove

To make sure you're feeling all the subdivisions strongly at all times, our audio tracks have a soft but continuous stream of *maraca* sounds. It's extremely important to get comfortable with this "click track" because the steady flow of subdivisions will keep you in the groove and help your timing. Every sound you'll be asked to sing, clap, play or dance to will fall precisely on one of these subdivisions. You might think of the click track and the sounds coming from the right speaker as the aforementioned "ringer" musician you've hired for the rest of the band to lean on.

Audio Track 1-2 consists of only this click track, gradually increasing in speed from 50 to 150 beats per minute (BPM), the basic range of Cuban music, from the slowest *bolero* to the fastest *rumba columbia*. The first subdivision of each four is slightly louder and the first of the whole group of 16 is slightly louder still.

Exercise 1-2: Visualizing the Groove • Audio Track 1-2

1. Listen to Audio Track 1-2 with your eyes closed, keeping your place in the 16-subdivision cycle. Try to describe your mental image of this grid as you move through it. There's no right answer. You might be counting numbers or visualizing squares, or stair steps, or – more likely – visualizing something so abstract that you can't even describe it in words. That's perfectly okay. This process is about feeling, not about thinking or understanding, and it doesn't matter what your personal mental image of "the grid" is. What *does* matter is the level of detail with which you perceive it.

2. Some highly-trained musicians – believe it or not – can actually picture standard music notation written out as they listen to music. Other musicians, including many of the greatest percussionists on the planet, don't know a thing about written music and are incapable of counting a rhythm or describing it in words. When called upon to teach, they teach by rote, as is the case in most of the world's musical cultures. They simply play the part over and over until the student either learns it or gives up. The fact that

these master percussionists have no verbal or written way of representing their music makes it harder to study with them, but it doesn't diminish their ability to play music in the least. If you were to play a difficult rhythm for such a musician, he or she would be able to effortlessly repeat the pattern, retain it, and play it again for you the next day, and to do so with exquisite timing, tone and feeling. But how can they do this without counting it or writing it down? They can remember any rhythm, but what is it that they're remembering and how are they remembering it? The answer is that the abstract, personal rhythmic grid in this person's head is extremely detailed and he or she can feel the details as if reaching out and touching a sculpture. It's not numbers, or words, or 8th notes and 16th notes, and it's probably very different from one master percussionist to the next, but whatever it is, it's crystal clear in that percussionist's mind – *so clear that he or she can instantly hear how any rhythm fits against it,* and retain a sharply detailed memory of that pattern for future reference.

3. With this in mind, close your eyes and listen to Audio Track 1-2 again. If your focus starts to wane, use your listening device to jump back and listen from the beginning at the slower tempo. Remember that the most common tempo for Latin dance music comes less than halfway through this gradually accelerating track. Let the details of your own personal internal grid come to you naturally as you passively observe the workings of your inner ear and whatever abstract image your mind creates as you keep your place in the 16-subdivision cycle. **As long as you know where you are in the cycle of 16, you're doing it right.** Get used to your own personal, non-verbal world of rhythm and spend as much time there as you can. The clearer your perception of which subdivision you're on at any given point, the better your rhythmic skills have become.

The next step is optional because it's quite possible to learn every rhythm in this course by simply listening, imitating, and visualizing what you hear against your mental grid. For some readers, this will be the easiest and most natural way to learn. For others, however, adding a visual representation makes learning easier. Try both ways and see which works best for you.

4. Now listen to Audio Track 1-2 with your eyes open, following along with each of the following four interchangeable diagrams:

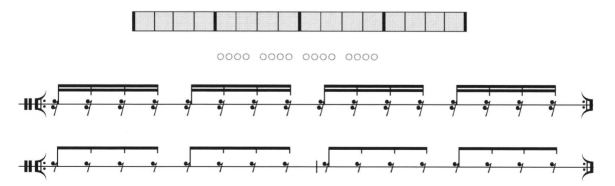

Try to keep your eyes on the square, the ○, or the rest symbol that corresponds to the maraca sound you're hearing. When you get to the end of the line, let your eyes loop back to the beginning. When the track gets too fast to do this comfortably, jump back to the beginning of the audio track. It's not necessary to reach the fastest tempo.

Now let's learn a short repeating rhythmic figure, or *rhythmic cell*. This one is called *main beats,* and consists of a percussive sound (or *stroke)* on the first of every group of four subdivisions. Listen to **Audio Track 1-3a** and/or **1-3b** while following along with each of the four diagrams. We provide two audio tracks of each rhythmic cell: "a" (faster) and "b" (slow motion). Later on, we'll add two others: fast and slow "c" and "d" versions using our special method of building rhythms event by event. If you prefer a different tempo, there are many free or inexpensive software programs that will allow you to change the tempo or loop sections to create longer practice tracks.

Exercise 1-3: main beats • Audio Tracks 1-3a and 1-3b

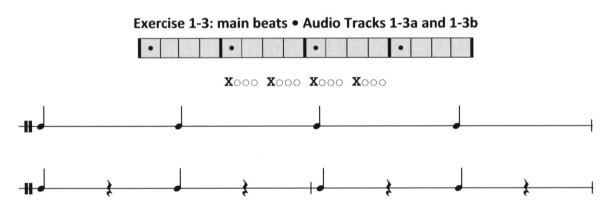

Note that not all types of music use this "four groups of four" type of grid. Three groups of four (e.g., waltz time, or 3/4) and four groups of three (e.g., shuffle time, or 12/8) are common and all sorts of other combinations occur in classical music, modern jazz, some pop, and many types of music from India and Eastern Europe. In every major genre of Latin popular music, however, it's always four groups of four. The only exception that we'll eventually need to concern ourselves with is Afro-Cuban folkloric music, which often uses four groups of three, but every *popular* music rhythm in this book can be expressed very clearly with these four-by-four grids. We'll study Afro-Cuban folkloric music in Listening Tour 4.

The rhythm section parts for the various Latin genres are built by layering rhythmic cells, with a different pattern for each instrument. The combination of all these patterns creates a recognizable, danceable groove upon which the voices and melodic instruments can build the larger phrases of the arrangement. So, if the leader of a band turns to his or her rhythm section and says *"let's play this song as a chachachá"*, this means something different for each player's part. The combination of all these special rhythm section parts, and the overall tempo, is what we mean when we say *chachachá, guaguancó, guaracha* and so on.

When a band routinely switches between several of these recognizable grooves within the same song – either by rehearsing them or invoking them with signals – we call them "gears", a central concept in this series, covered in great detail in *Beyond Salsa Percussion, Volume 3: Timba Gears.*

The Audio File Method

Two groups of audio files for this book can be found at timba.com/audio. The first set can be downloaded free of charge. **Please download these and load them into your music player before reading the rest of this chapter.** The more advanced second set is a separate $10 product. The audio method I'm about to explain is an unusual approach that some people find incredibly valuable – myself included – but not everyone who tries it likes it, so try the free download first to see how it works for you. The free download includes 107 tracks selected from each Rhythm Exercises section.

Here's how the audio file method works and why it's designed the way it is. The premise is simple:

- Every rhythm – no matter how complex or difficult – consists of a series of individual task or events.

- If you're asked to sing, clap, or play only the first sound of the pattern, it's very easy.

- Once you master the first sound, adding just the second sound will be equally easy.

- As long as this process is done with a steady rhythmic accompaniment, it's relaxing and enjoyable and you always learn the rhythm with the correct orientation from the very beginning.

Most of the exercises in this book consist of only one part, but you'll be asked to do two things at once in some of our more advanced books and it's a lot of fun. To show how our method works, we'll use one of the more difficult "two things at once" scenarios: tapping your foot on the beats while clapping or singing the clave. Box notation is the method of choice for seeing how multiple parts align in time but we'll show the exercise in our usual four methods.

Exercise 1-4: main beats + 3-2 son clave • Audio Tracks 1-4a-d

3-2 son clave	•			•			•			•			•			•		
foot taps	•						•						•						•	
individual tasks:	1				2	3		4		5		6		7		

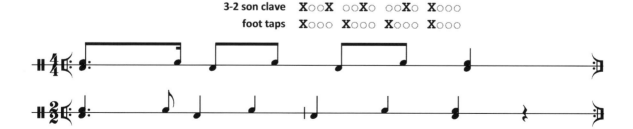

Instead of imagining the superhuman task of "doing two things at once", let's look at it another way: all we have to do is seven *single* tasks, one at a time. Task 1 is to tap your foot at exactly the same time that you clap your hands. Not so hard, eh? It's not two things at once – it's just one body movement. Try it – clap and stomp in one movement – just as you would at the end of a great concert when everyone is calling for an encore *("otra! otra! otra!")*.

Task 2 is to clap your hands *without* tapping your foot. So you're going from clapping and stomping to just clapping. This may take a tiny bit of coordination, but after a minute you'll be able to do both tasks as easily as you were able to do just Task 1.

Task 3 is to just tap your foot without clapping. So now it's "both, clap, stomp". These three tasks are then repeated over and over until you can do them in your sleep.

When doing the exercises, make absolutely sure you've mastered each task before proceeding! "Overkill" at each stage is the secret to this type of learning. At this point, take a short break and do something else to clear your short-term memory.

When you come back from your break, repeat the original steps until you can again perform the first three tasks as effortlessly as you performed just the first and until you can repeat it immediately after coming back from a break. Task 4 is another clap:

Task 1	both
Task 2	clap hands
Task 3	tap foot
Task 4	clap hands
Task 5	tap foot
Task 6	clap hands
Task 7	both

And that's a hard one! Most of the exercises are easier because there's only one part.

There's no one task that isn't easy to add by itself. In *Beyond Salsa Percussion, Volume 1,* we'll use the same method to play *three* different parts at once (e.g., kick drum, bell and clave), and even this isn't very hard once you get used to the method.

The audio files add a maraca part to keep you in rhythm. We take advantage of stereo recording to make it even easier by providing you with a "tutor", or "coach", in the right speaker to help you be sure you're doing the exercise correctly. Think of the right speaker, or right headphone channel, as a friendly personal trainer who doesn't make you do sit-ups or charge you $60 an hour.

The exercise is presented here to show you how the method works with a 2-part exercise, but try the easier exercises in the next two Rhythm Exercise sections before you "try this at home".

Track Naming Conventions

There are four audio tracks for each exercise. The first number is the number of the section, the second is the number of the exercise, followed by a letter, a, b, c, or d (see below for an explanation of the letters), followed by the clave direction and a brief description, and finally the tempo.

1-4a-3-2 main beats + clave-fast.mp3

1	4	a	3-2	main beats + clave	fast
section→	exercise→	type (see below) →	clave direction→	description→	tempo→

1-4a	"a" = the full pattern, full speed
1-4b	"b" = the full pattern, slow motion
1-4c	"c" = task-by-task training, full speed
1-4d	"d" = task-by-task training, slow motion

If you have the patience to start with the slow versions, you'll get much better results, but some people can't stand to listen to music in slow motion. Note that there are many free and inexpensive computer programs that will allow you to change the speed, loop points and durations of these files to your own specifications if you find yourself wishing these were faster, slower, or longer.

How the Audio Files Work

The Pocket

As explained above, the key to all things musical is to feel the "groove" or "pocket" created by the subdivisions. Each of our audio tracks has a soft but steady stream of maraca sounds with slight accents on the beats. The track opens with a loud bell count-off ("1, 2, 3, and, 4, and") and then the exercise begins. Use this count-off to lock yourself as deeply as possible into the groove of the subdivisions. Keep your finger on the rewind button and use it often.

The "Teacher" and the "Tutor"

The left speaker of your playback device is your "teacher". The routine is to listen to the teacher, then groove with the subdivisions for rest of the four beat section (or two beat section in the Rhythm Exercises 2 chapter), and then copy the teacher exactly (reinforced by the right channel).

The right channel is your "tutor", playing the answer exactly as you should be playing it. Think of this as riding with "training wheels". When you get more confident, you can turn the balance control all the way to the left and try it without the tutor. The tutor gives you instant feedback, saving you from ever learning a rhythmic cell incorrectly and then having to spend twice as long unlearning it.

The exercise is built one "task" at a time, with each task repeated twice by the teacher. When the pattern is complete, the teacher plays it over and over for at least a minute so you can play along, repeating the part continuously as you would in a real playing situation. The "a" and "b" versions of each audio file contain the full pattern from the beginning, while the "c" and "d" versions use the task-by-task method described here. An issue that comes up with the "c" and "d" versions is that people master the first half of the pattern and then, when having trouble with something in the second half, they get bored repeating the first half. To address this, there are many audio programs that will allow you to see the waveform, select the second half, and start from that point every time. For even more control, try a program like Sony Acid™ or E-mu Emulator X™. These miracles of modern technology will allow you to make custom loops that start on any beat and loop seamlessly.

The Psychological Stages of Learning
Frustration → Boredom → **Mastery**

Our method allows you to completely remove the Frustration stage. As soon as you experience even the slightest pang of frustration, hit the button that jumps back to the beginning of the track and restart the exercise. Boredom, however, is unavoidable with any musical method and this basic fact of life is especially true when it comes to learning to dance or play in a rhythm section. Think about your favorite drummers. I'm not talking about soloists – I'm talking about accompanists – the guys who lay down the groove that makes the melodies, lyrics and harmonies sound so good and makes the audience want to dance. For the most part, these drummers are playing one repeating part over and over and over. Why isn't this boring? Why are they, and everyone else in the room, smiling from ear to ear? It's because they've passed *through* the "boredom" stage and come out on the other side.

You'll never experience being in that magical pocket until you can dance the step or clap the rhythm without thinking or trying, and you'll never reach *that* point without experiencing boredom.

When most people get bored, they instinctively look for something more challenging. Avoid this temptation. Embrace the boredom! Boredom does *not* mean that you've mastered the rhythm and you're ready to move on. Boredom means you're getting *close* to mastering the rhythm. When you actually master it, the feeling you experience will be closer to euphoria than boredom, so instead of trying to add something harder, just enjoy the accents and the feeling in your body as you effortlessly repeat a simple rhythm.

Suggested Listening: Prince: *Joy in Repetition*

Hitting rewind on your audio device is a foolproof method for avoiding the frustration of not being able to keep up, but for some people, rewinding creates its own form of frustration: *"Arggggh! … now I have to do just the kick drum four times, and then just the kick and the bell, and then after about a minute I'll finally get back to the part I was having trouble with."* Of course, you don't have to rewind all the way to the beginning but I recommend doing so, and using the "boring" opening strokes to focus ever more deeply on the sound and feel of the subdivisions.

The next time you're at a live Afro-Cuban folkloric performance, watch the person with the *chékere* (a large gourd in a net of beads). Often, while everyone else is playing wild syncopations, this person is simply playing the first main beat of each side of the clave. How boring is that? And yet, when it's done properly, the result is thrilling rather than boring.

That said, the chékere can also be played with dazzling virtuosity, as in the cases of Eladio "Don Pancho" Terry and his son Yosvany.

Chékere Masters – Don Pancho Terry and his son Yosvany – Yerba Buena Gardens – photos by Tom Ehrlich

Listening Tour 2: Post-Revolution (1959-1989)

Category	Year	Song	Source
salsa	1978	*Plástico*	Rubén Blades and Willie Colón: *Siembra* – Fania
mozambique	1965	*Nace en Cuba el mozambique*	Pello el Afrokán: *Nace en Cuba el mozambique* – Orfeon
songo	1972	*Ponte para las cosas*	Los Van Van: *Colección, Vol. 2* – EGREM
modern charangas	1987	*Baila si vas a bailar*	Ritmo Oriental: *La historia de la Ritmo, Vol. 2* – QBADisc
modern jazzbands	1974	*Bacalao con pan*	Irakere: *Bacalao con pan* – Escondida
modern conjuntos	1978	*A Bayamo en coche*	Son 14: *Grandes éxitos* – EGREM
charangón	1987	*Changüí clave*	Elio Revé y su Charangón: *Volume 2* – BIS

Our second listening tour covers the period between the 1958 Cuban Revolution and the fall of the Berlin Wall. Before getting into the music, let's briefly try to understand why these non-musical historic events bookend musical eras so conveniently.

Politics, Economics and Music

Most of history's great music has been produced in bursts, during those unlikely periods when politics, economics, and talent have come into perfect alignment – however briefly – at the right time and in the right place. I like to call this rare and wonderful type of phenomenon a "scene". Most people, in most places, at most times, can be heard to complain bitterly that *"music is in a slump here – I remember the good old days when ..."*. The depressing reality is that music being "in a slump" is the normal state of affairs. A "scene", on the other hand, is an aberration, but one that always leaves a lasting impression on those lucky enough to experience it first-hand. The "scene" I stumbled into in 1999 Havana continues to provide me with the motivation to write these books.

As an example, such a scene occurred in the 1930s, during the Prohibition era, when Kansas City was under the control of corrupt politicians who bribed prosecutors in order to keep the booze flowing, resulting in a thriving nightclub scene that attracted top musicians from all over the country, a country that was otherwise deep in the doldrums of the Great Depression.

It was in Kansas City in the mid-1930s that a young saxophonist named Charlie Parker used to sneak into the balcony of the dance hall to study his idol, Lester Young, as he played with the Count Basie Orchestra. The social conservatives and politicians who brought us Prohibition and the gangsters who ran Kansas City inadvertently conspired to make it possible for a community of brilliant artists to come together and produce the scene that inspired Parker's development and subsequent breakthroughs. Charlie Parker went on to become one of the great geniuses of the 20th Century, but his genius might never have come to fruition if he'd lived in Des Moines, Iowa, where no such "scene" happened to be occurring during his formative years. Of course, he might have been inspired to find his way from Des Moines to Kansas City, but what if the Kansas City scene had never occurred in the first place?

There were few jazz fans among the politicians who instigated and later rescinded Prohibition, and the gangsters who created the Kansas City nightclub scene did so for financial reasons having nothing to do with creating a fertile environment for the birth of modern jazz. In retrospect, we had various groups of bad people, doing bad things for bad reasons, and, by sheer chance, creating the necessary conditions for an explosion of musical progress and creativity.

The same story – with different geniuses, different heroes and villains, and different political and economic circumstances – could be told about Vienna from 1780 to 1810, New York from 1942 to 1949, London from 1963 to 1970, Detroit from 1960 to 1967, or Havana in the late 1920s, late 1940s or the 1990s. Throughout history, music has been like a leaf in the wind, blown about randomly and uncaringly by wars, revolutions, depressions, religious movements, the slave trade, the Industrial Revolution, and now, by the turmoil created by the advent of digital recording and the rise of the internet. Every macro event creates unique musical opportunities and snuffs out others.

Further Reading:
Ned Sublette: *Cuba and its Music* – Chicago Review Press
Robin D. Moore: *Music and Revolution* – University of California Press

In *Cuba and its Music,* Sublette recounts the relentlessly gory and unfair political history of Cuba. Most often, political and economic circumstances tended to make life miserable for musicians and music fans, but every so often, some concurrence of corruptly-motivated internal and external power plays would inadvertently, and temporarily, create an environment for musicians to thrive. When this coincided with the presence of a particularly talented generation of musicians, with a particularly combustible chemistry among them, a "scene" would emerge, producing a burst of wonderful music before the next wave of non-musical events drew the party to a premature close.

Sublette's book ends six years before the 1958 revolution but the random effects of politics and economics on musical scenes never ends, and is endlessly fascinating. For those left hanging by the absence of the long-awaited second volume of *Cuba and its Music,* the story is picked up by Robin D. Moore (no relation to the author of this book) in his excellent *Music and Revolution.*

Before returning to the music, let's briefly summarize the effects of the Cuban Revolution on the music of the 1960s:

- It artificially separated the Cuban musical community from those of New York and Puerto Rico, with profound effects on each.

- It set in place a music conservatory system in Cuba that would have a profound impact on future generations of Cuban musicians, but had little immediate effect of the working musicians of the 1960s.

- It removed the financial infrastructure that had supported Cuba's nightclub scene and recording industry and – even by the end of the 1960s – had still only begun (in unpredictable and rapidly changing fits and starts) to create a new infrastructure in its place.

So, at this point we have to break with our linear chronology and deal with salsa and the 1960s in Cuba in separate sections.

Salsa

highlighted track: *Plástico* (1978) – Rubén Blades and Willie Colón: *Siembra* – Fania

time	tempo	comments
0:00	84	intro: R&B/disco groove
0:47	101	cuerpo A: changes from normal cáscara and bongó (*marcha abajo*) to bomba sicá at 0:56, 1:27, 1:58, 2:29
2:51		cuerpo B: marcha abajo
3:46	105	montuno – coro 1: timbalero and bongosero switch to bells (*marcha arriba*)
4:08		mambo 1
4:48		coro 1
5:19		mambo 2
5:38		coro 2
6:04		coda: motivo (piano doubles bass)

By the end of 1958, the global popularity of Cuban music had reached its all time high. In Cuba, Celia Cruz, Beny Moré, Pérez Prado, Aragón and Chappottín were at the peaks of their careers. Outside Cuba, everyone – Latino and otherwise – danced to chachachá and mambo. Desi Arnaz and his Cuban big band were featured on the world's top television show. As accurately depicted by the *current* television show, *Mad Men,* white Madison Avenue executives danced (albeit badly) to Cuban music at their Christmas parties. Musicians traveled freely between Cuba and the U.S. and thousands of Puerto Ricans emigrated to New York each month, adding to the growing audience that supported big bands like those of Tito Puente and Tito Rodríguez at huge venues like the Palladium Ballroom. Even rock and R&B, which also developed during this period, were based on Cuban music to a much greater degree than most people realize, as explained in detail in Sublette's essay, *The King's Men and the Cha-Cha-Chá,* from the anthology *Listen Again.*

Then, on New Year's Eve, 1958, the lines of cultural communication between Cuba and the rest of the pop music world were abruptly and almost completely severed. The music scene outside Cuba continued as before, but without fresh input from the island, and the musicians who remained there were suddenly operating in a completely different socio-economic environment that was changing quickly and unpredictably.

Cuban music developed erratically, eclectically, and in many directions at once – from Pello el Afrokán's *mozambique,* to Enrique Bonne and Pacho Alonso's *pilón* and *simalé,* to Revé's *changüí-68,* Los Van Van's *songo,* Ritmo Oriental's modernized charanga, and Irakere's fusions of jazz, classical music, rumba and Afro-Cuban folkloric music. Very little of this music was heard outside Cuba. The New York-based Típica 73 recorded a Van Van cover *(La candela)* and another from Ritmo Oriental *(Yo bailo de todo),* but by and large, the rest of the world was even more cut off from Cuba than the Cubans were from the rest of the world.

Due to the U.S. embargo, Cuban music continues – even in 2012 – to fly well under the radar of most North American listeners and musicians, but the 1980s witnessed a major surge of interest among Cubans in what the rest of the world had been doing with their music in the 20 years since they'd last checked. They liked what they heard. The 1960s and 1970s had been characterized in Cuba by experimentation with non-Latin genres, balanced with new infusions of Afro-Cuban folkloric music, but the pendulum swung back to more traditionally Latin approaches in the 1980s, inspired by the global popularity of salsa and merengue. Rubén Blades' *Siembra* was one of the most popular albums in Cuba in the early 1980s and I've yet to talk to anyone who lived in Cuba in the 1980s who didn't immediately and emphatically bring up the impact of Oscar d'León's Cuban tour of 1983. As Orlando Fiol points out, d'León, a Venezuelan citizen, wasn't subject to the restrictions of the embargo, and was ideally suited to the task of helping to repopularize traditional Cuban music – now repackaged as salsa – in Cuba. In the case of Rubén Blades, his songwriting is of such a high level of originality and creativity as to transcend genre considerations. Quotes from *Siembra* are still heard regularly in the timba era. For example, *Plástico* is quoted by Manolín in *Dios sabe* and by Mayito Rivera in Los Van Van's *Llévala a tu vacilón,* and *Pedro Navaja* is quoted by Los Que Son Son's Mandy Cantero on *Qué cosas tiene la vida.*

The term *salsa* is – or at least was – a controversial one, with some purists decrying it as nothing more than a marketing term for Cuban music played by Nuyoricans. On the other hand, a competing group of purists hold that *timba* is nothing more than Nuyorican salsa played by Cubans. After looking at it from all the angles, I agree with the premises, but disagree with with the conclusions of both groups of purists. Salsa is neither conjunto nor charanga. Conjuntos use bongó and congas and charangas use timbal and congas, but salsa uses all three in a consistent way. For cuerpos, the timbales play cáscara and the bongosero plays bongó (i.e. *marcha abajo),* and for montuno sections, the timbalero plays contracampaneo while the bongosero's hand bell plays campaneo (i.e., *marcha arriba).* The bassist plays continuously and concentrates on the bombo-ponche rhythm, while the piano part has its own clave-aligned rhythmic formula. All of these elements, (which we'll learn to sing and clap in the Rhythm Exercises 3 section), can of course be found in pre-Revolution Cuban music, but not until salsa was this particular combination standardized and used consistently in these ways. So "salsa" can describe a distinct way of handling the rhythm section, and it also has its own very distinct time feel and styles of singing, lyric-writing, and arranging.

Although salsa is more than a marketing term, it was nevertheless marketed quite brilliantly for an extended period of time. I wouldn't be surprised if more records were recorded by salsa artists between 1960 and 1990 than have been recorded in the entire history of Cuba.

The purists who say that timba is just Cuban salsa are even farther off the mark. They're correct that in terms of handling the rhythm section and overall arrangement, timba has more in common with salsa, its cousin-once-removed, than with its immediate family relatives in the conjunto and charanga categories. But, as we'll see in Listening Tour 3, the timberos unleashed a torrent of innovations in all aspects of music creation that rivals Arsenio's breakthroughs of the 1940s.

The *"Beyond Salsa"* series – as its title implies – assumes that many readers will be coming from a salsa background. For them, this "salsa" section of our listening tour will be familiar territory, but for those coming from a more Cuba-centric background, acquiring a good knowledge of salsa can be an overwhelming project for the simple reason that there's so much of it.

The good news for newly-anointed salseros is that salsa is much easier to find and collect than Cuban music, and the massive and brilliantly-executed Fania remastering project has made the task much more pleasant with excellent documentation and audio quality. If only Cuba's EGREM label would do the same with its own prodigious catalog.

One logical way to break the vast body of salsa music into categories is to divide the artists geographically: Puerto Rican (e.g., Sonora Ponceña, Cortijo, Roberto Roena, Willie Rosario, Gran Combo, Bobby Valentín, Gilberto Santa Rosa, etc.); Nuyorican (Ray Barreto, Eddie Palmieri, Larry Harlow, Willie Colón, Johnny Pacheco, Marc Anthony, Spanish Harlem Orchestra, etc.); Venezuelan (Oscar d'León, Guaco, etc.); and so on.

To avoid filling the Further Listening list with Rubén Blades songs, I'll make a separate Further Listening list for Blades here: *Pablo Pueblo, Buscando guayaba, Pedro Navaja, Todos vuelven, Tiburón, Dime, Como un huracán, Oye, No hay chance.*

Further Listening Recommendations for Salsa

Year	Song	Source
1957	*Complicación*	Tito Puente: *Dance Mania* – RCA
1958	*El chivo de la campana*	Cortijo y su Combo (vocal: Ismael Rivera): *Baila con Cortijo* – Seeco
1960	*Mamá Güela*	Tito Rodríguez: *At the Palladium* – United Artists
1965	*Azúcar*	Eddie Palmieri: *Azúcar pa' ti* – Tico (reissued by Fania)
1967	*Tengo máquina y voy a sesenta*	Charlie Palmieri: *Tengo máquina y voy a sesenta* – Alegre
1969	*La revolución*	Larry Harlow: *Electric Harlow* – Fania
1969	*Que me castigue Dios*	Roberto Roena y su Apollo Sound – Fania

Year	Song	Source
1970	*Huracán*	Bobby Valentín: *Algo nuevo* – Fania
1971	*Brujería*	Mark Dimond: *Brujería* – Vaya
1972	*Y no hago más na'*	El Gran Combo: *25th Anniversary* – Combo Records
1972	*Pa' bravo yo*	Justo Betancourt: *Pa' bravo yo* – Fania
1973	*Juventud siglo 20*	Willie Rosario: *Infinitivo* – Inca
1973	*Indestructible*	Ray Barretto: *Indestructible* – Fania
1973	*Puerto Rico*	Eddie Palmieri: *Sentido* – Fania
1974	*Canto a La Habana*	Johnny Pacheco (vocal: Celia Cruz): *Celia & Johnny* – Fania
1974	*Un toque pa' Yambaó*	Pete "El Conde" Rodríguez
1975	*La escoba barrendera*	Típica 73: *La candela* – Inca
1976	*Guajira típica*	Típica 73: *Rumba caliente* – Inca
1976	*Anacaona*	Cheo Feliciano: *Cheo* – Vaya
1977	*Salsa Suite (orig. title: Sabrosito rumbón)*	Típica 73: *Two Sides* – Inca
1977	*La botija de abuelito*	Típica 73: *Two Sides* – Inca
1977	*Boranda*	Sonora Ponceña: *El gigante sureño* – Fania
1979	*Al ver sus campos*	Ray Barretto: *Rican-Struction* – Fania
1979	*Mi bajo y yo*	Oscar d'León: *El más grande* – Trébol
1979	*Fiesta de tambores*	Típica 73: *Intercambio cultural* – Fania
1980	*Ublabadú* (vocal: Héctor Lavoe)	Fania All Stars: *Commitment* – Fania
1981	*Se le ve*	Batacumbele: *Con un poco de songo* – CMT
1982	*El bohemio*	Luis Perico Ortiz: *Sabroso* – RYQZ
1983	*Fuiste tú*	Mulenze: *Otra vez* – Proyecciones DC
1988	*Bamboleo* (vocal: Celia Cruz)	Fania All Stars: *Bamboleo* – Fania
1991	*Llora timbero*	Conjunto Libre: *Ritmo sonido y estilo* – Montuno Records
1995	*Se me sigue olvidando*	Marc Anthony: *Todo a su tiempo* – Soho Sounds
1997	*Que se lo lleve el río*	Gilberto Santa Rosa: *De corazón* – Sony U.S. Latin
2008	*Ten cuida'o*	José Lugo Orchestra (vocal: Victor Manuelle): *Guasábara* – BMG
2010	*Como baila mi mulata*	Spanish Harlem Orchestra: *Viva la tradición* – Concord Picante
2011	*Canela bella*	Mambo Legends Orchestra: *Ten cuida'o* – Zoho

Further Reading on Salsa

There are many resources, in print and on the internet, for further study on salsa. My top book recommendations are *Salsa!* by Charlie Gerard and Marty Sheller and *Mambo Kingdom* by Max Salazar. Another fantastic resource is the descarga.com website. Click on "Meet the Writers" in the left column. If you work through that section patiently, you'll find *at least* a book's worth of excellent history, analysis and interviews. The liner notes of the Fania reissue series are also very good. There are also many excellent documentaries such as *Latin Music USA* from PBS.

Cuba in the 1960s

highlighted track: *Nace en Cuba el Mozambique* (1965)
Pello el Afrokán: *Nace en Cuba el Mozambique* – Orfeon

time	tempo	comments
0:00	111	intro: layered percussion entries
0:18		cuerpo A
0:31		cuerpo B
0:57		cuerpo A
1:10		cuerpo B
1:36		coro 1: alternating with percussion
2:40		bloque
2:50	113	coro 2: alternating with percussion
3:17		coda: percussion

Cuba produced even fewer recordings in the 1960s than in the 1930s and most are even harder to find. The decade did, however, produce more than its share of new rhythms and genres. *Changüí-68* and *songo* are discussed in the next section and *mozambique, pilón, simalé* and *upa-upa* are covered in great detail by Calixto Oviedo in Volume 2 of *Beyond Salsa Percussion*, and from a keyboard perspective in Volume 3 of *Beyond Salsa Piano*.

Further Listening Recommendations for 1960s Cuba

Year	Song	Source
1964	*María caracoles*	Pello el Afrokán: *Nace en Cuba el mozambique* – Orfeon
1964	*Tú no sabes de amor (guasón)*	Pacho Alonso: *Yo no quiero piedra en mi camino* – EGREM
1965	*Rico pilón*	Pacho Alonso: *Rico pilón* – Areíto (vinyl)
1965	*La pianola de Manola*	Pacho Alonso: *Rico pilón* – Areíto (vinyl)
1965	*El pilón de María Cristina*	Pacho Alonso: *Rico pilón* – Areíto (vinyl)
1968	*Te lo ganaste*	Orquesta Revé – Areíto (vinyl)
1971	*Simalé a lo Bonne*	Pacho Alonso y sus Pachucos – Areíto (vinyl)
1974	*No me critiques*	Pacho Alonso: *Upa upa* – Produfon

Los Van Van (songo era)

highlighted track: *Ponte para las cosas* (c. 1972)– Los Van Van: *Colección, Vol. 2* – EGREM

time	tempo	comments
0:00	109	cuerpo A1: (vocals with only strings and percussion)
0:24		cuerpo A2: (full rhythm section)
0:46		cuerpo B
1:01		cuerpo A3
1:21	112	montuno section: (coro with only percussion)
1:32		add string counter theme
1:46	114	add keyboard counter theme
1:58		add bass
2:18		coro with percussion and orchestrated punches
2:32	115	flute solo with coro ... fades

Juan Formell made his first big impact on the Cuban music scene as Orquesta Revé's musical director in 1968, creating a quirky, rock-influenced genre he called *changüí-68*. In 1969, Formell left to form Los Van Van, taking most of the band with him, including pianist César "Pupy" Pedroso. The first Los Van Van album was in a similar style, but now Formell called it *songo,* possibly named after a small town between Guantánamo and Santiago de Cuba. In 1970, the original drummer, Blas Egües (brother of flutist Richard Egües of Aragón) was replaced by José Luis "Changuito" Quintana, whose pivotal innovations we'll encounter with great regularity over the course of these books.

By the time Los Van Van returned to the studio – with a series of game-changing singles beginning around 1970 – they were no longer imitating rock, or even "fusing" it with Cuban music. They had cracked the code and created an entirely original genre, full of pop masterpieces like *Ponte para las cosas, Chirrín chirrán, Pero a mi manera* and *La candela.* Los Van Van has continued unabated at the top of the Cuban music scene ever since, changing and adapting each year and never resting on their laurels or becoming a heritage act. It's rare enough for a pop music artist who's achieved fame and creative success at the age of 20 to continue producing new hits and innovations well into middle age and beyond, but Van Van had three such figures in Formell, Changuito and Pupy Pedroso. In 2001, Changuito helped Pupy create a new band, Los Que Son Son, with a strikingly innovative rhythmic style quite different from Van Van's. In 2012, both bands remain dominant forces in the competitive Havana music scene. We'll cover the current Los Van Van and Los Que Son Son in Listening Tour 3, but there's still much to be said about the original songo era group.

As lyricists, Formell and Pedroso have always seen themselves as "social chroniclers", writing in a candid, genuine and unglorified way about the everyday lives of everyday people in Cuba. Their songs, laced with humor, irony and double entendre, introduce a huge ensemble cast of colorful characters from the various neighborhoods of Havana, as well as the more remote provinces, facing all the strange and unique joys and problems of life in the constantly changing, topsy-turvy world of post-revolutionary Cuba.

From a musical point of view, Van Van created its own revolution in terms of harmony, rhythm, and form. Listen again to *Ponte para las cosas.* Many previously universal elements of Cuban popular music are absent – there are no bells, timbales, bongó, or call and response vocals. Conversely, many previously unheard-of elements are added: snare drum, kick drum, hihat and electric keyboards. Large sections have no piano tumbao and many other Van Van songs from this era have no piano tumbao at all. The bass drops out in several places, a powerful effect that didn't happen with regularity in Latin music until the timba era. There's a conga marcha, but it's not one that anyone had ever used prior to 1969. Formell borrowed harmonies from The Beatles and other rock artists (and invented many of his own) that no previous Latin dance music songwriter would have dreamed of using. As important as the music itself was the fact that Los Van Van broke all the rules and shattered all the norms, leaving the field wide open for future generations (and future incarnations of Van Van itself) to put the pieces back together in a variety of interesting ways.

Further Listening Recommendations for Los Van Van (songo era)

Year	Song	Source
1969	La lucha	La Colección, Vol. 1 – EGREM
c. 1972	Aquí se enciende la candela	Colección Havana Club – EGREM
c. 1972	Pero a mi manera	La Colección, Vol. 2 – EGREM
1974	Chirrín chirrán	La Colección, Vol. 2 – EGREM
1974	Uno solo fuerte	La Colección, Vol. 2 – EGREM
1974	Llegué llegué (Güararey)	La Colección, Vol. 3 – EGREM
1974	A ver que sale	La Colección, Vol. 3 – EGREM
1974	Y no le conviene	La Colección, Vol. 3 – EGREM
1975	Te traigo	La Colección, Vol. 4 – EGREM
1975	Dale dos	La Colección, Vol. 4 – EGREM
1975	Mi son entero	La Colección, Vol. 4 – EGREM
1975	Por qué lo haces	La Colección, Vol. 4 – EGREM
1979	Con el bate de aluminio	La Colección, Vol. 5 – EGREM
1979	Tal como empezó	La Colección, Vol. 5 – EGREM
1979	Si a una mamita	La Colección, Vol. 5 – EGREM

In the 1980s, Changuito switched from drumset to timbales (with kick drum), a trombone section was added, and many traditional elements of Latin dance music were reintroduced, although the group continued to introduce new elements and new influences from non-Cuban music. Van Van put out an album every year of the 1980s and was more popular than ever, as evidenced by the following list of well-known classic hits (and lesser-known treasures). The music of this period – and Pupy Pedroso's unique piano style – are covered in great detail in Volumes 10 and 11 of *Beyond Salsa Piano*.

Further Listening Recommendations for Los Van Van (1980s)

Year	Song	Source
1980	*Tú tranquilo*	*La Colección, Vol. 6* – EGREM
1980	*De la Habana a Matanzas*	*La Colección, Vol. 6* – EGREM
1982	*Somos Los Van Van*	*La Colección, Vol. 7* – EGREM
1982	*Hoy se cumplen seis semanas*	*La Colección, Vol. 7* – EGREM
1983	*Por encima del nivel (Sandunguera)*	*La Colección, Vol. 8* – EGREM
1983	*Qué palo es ese*	*La Colección, Vol. 8* – EGREM
1983	*Después que te casaste*	*La Colección, Vol. 8* – EGREM
1984	*Será que se acabó*	*La Colección, Vol. 9* – EGREM
1984	*La Habana no aguanta más*	*La Colección, Vol. 9* – EGREM
1985	*La duda de Belén*	*La Colección, Vol. 10* – EGREM
1985	*Quien bien te quiere te hará llorar*	*La Colección, Vol. 10* – EGREM
1985	*El buenagente*	*La Colección, Vol. 10* – EGREM
1985	*Se muere la tía*	*La Colección, Vol. 10* – EGREM
1986	*No es fácil, que no que no*	*La Colección, Vol. 11* – EGREM
1986	*Si quiere que llegue pronto*	*La Colección, Vol. 11* – EGREM
1987	*La titimanía*	*La Colección, Vol. 12* – EGREM
1988	*Me gusta y no puede ser*	*La Colección, Vol. 13* – EGREM
1988	*El negro no tiene na'*	*La Colección, Vol. 13* – EGREM
1988	*Se acabó el querer*	*La Colección, Vol. 13* – EGREM
1989	*Yo sé que Van Van*	*La Colección, Vol. 14* – EGREM
1989	*No soy de La Gran Escena*	*La Colección, Vol. 14* – EGREM
1989	*Tranquilo, Mota*	*La Colección, Vol. 14* – EGREM
1990	*Aquí el que baila gana*	*La Colección, Vol. 15* – EGREM
1990	*Esto está bueno*	*La Colección, Vol. 15* – EGREM
1990	*Me basta con pensar*	*La Colección, Vol. 15* – EGREM
1990	*Deja la bobería*	*La Colección, Vol. 15* – EGREM
1990	*Mis dudas*	*La Colección, Vol. 15* – EGREM
1990	*Se acabó la tristeza*	*La Colección, Vol. 15* – EGREM

Irakere and other Modernized Jazzbands

highlighted track: *Bacalao con pan* (1974) – Irakere: *Bacalao con pan* – Escondida

time	tempo	comments
0:00	114	introduction
0:16	115	cuerpo A (electric guitar)
0:51	116	cuerpo B (vocal, then horns)
1:49	121	piano tumbao with efectos but no bass or congas – This was a singular, song-specific stroke of arranging inspiration that years later would become a critical part of timba arranging – *presión* gear.
1:57		montuno section: coro and lead vocal
2:13		mambo 1
2:29		percussion breakdown
2:45		bloque
2:49		coro with trumpet solo
3:06	123	mambo 2; fade to end

Irakere's repertoire was an eclectic mix of styles, each style an eclectic mix of genres. The excellent DVD, *Irakere: Latin Jazz Founders,* is full of candid interviews in which leader Chucho Valdés and his team of virtuosi explain that their passion was to fuse Afro-Cuban folkloric music with modern jazz and classical influences, a pursuit that they financed with periodic ventures into dance music. Intent notwithstanding, many of their dance tracks were quite brilliant in their own right and still sound fresh and vibrant today – especially *Bacalao con pan, Santiaguera* and *Rucu-rucu in Santa Clara.*

Our highlighted track, *Bacalao con pan,* is based on a rhythm Irakere called *batumbatá,* invented largely by their founding conguero Lázaro "Tato" Alfonso. Tato mounted a cowbell on one conga, playing the bell and conga with a stick while playing a second conga barehanded. Not expecting Irakere's experimental approach to catch on, Tato (who was much better at inventing rhythms than predicting commercial success) moved on to seek more gainful employment after the first Irakere album, passing his job on to his brother, the late Jorge "El Niño" Alfonso. El Niño was followed by two other legendary congueros: the late Miguel "Angá" Díaz and Andrés "El Negrón" Miranda, the latter now touring regularly with Wil Campa y su Gran Unión.

A particularly prescient part of the *Bacalao con pan* arrangement occurs at 1:49, where the bass, congas and bell drop out to expose a catchy, song-specific piano tumbao, further intensified by rhythmic breaks *(efectos)*. Los Van Van had a similar passage around the same time in *Aquí se enciende la candela,* but strangely, no other bands, including Irakere or Van Van, made regular use this incredibly effective device for another 15 years, at which time it became standard practice as the timba "gear" that we call *presión* – that *"manos pa' arriba"* moment of euphoric rhythmic release that's so central to timba dancing and the timba experience in general. (See Listening Tour 3 for more on this subject.)

Many of Cuba's greatest virtuosi have passed through Irakere, among them Carlos d'Puerto, Enrique Pla, Alain Pérez, Oscar Valdés, Andrés "El Negrón" Miranda, Arturo Sandoval, Paquito d'Rivera, José Miguel, Germán Velazco, Orlando "Maraca" Valle, Elpidio Chappottín (son of the famous son montuno trumpeter) and José Luis "El Tosco" Cortés, who would later form the first timba band, NG La Banda, around a nucleus of ex-Irakere horn players.

Most notable among the many modernized jazzbands that followed in Irakere's wake were *Grupo AfroCuba, Opus 13,* and *Orquesta 440.*

Further Listening Recommendations for Modernized Jazzbands

Year	Song	Source
1974	*Quindiambo*	Irakere: *La colección, Vol. 1* – EGREM
1977	*Xiomara*	Irakere: *La colección, Vol. 3* – EGREM
1977	*Juana 1600*	Irakere: *La colección, Vol. 3* – EGREM
1980	*Si pregunta por mí dile que vuelvo*	Grupo AfroCuba: *Smooth Jazz Moods* – RMM
1980	*Qué sensación cuando la ví*	Grupo AfroCuba: *Smooth Jazz Moods* – RMM
1981	*Ese atrevimiento*	Irakere: *La colección, Vol. 5* – EGREM
1985	*Rucu rucu a Santa Clara*	Irakere: *Bacalao con pan* – Escondida
1986	*Santiaguera*	Irakere: *Bacalao con pan* – Escondida
1988	*Ven sígueme*	Orquesta 440: *Ven sígueme* – RMM
1985	*Oiga usted señora*	Opus 13: *Que llueva de una vez* – vinyl – Areíto
1987	*Tú no eres el mejor (solo: Angá)*	Opus 13: *Merengue y quilo* – vinyl – Areíto
1991	*La dama del son (bongó: Carlos Caro)*	Opus 13 with Jacqueline Castellanos: *Sólo vivo por ti* – EGREM
1991	*Tú no me calculas*	Opus 13 with Paulito FG: *Reclamo tu cuerpo* – RMM
1992	*Acontecer*	Grupo AfroCuba: *Acontecer* – Discmedi Records

Suggested Viewing: Malanga Films: *Irakere – Latin Jazz Founders*

This is the definitive Irakere history including extensive subtitled interviews with all the major members and lots of great performance footage.

Ritmo Oriental and other Modernized Charangas

highlighted track: *Baila si vas a bailar* (1987) – Ritmo Oriental: *La historia de la Ritmo, Vol. 2* – QBADisc

time	tempo	comments
0:00	110	intro: flute and strings
0:17	*	efecto (*Ritmo Oriental was famous for stretching the tempo during efectos)
0:19	111	cuerpo
0:35		piano solo
0:44		efecto
0:45	116	coro 1:
1:01		efecto
1:03	115	flute interlude
1:07		efecto
1:11		drum/timbal solo
1:31		efecto
1:33		coro 2: with congas but no bass tumbao *(i.e., masacote)*
1:42	117	coro 2 continues with normal accompaniment
2:23	118	flute solo
2:38		efecto
2:43	120	coro 3:
3:15		flute solo
3:27	124	coro 4: breakdown with congas but no bass tumbao *(i.e., masacote)*
3:42		efecto
3:47		coro 4 with flute solo
4:06		coro 2
4:18		efecto
4:23		coda: masacote breakdown with a cappella coro, efecto

Van Van and Irakere were proactive musical revolutionaries, consciously dismantling tradition and replacing it with a plethora of bold, new experimental ideas, some of which have stood the test of time better than others. Ritmo Oriental's revolution was more subtle, more insidious, and more organically Cuban. The resulting musical style was every bit as original, but they arrived at it by working more within the system, starting as a pure 1950s charanga and gradually morphing into one of the most unique and consistently brilliant pop groups of all time. The masterpieces they churned out steadily between 1974 and 1987 sound as fresh and timeless today as those of Arsenio Rodríguez and the original Muñequitos de Matanzas.

Ritmo Oriental, or *La Ritmo,* began as a spinoff from Revé in 1958 and played traditional charanga until about 1970 when their incredibly creative style began to emerge. If you're wondering, as I did, why it's "la" Ritmo even though Ritmo ends with "o", it's short for "La Orquesta Ritmo Oriental", as is the case with "La Revé". Similarly, it's "la foto" because "foto" is short for "fotografía". (See Appendix 2 for more remedial Spanish tips.)

La Ritmo's Percussion Section

Daniel Díaz's percussion setup – photos by Will Douglas

Among life's great mysteries, we have:

"Is there a God?"

"Is there life on other planets?"

"What exactly is drummer Daniel Díaz playing on all those early Ritmo Oriental records?"

And not necessarily in that order. The rhythm section mix on the critical 1970s Ritmo Oriental recordings accentuates leader Enrique Lazaga's güiro, the congas of Juan Claro Bravo, and a pair of hand held claves played by one of the singers. Buried in the mix is one of Cuba's most innovative drummers, Daniel Díaz, who passed away in the 1990s and was never adequately captured on video. Played from a seated position, his kit includes three timbales (two normal and one extra low), two toms (one low enough to almost sound like a kick drum), a very frequently used snare and six assorted bells, plus a seventh bell played with a foot pedal, using a felt mallet, making it still harder to pick it out of the mix. The bells are easier to hear on some 1980s tracks but his style had also changed by that point. The details of Díaz's 1970s style, like the non-solo piano parts on Arsenio's early mono recordings, remain high on my research list if and when time travel becomes available.

Elsewhere in this book we discuss the highly improvisational styles of Los Que Son Son drummer Bombón Reyes and Manolín's conguero Alexis "Mipa" Cuesta. In each case, other members of the rhythm section play relatively stable parts to enable these players to play in a state of constant controlled improvisation (studied in great detail in the later volumes of this series). With Díaz and Ritmo Oriental, the contrast is at least as extreme, with snare, ghost snare, and all manner of bells and toms glistening through the fabric of the music in a myriad of unpredictable, but always musically sublime ways.

For further study, I've written a long history and discography of Ritmo Oriental on timba.com with many audio clips and transcriptions. La Ritmo is also featured prominently in my free online book, *The Roots of Timba,* also on timba.com. There's also a very long interview with Enrique Lazaga.

Ritmo Oriental's music and success inspired a new wave of modernized charangas in the late 1970s and 1980s, including Maravilla de Florida, Orquesta Aliamén, Original de Manzanillo, Unión Sanluisera and Orquesta Típica Juventud. Even Orquesta Aragón caught the modernized charanga fever in the late 70s with their two excellent *cha-onda* releases. If you like Ritmo Oriental, all of these other groups are worth seeking out as well. Much more historical and discographical detail on all of them can be found in the timbapedia section of timba.com.

For timba fans learning about the roots of their favorite genre, it's interesting how many famous timberos got their starts with the bands covered in this listening tour. Here's a very abridged list:

1980s Band	Artist	Instrument	Timba Band
Ritmo Oriental	Tony Calá	voice	NG La Banda
Ritmo Oriental	David Calzado	violin, composer	Charanga Habanera
Maravilla de Florida	Manolito Simonet	piano, composer	Manolito y su Trabuco
Irakere	José Luis "El Tosco" Cortés	flute, composer	NG La Banda
Irakere	Germán Velazco	sax	NG La Banda
Irakere	Elpidio Chappottín	trumpet	NG La Banda
Irakere	José "El Greco" Crego	trumpet	NG La Banda
Irakere	Carlos Averhoff, Sr.	sax	NG La Banda, Issac Delgado
Orquesta Aliamén	Sixto "El Indio" Llorente	voice	Manolito y su Trabuco
Pachito Alonso	Issac Delgado	voice, composer	NG La Banda
Opus 13	Paulito FG	voice, composer	Paulito FG y su Élite
Opus 13	Juan Ceruto	sax, arranger	Paulito FG, etc.
Opus 13	Joaquín Betancourt	arranger	Issac Delgado, etc.
Adalberto Álvarez	Calixto Oviedo	drums	NG La Banda
Adalberto Álvarez	Hugo Morejón	trombone, arranger	Los Van Van
Elio Revé y su Charangón	Juan Carlos Alfonso	piano, composer	Dan Den

Further Suggested Listening for Ritmo Oriental

Year	Song	Source
c. 1970	*Sabroseao con la Ritmo*	(vinyl only)
1974	*Mi socio Manolo*	*La historia de la Ritmo, Vol. 1* – QBADisc
1974	*Adiós no estoy loco*	*La historia de la Ritmo, Vol. 1* – QBADisc
1975	*Yo bailo de todo*	*La historia de la Ritmo, Vol. 1* – QBADisc
1975	*La chica Mamey*	*La historia de la Ritmo, Vol. 1* – QBADisc
1975	*Ahora sí, voy a gozar*	*La historia de la Ritmo, Vol. 1* – QBADisc
1975	*Y se baila así*	*La historia de la Ritmo, Vol. 1* – QBADisc
1975	*Un matrimonio feliz*	*La historia de la Ritmo, Vol. 1* – QBADisc
1977	*La ritmo suena a Areíto*	*La Ritmo Oriental te está llamando* – Globe Style
1977	*Qué rico bailo yo*	*La Ritmo Oriental te está llamando* – Globe Style
1977	*El son Claro*	*Cuba Gold 4* – QBADisc
1977	*Al que le tocó le tocó*	*Cuba Gold 4* – QBADisc
1978	*Maritza*	*La Ritmo Oriental te está llamando* – Globe Style
1978	*Nena, así no se vale*	*La Ritmo Oriental te está llamando* – Globe Style
1978	*Tiene nivel*	*La historia de la Ritmo, Vol. 2* – QBADisc
1981	*Cuida'o con la percusión*	*Cuba Gold 2* – QBADisc
1983	*Barrios de rumberos*	*La historia de la Ritmo, Vol. 2* – QBADisc
1983	*El agua no me llevó*	*La historia de la Ritmo, Vol. 2* – QBADisc
1983	*Conmigo candela brava*	*La historia de la Ritmo, Vol. 2* – QBADisc
1985	*Baila azúcar*	*Guarachando* – ARTEX
1987	*Azúcar a granel*	*La historia de la Ritmo, Vol. 2* – QBADisc
1987	*Bailadores*	*La historia de la Ritmo, Vol. 2* – QBADisc

Further Suggested Listening for Other Modernized Charangas

Year	Song	Source
1975	*Operación sitio*	Típica Juventud: *Presencia cubana* (vinyl) – Areíto
1979	*Baila güiro son wambarí*	Maravilla de Florida: (self-titled vinyl) – Areíto
1980	*Oiga como suena el son, compay*	Orquesta Aliamén: *La cumbancha* – Salsa Center
1980	*Traigo un tumbaíto sabroso*	Orquesta Aliamén: *La cumbancha* – Salsa Center
1982	*Mi decisión no cambiará*	Típica Juventud: *Mi orquesta sigue igual* (vinyl) – Areíto
1983	*Apártate que te piso*	Unión Sanluisera: *Un meneíto sabroso* – (vinyl) – Siboney
1986	*Oye bien guagüero*	Maravilla de Florida: *Puros como el son cubano* (vinyl) – Areíto
1988	*Tembló la calle*	Orquesta Aliamén: *Haciendo bailar al pueblo* – (vinyl) – Areíto
1990	*Un compositor confundido*	Maravilla de Florida – *El agua coge su nivel* – Salsa Center
1992	*A la hora que me llamen voy*	Original de Manzanillo: *A la hora que me llamen voy* – (vinyl) – Areíto

Modernized Conjuntos

highlighted track: *Bayamo en coche* **(1979) – Son 14:** *Grandes éxitos* **– EGREM**

time	tempo	comments
0:00		spoken intro
0:25	120-125	a cappella coro 1 with vocal and clapping guaguancó
1:10	118	horn intro
1:19		cuerpo A
1:37	115	cuerpo B
2:02	118	horn bridge
2:09	121	coro 1
2:48	125	mambo 1
2:54	128	coro 2
3:13		mambo 2
3:27		coro 3
3:58		mambo 3
4:09	135	coro 4 with muela (singer talks to virtual audience)
4:58		mambo 4
5:21		coro 4 to coda

The bongó- and trumpet-driven conjunto format experienced a revival in the 1980s. Juan d'Marcos captured the imagination of the younger generation with Sierra Maestra, a group of young, conservatory-trained musicians who began by playing faithful transcriptions of Septeto Nacional and Arsenio Rodríguez before branching out into original material. After leaving Sierra Maestra, d'Marcos repeated his success on a global level as the musical director of the phenomenally popular *Buena Vista Social Club* project. He now tours regularly with the Afro-Cuban All Stars.

Rumbavana and Son 14 modernized their conjuntos with creative arrangements that expanded the harmonic palette, arsenal of rhythms, and tempo range. In 1984, pianist/composer Adalberto Álvarez broke away from Son 14 to form Adalberto Álvarez y su Son, adding trombones and drummer/timbalero Calixto Oviedo (subject of Volumes 2 and 3 of *Beyond Salsa Percussion).*

Further Listening Recommendations for Modernized Conjuntos

Year	Song	Source
1979	*Agua que cae del cielo*	Son 14: *Grandes éxitos* – BIS
1980	*El son del campeón*	Rumbavana: *Conjunto Rumbavana* – Areíto (vinyl)
1980	*Negro de sociedad*	Rumbavana: *Conjunto Rumbavana* – Areíto (vinyl)
1981	*Juana Peña*	Sierra Maestra: *El guanajo relleno* – Prodisc Records
1983	*El son de la madrugada*	Son 14: *Grandes éxitos* – BIS
1983	*Que baile sola el son*	Rumbavana: *Déjala que baile sola* – Vitral
1983	*En el casa de Pedro el Cojo*	Rumbavana: *Déjala que baile sola* – Vitral
1985	*Esperando que vuelva María*	Adalberto Álvarez y su Son: *Grandes éxitos* – EGREM
1986	*El regreso de María*	Adalberto Álvarez y su Son: *Grandes éxitos* – EGREM
1986	*Oye la rumba está buena*	Rumbavana: *30 aniversario* – Siboney (vinyl)
1987	*Cántalo pero baílalo*	Adalberto Álvarez y su Son: *Grandes éxitos* – EGREM
1988	*Si me habían de ti, tío*	Rumbavana: *De nuevo con Rumbavana* – Siboney (vinyl)
1990	*Si la guagua está llena*	Adalberto Álvarez y su Son: *Grandes éxitos* – EGREM
1993	*Y qué tú quieres que te den*	Adalberto Álvarez y su Son: *Grandes éxitos* – EGREM
1999	*Si no vas a cocinar*	Adalberto Álvarez y su Son: *Jugando con candela* – Havana Caliente

El regreso de María – the 1986 vinyl release of Adalberto Álvarez y su Son
(Calixto Oviedo is in white beret at lower right of bus window)

Elio Revé y su Charangón

highlighted track: *Changüí clave* (1987) – Elio Revé y su Charangón: *Volume 2* – BIS

time	tempo	comments
0:00	96	intro: coro 1, a cappella, with unison interjections by band
0:15		guaguancó with orchestration and improvisations by bass and tres
1:47	111	intro reprise
2:07	117	montuno (coro 1)
2:27	118	trombone mambo 1
2:40		coro 1
2:55	119	trombone mambo 2
3:11	109	intro reprise
3:16	112	coro 2 in 12/8 with batás
3:51	121	coro 2 in 4/4
4:07		efecto
4:26		muela section (band drops down for lead singer to talk, as if to crowd – notice the interlocking piano and tres tumbaos)
4:43	123	coro 2 – normal marcha gear (at 5:00, listen for Elio Revé's signature vocal interjection)
5:02		trombone mambo 3 (into coda)

As detailed in the changüí section of Listening Tour 4, the Revé group, in its many incarnations, has stayed in top tier of the Cuban music scene for over half a century. The 2012 group may be the strongest yet from a purely musical standpoint, but in terms of game-changing innovations, the two 1980s groups were arguably the most important. It was at this point that Revé introduced the *charangón* format, beginning with a charanga instrumentation, then adding tres and bongó from changüí, quinto and batá from folkloric music and a trombone section for good measure.

Elio Revé's skill as a talent scout is the stuff of legends. Among the groups formed by departing Revé musicians are Ritmo Oriental (1958), Los Van Van (1969), Grupo Layé and Orquesta 440 (1970s), and Dan Den (1988). Individual ex-Revé musicians include Chucho Valdés, Yumurí and Félix Baloy.

Revé's first charangón group recorded only one album – *Elio Revé y su ritmo changüí* (1980) – a masterpiece that was inexplicably never reissued on CD – even in Cuba. It's one of the most important albums of the era and well worth seeking out. The key arrangements were by pianist Ignacio Herrera (father of current Latin jazz star Nachito Herrera), and the singer was the great Félix Baloy who subsequently gained great fame with Adalberto Álvarez and still later with the Afro-Cuban All Stars. Several black and white television clips of this group can be found on YouTube.

The second charangón (c. 1984-1988), directed by pianist Juan Carlos Alfonso, featured three great vocalists: Héctor Valentín, Ricardo "Alfonsito" Alfonso and William "El Padrino" Esquivel.

In the late 1980s, only Los Van Van was as popular in Cuba as Elio Revé y su Charangón so there was a great uproar when Juan Carlos Alfonso broke away to form Dan Den, taking, among others, two of the lead singers (Valentín and Alfonsito). Dan Den was a great success, but Revé was undaunted, and quickly assembled his third great charangón, releasing the big hit *Suave suave*, with lyrics addressing the breakup, and then perhaps the biggest hit of his career, *Mi salsa tiene sandunga*, used as the theme song for Cuban television's best and classiest music program, *Mi Salsa*. Some of the best live Cuban video comes from this long-running show, which, *gracias a Dios*, never resorted to lip-synching, a practice that has marred so much music on television in Cuba and elsewhere.

This third great charangón (c. 1988-1993) added musical director/pianist Tony Gómez, retained El Padrino, and added two new singers of the highest calibre in Yumurí Valle and Juan Miguel "El Indio" Díaz (one of many great musicians with that nickname, among them Sixto "El Indio" Llorente of Orquesta Aliamén and Manolito y su Trabuco).

Elio Revé died tragically in a traffic accident while on tour in 1997 and the group was inherited by his son Elito, who has taken them to new heights in the timba era (see Listening Tours 3 and 4).

Further Listening Recommendations for Elio Revé y su Charangón

Year	Song	Source
1980	*Negra con pelo*	*Elio Revé y su ritmo changüí* – Siboney (vinyl)
1980	*Oyan coro*	*Elio Revé y su ritmo changüí* – Siboney (vinyl)
1980	*Vamos a Artemisa*	*Elio Revé y su ritmo changüí* – Siboney (vinyl)
1980	*Manye pa' Catalina*	*Elio Revé y su ritmo changüí* – Siboney (vinyl)
1985	*Rumberos latinoamericanos*	*Elio Revé y su charangón – Vol. 2* – BIS
1985	*Yo sé que tú sabes que yo sé*	*Rumberos latinoamericanos* – Disques DOM
1985	*Changüí campanero*	*Elio Revé y su charangón – Vol. 2* – BIS
1987	*No me cojan para eso*	*Rumberos latinoamericanos* – Disques DOM
1988	*La gente no se puede aguantar*	*La explosión del momento* – Realworld
1988	*Más viejo que ayer, más joven que mañana*	*La explosión del momento* – Realworld
1990	*Suave suave*	*Elio Revé y su charangón – Vol. 1* – BIS
1991	*Mi salsa tiene sandunga*	*Elio Revé y su charangón – Vol. 1* – BIS
1991	*El Ibiano*	*Elio Revé y su charangón – Vol. 1* – BIS

Rhythm Exercises 2: Two-Beat Rhythmic Cells

In this section we'll learn the most common rhythmic cells that repeat after only two beats. If you look carefully at each exercise, you'll see that the first half is identical to the second half. So why don't we just show the first half? The reason is that these two-beat cells are always used in combination with other instruments that are playing clave-aligned, four-beat cells, such as *cáscara*, *contracampaneo* and of course *clave* itself. So, we'll learn the two-beat cells against the same four-beat grid we introduced in the Rhythm Exercises 1 section.

Jorge Luis Guerra of Manolito y su Trabuco is the most electrifying güirero I've ever heard.
photo by Tom Ehrlich – San Francisco – 2010

Exercise 2-1 is probably the most common time-keeping figure in Latin music. It's the primary pattern for the *güiro* (the sound used on the audio track), and it's also commonly used for the hand bell (aka, *campana, "bongo bell")*, and the hihat of the drumset. When used on hihat and bell, it's usually altered to "mark the clave", turning it into a four-beat cell (see Exercises 3-13 through 3-16). Shown in Exercise 2-1 in its purest form, it's actually only a one-beat cell.

Exercise 2-1: güiro time-keeping pattern • Audio Tracks 2-1a-d

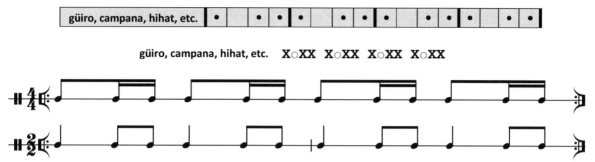

Exercise 2-2 is commonly called *tresillo.* It creates the feeling of "three-over-two" but the durations have to be "squared off" to fit into eight subdivisions, with a spacing of 3-3-2.

Exercise 2-2: tresillo • Audio Tracks 2-2a-d

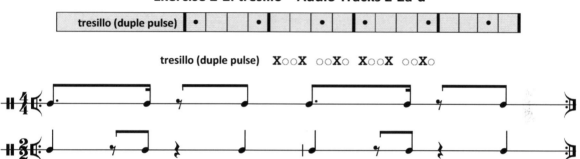

As a looped two-beat cell, tresillo and its close relative cinquillo (Exercise 2-4) are the core rhythmic feel of many genres, such as *makuta, calypso, rumba flamenca, reguetón* and the *masón* section of *tumba francesa*. Tresillo is also half (the "3-side") of the *son clave* rhythm, discussed in the Rhythm Exercises 3 section. We won't cover clave in this section because it lasts four beats before repeating.

tresillo	•			•			•		•			•			•		
3-2 son clave	•			•			•			•		•					

Tresillo also means "triplet" in Spanish, in which case it refers to the following 12/8 cell, with three strokes of equal length, spaced 2-2-2.

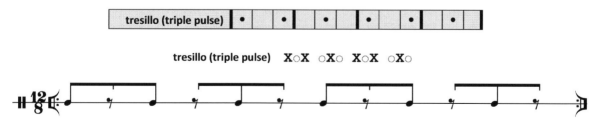

As explained earlier, this "four groups of three" grid is used in more than half of the rhythms of Afro-Cuban folkloric music (See Listening Tour 4), but almost never in Latin popular music.

Exercise 2-3 uses the same sequence of durations as tresillo but is "displaced" so that it starts on beats 2 and 4 instead of beats 1 and 3. If you start on the shaded subdivisions, you'll hear that it's the same rhythm as Exercise 2-2, starting in a different place.

Exercise 2-3: displaced tresillo • Audio Tracks 2-3a-d

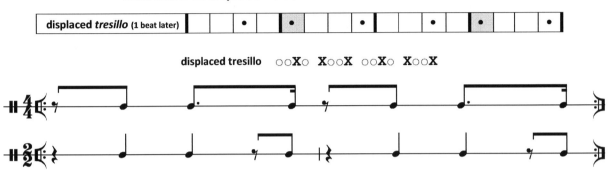

There are eight different ways that tresillo (or any other two-beat rhythm) can be displaced, but Exercise 2-3 is particularly fascinating because it outlines the rhythm of the 2-side of clave while normal, non-displaced tresillo (Exercise 2-2) outlines the rhythm of the 3-side.

displaced *tresillo* (1 beat later)			•		•			•				•		•			•
3-2 son clave	•				•			•				•	•					

Displacement is one of the most fascinating aspects of rhythm. The idea is to start playing a recognizable rhythm at a different point in the 16-subdivision cycle. Let's look again at the pattern of tresillo. There are two empty subdivisions between each of the three strokes, and then only one single subdivision (shaded) before the pattern starts again:

tresillo	1			2			3		1			2			3	
displaced tresillo			3		1			2			3		1			2

> **Suggested Reading:** David Peñalosa's *The Clave Matrix* uses a study of these tresillo patterns to generate a wealth of revelations on the origins of the clave rhythm and the relationships between triple pulse (12/8) and duple pulse (4/4) grooves.

Exercise 2-4 is commonly called *cinquillo.* Just as the term *tresillo* can also mean "triplet" (three equally spaced strokes), *cinquillo* can also mean "pentuplet" (five equally spaced strokes). But when "squared off" to fit the four-by-four grid, cinquillo becomes another of the most important rhythms in Latin music.

Exercise 2-4: cinquillo • Audio Tracks 2-4a-d

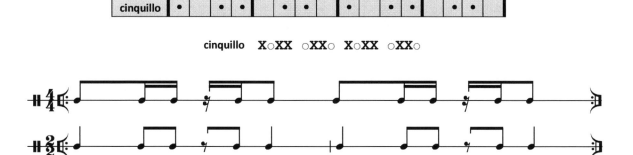

cinquillo **X**○**XX** ○**XX**○ **X**○**XX** ○**XX**○

Cinquillo can be thought of as a decorated version of tresillo.

cinquillo	•		•	•		•	•		•	•		•	•
tresillo	•			•			•			•			•

Here are two great exercises to practice: alternating between tresillo and cinquillo every other time, and playing cinquillo with your right hand while playing tresillo with your left.

Cinquillo also forms half of the clave-aligned *baqueteo* cell we'll study in the next section:

cinquillo	•		•	•		•	•		•		•	•	
baqueteo	•		•	•		•	•		•		•		•

Exercise 2-5 is the main motif of the Puerto Rican rhythm *bomba sicá,* borrowed and reworked by Cuban bands of the early 1990s.

Exercise 2-5: bomba sicá • Audio Tracks 2-5a-d

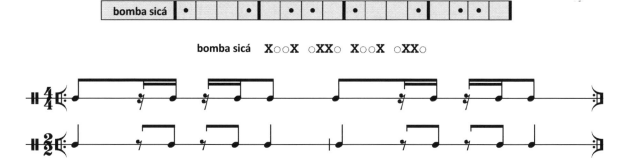

bomba sicá **X**○○**X** ○**XX**○ **X**○○**X** ○**XX**○

Like tresillo, bomba sicá is a subset of cinquillo:

bomba sicá	•			•		•	•		•			•		•	•	
cinquillo	•		•	•		•	•		•		•	•		•	•	

SF Bay Area percussionist José Reyes playing bomba in his native Ponce, Puerto Rico – photo by Bob Krist, bobkrist.com

Exercise 2-6 is a common drum figure in Afro-Cuban folkloric music, a common bass tumbao in various Cuban genres, and by far *the* most common bass tumbao in salsa (a *tumbao* is a syncopated loop or *ostinato*). Exercise 2-6 is sometimes called *bombo-ponche* or given the onomatopoeically-derived name "king-kong".

Exercise 2-6: bombo-ponche • Audio Tracks 2-6a-d

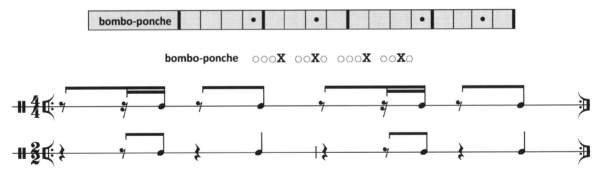

As you can see, bombo-ponche is simply tresillo without the first stroke.

bombo-ponche			•		•				•		•	
tresillo	•		•		•		•		•		•	

If we examine the basic rhythms and a cross-section of recordings, we can see the importance and omnipresence of tresillo and its two syncopated subdivisions, the *bombo* and *ponche*.

In *The Clave Matrix,* Peñalosa takes this a step further and offers the explanation that rhythms like tresillo and bombo-ponche are based on the 12/8 folkloric roots of Cuban music. Let's take a quick look at this fascinating connection.

As explained in the Rhythm Exercises 1 section, and shown below, the rhythmic grid of 12/8 is four groups of three, rather than the four groups of four on which all the popular music rhythms we're learning are based.

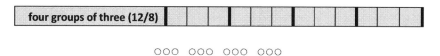

four groups of three (12/8)												

○○○ ○○○ ○○○ ○○○

The next logical layer of syncopation is to play three equally spaced strokes in the space of two beats, which Peñalosa terms the *"secondary beat cycle",* (the *primary beat cycle* consisting of the main beats themselves):

	1	2	3	4	5	6	7	8	9	10	11	12
12/8 primary beat cycle	•			•			•			•		
12/8 secondary beat cycle	•		•		•		•		•		•	

But popular music is in 4/4, or four groups of four, and since there's no way to divide eight or sixteen subdivisions into equal groups of three, the rhythms wind up getting "squared off", using a 3-3-2 spacing. Peñalosa calls the resulting rhythm the *"duple pulse correlative",* i.e., it serves the same essential rhythmic function, but in 4/4 instead of 12/8.

	1	2	3	4	5	6	7	8	9	10	11	12	13	14	15	16
4/4 primary beat cycle	•				•				•				•			
4/4 secondary beat cycle	•			•			•		•			•			•	

This connection becomes even more clear in faster genres such as *guaguancó, rumba columbia* and fast *songo,* played by Cuban musicians with a "swing", or as Spiro calls it, a "fix" (<u>f</u>our + s<u>ix</u>) time feel. In these cases, the 4/4 rhythms are pulled inward toward the triplet subdivisions. At a certain tempo the swing effect is so extreme that it becomes almost impossible to say whether a given performance is in 12/8 or 4/4.

The following chart shows the similarities and differences among the family of rhythms built on the secondary beat cycle concept.

	1	2	3	4	5	6	7	8	9	10	11	12	13	14	15	16
bombo-ponche				•			•				•				•	
tresillo	•			•			•		•						•	
cinquillo	•		•	•		•	•		•		•			•	•	
bomba sicá	•			•		•	•		•					•	•	
				bombo			ponche				bombo				ponche	

Exercise 2-7, *bota,* is a two-beat member of the *songo* family of rhythms created for Los Van Van by José Luis "Changuito" Quintana, one of the most important rhythmic innovators in the history of Cuban popular music. In 1998, the rhythm was adapted by conguero Tomás Cruz, of Paulito FG y su Élite, for use in a type of breakdown, sometimes known as *songo con efectos* (part of what we call the timba *masacote* gear family). It's interesting that both the bombo *and* ponche are absent from the bota cell.

José Luis "Changuito" Quintana with Los Van Van – mid 1980s – Pupy Pedroso on keyboard – photo by Brett Gollin

Exercise 2-7: bota • Audio Tracks 2-7a-d

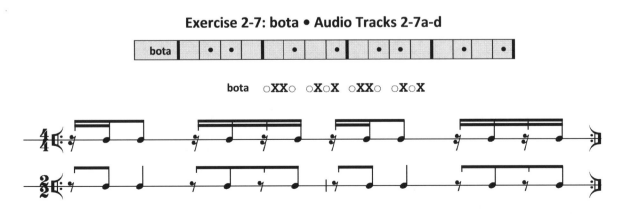

All of these cells are meant to be played as continuous loops and as such don't really have a "beginning" or "end", but there's a tendency to assume that if a cell doesn't include Beat 1 itself, it should start on the first subdivision after "1". However, depending on the musical context, these rhythms often sound more natural if you think of them as beginning on the last subdivision *before* "1" (in this case, on the last stroke shown in the diagram). *Bota* is an example of this – a rhythm that sounds more natural starting on the anticipation of "1". Try accenting the pattern in different ways and see which perceived beginning points sound best to you.

Exercises 2-8 and 2-9 are very simple and of interest primarily for historical reasons and for older-style bass tumbaos, but they generate a very important modern rhythm (Ex. 2-10) when we remove the first stroke, just as we did earlier to get from tresillo (Ex. 2-2) to bombo-ponche (Ex. 2-6).

Exercise 2-8 was the first bass tumbao to come into common usage in Cuban music in the early part of the 20th Century. It's still used for *bolero,* Dominican *bachata* and many other world genres.

Exercise 2-8: bolero bass • Audio Tracks 2-8a-d

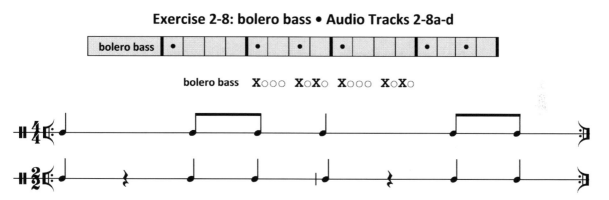

Coincidentally, the bolero bass figure uses the same rhythm as the "on 3" dance step that we'll be learning in the Rhythm Exercises 3 section.

Exercise 2-9, the famous *habanera* rhythmic cell, played a critical role in the Cuban music of the 1800s and early 1900s. It's also a common traditional bass tumbao, e.g., in *El bodeguero,* an early 1950s classic by Orquesta Aragón. The rhythm is also sometimes called *tango.*

Exercise 2-9: habanera • Audio Tracks 2-9a-d

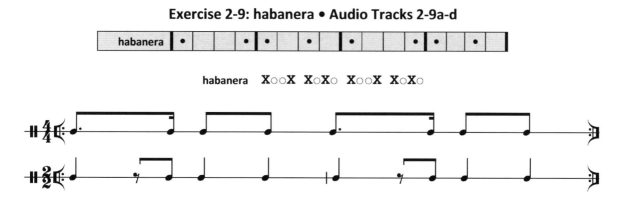

Exercise 2-10 has two important uses in modern Cuban music and deserves its own special name, but I've never been able to find or invent a good one. Its first important use is as a bass tumbao, creating the same anticipated bass effect as bombo-ponche (Exercise 2-6), but with its own very distinct flavor. It's also the most common part for the kick drum during the breakdown sections of Cuban timba.

Exercise 2-10: common bass and kick cell • Audio Tracks 2-10a-d

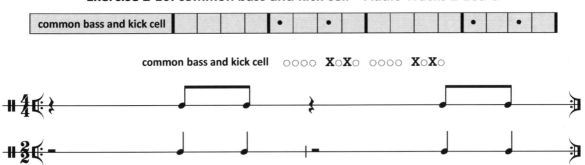

Giraldo Piloto – brilliant composer, ex-drummer of NG La Banda and Issac Delgado, now drummer and leader of Klímax – photo by Chuck Silverman

More on Bass Tumbaos

**Alain Pérez, subject of *Beyond Salsa Bass, Vols. 6-9* – sitting in with Havana d'Primera
drums: Keisel Jiménez, timbales: Güillermo del Toro** – Yoshi's San Francisco – 2012 – photo by Kevin Moore

In the early 1900s, the most common bass tumbao in Cuban popular music was the bolero bass figure (Exercise 2-8). During the *son* explosion of the 1920s, the syncopated tresillo bass tumbao (Exercise 2-2) became more and more common. The next major leap towards more syncopation occurred when bassists started leaving out the first stroke, i.e., using bombo-ponche (Exercise 2-6) for bass tumbaos and later converting Exercise 2-8 to Exercise 2-10 in the same way. In both cases, since the harmony normally changes on the first beat, the new chord was now played on the ponche, creating the wonderful and dramatic effect of the bass anticipating the harmonic change by two full subdivisions and then ringing "over the bar line" as the voice and other instruments caught up with it. For more on the anticipated bass, see Exercise RP-02 and RP-03. The bombo-ponche bass tumbao became very dominant in salsa, but it's only one of several important bass tumbao styles in post-1940 Cuban music, which was also often modeled on the song-specific, clave-aligned "singing bass" tumbaos of Arsenio Rodríguez y su Conjunto.

Suggested Reading: To learn more about the history and influence of these rhythms, see Peter Manuel's *The Anticipated Bass in Cuban Popular Music, From Contradanza to Son*, and *Creolizing Contradance in the Caribbean,* Orlando Fiol's *Transforming The Bass – Phenomenology, Aesthetics and Cultural Identity*, and Robert Fernández's *The Afro-Cuban Folkloric Musical Tradition.* To acquire a panoramic view of Cuba's role in the history of music my top recommendation is Ned Sublette's extraordinary *Cuba and its Music: From the First Drums to the Mambo. Beyond Salsa Bass, Volumes 1-5* (2013) will trace the development of bass tumbaos in detail.

Exercise 2-11 represents the main accents, or "speaking tones", of the simplest and most common conga *marcha* (i.e., accompaniment pattern; sometimes called *tumbao)*. Played with a different time feel, this is also the most common marímbula part in changüí. When used in the standard conga marcha, the conguero plays these strokes with his or her strong hand and fills in the other subdivisions with softer time-keeping strokes (sometimes called *manoteo)*. The hand rocks back and forth between a stroke alternately called *palm, bass* and *heel,* and another stroke alternately called *tip, finger* and sometimes even *toe.* I've yet to find any two books on congas that use the same pair of terms for these, but whatever you *call* them, they're very important because they allow the conguero to churn out all the subdivisions. When the band is playing loudly, the manoteo is partially masked by louder timbres, with the result that what you mostly hear is the slap and open tone pattern notated below, but the conguero and musicians on stage definitely hear and *feel* the subdivisions. Our audio tracks layer in the manoteo part after establishing the speaking strokes.

Exercise 2-11: 2-beat conga marcha cell • Audio Tracks 2-11a-d

2-beat conga marcha cell			S			O	O		S			O	O

2-beat conga marcha cell   ooSo ooOO ooSo ooOO

In the Rhythm Exercises 3 section, we'll learn several ways that the conga marcha was extended to a 4-beat cell. Conga parts became much more varied in the 1970s with the *songo* marchas of Raúl "El Yulo" Cárdenas and Changuito of Los Van Van, Juan "Claro" Bravo of Ritmo Oriental and Lázaro "Tato" Alfonso of Irakere. Then, in the 1990s, the art of the conga marcha experienced another quantum leap forward at the hands of such masters as Juan "Wickly" Nogueras of NG La Banda, Alexis "Mipa" Cuesta of Manolín el Médico de la Salsa, Orlando Mengual of Charanga Habanera, and Tomás Cruz of Paulito FG, the latter pioneering the idea of composing specific marchas for specific songs, often of eight or even sixteen beats in duration.

Afro-Cuban folkloric dance troupe, Raíces Profundas – 2012 – San Francisco – photo by Peter Maiden – maidenfoto.com

Listening Tour 3: Timba

Group	Year	Song	Source
NG La Banda	1994	*Picadillo de soya*	*Simplemente lo mejor de NG La Banda* – BIS
Charanga Habanera	1996	*Nube pasajera*	*Pa' que se entere La Habana* – Caribe
Issac Delgado	1997	*Se te fue la mano*	*Exclusivo para Cuba* – Ciocan
Paulito FG	2000	*Enredadera de amor*	*Una vez más … por amor* – PROMUSIC
Manolín el Médico	1997	*Pegaíto, pegaíto*	*De buena fe* – Metro Blue (Caribe)
Manolito y su Trabuco	2007	*Hablando en serio*	*Hablando en serio* – EGREM
Klímax	1997	*Consejo a una amiga*	*Concierto Eurotropical I* – Eurotropical
Bamboleo	1999	*Ya no hace falta*	*Ya no hace falta* – Ahí Namá
Azúcar Negra	1998	*Te traicionó el subconciente*	*Azúcar Negra* – MP3.com (Havana radio demo)
Los Van Van	1997	*Esto te pone la cabeza mala*	*Te pone la cabeza mala* – Caribe
Los Que Son Son	2004	*De la Timba a Pogolotti*	*Mi timba cerrá* – EGREM
Elito Revé y su Charangón	2005	*Dale agua al dominó*	*Se sigue comentando* – BIS
Havana d'Primera	2009	*Cosas de un amigo*	*Haciendo historia* – Ahí Namá

It's a tempting generalization to say that the timba era began in 1989 with NG La Banda's *En la calle*. It's like saying – as many historians do – that the classical era began in 1750 with the death of J.S. Bach and ended abruptly on the evening of April 7, 1805 when Beethoven's Eroica Symphony was first performed. It's neat and clean and sounds appropriately dramatic, but the reality is that changes in musical styles occur at a somewhat more glacial pace.

NG La Banda, Charanga Habanera, Manolito y su Trabuco, and Paulito FG y su Élite were created by the same musicians who had been experimenting with timba-related musical ideas throughout the 1980s in groups like Ritmo Oriental, Irakere, Opus 13, Maravilla de Florida and Pachito Alonso y su Kini Kini – and many of the innovations now associated with timba didn't fully emerge until well into the 1990s and even in the 2000s, with new groups like Los Que Son Son and Havana d'Primera.

These caveats notwithstanding, "The Cuban Timba Revolution" was a major and far-reaching sea change – musically and culturally. So, what caused it? What changed?

It's hard to find a major musical movement that isn't inextricably linked to non-musical trends and events. Beethoven's incredible reinvention of music was inseparable from the societal changes of his age: The Enlightenment, the French Revolution, the Napoleonic Wars, the decline in influence of churches and monarchies, and the rise of the middle class.

In the case of timba, the immediate external catalyst was the collapse of the Soviet Union and the abrupt end to the massive subsidies it had provided to Cuba's economy, resulting in an economic depression – dubbed "The Special Period" – from which Cuba has yet to fully recover.

The desperate need for cash flow into Cuba resulted in new importance being placed on tourism, leading to major changes in the entertainment industry and major financial incentives for musicians, along with significant reductions in censorship and other types of governmental interference. A wild nightclub scene emerged, centered around venues like El Palacio de la Salsa in the Hotel Riviera.

Meanwhile, the Soviet-style conservatory system was entering its fourth decade and turning out hundreds of highly trained young virtuosi to compete fiercely in the suddenly lucrative music scene. Attempts by the government to discourage interest in music from the United States had also subsided and the new generation voraciously consumed jazz, rock, salsa, and most importantly, R&B and funk. At the same time, Cuba's African heritage had come farther out of the shadows than ever before, allowing musicians to balance outside musical influences with copious amounts of *rumba* and *Santería* music, thus producing a vastly more sophisticated style of songwriting and arranging without sacrificing the unique national identity and *cubanismo* of their music.

Among the revolutionary aspects of timba were a greatly increased harmonic palette, longer montuno sections with multiple chord progressions, much greater use of pre-rehearsed rhythm section breaks (i.e., *bloques* and *efectos),* asymmetrical phrasing of lead and backup vocal parts, and the complete integration of the drumset – especially the kick drum – into the texture of Latin dance music. But the two most dramatic innovations were song-specific accompaniment parts and rhythm section gears, described in more detail in the sections below.

Song-specific Accompaniment Parts

Sometimes an audio file is worth a thousand words, so let's start by listening to **Listening Tour 3-1.mp3**, part of the free audio download for this book, available at timba.com/audio. The track plays a common vamp four times with generic conga, piano and bass parts. It then segues into the parts used on the 1997 timba classic *De la Habana* by Paulito FG y su Élite. As you can hear, each part has its own unique melodic "hook" – a listener familiar with the song would be able to identify it by listening to only one part, even the conga marcha. This conga part was originally invented by Tomás Cruz. The bass tumbao is by either Frank Rubio or Joel Domínguez and the piano part was originally invented by Emilio Morales, further developed by Sergio Noroña and played here, with substantial further modifications, by Rolando Luna.

Now that you have an auditory sense of what "song-specific" means, we'll move on to those pesky thousand words.

In 1781, Haydn turned the Viennese music world on its ear with his Opus 33 string quartets, which he boasted were "written in an entirely new and special style". No, he didn't add clave – but what he did add makes for an irresistible analogy to our discussion of timba. Up to that point, the important musical ideas of a classical string quartet were played by the first violin, with the other three instruments providing relatively generic, formulaic accompaniments. Haydn gave the cello, viola and second violin their own melodic parts, based on thematic material, resulting in a four-way conversation in which each part was unique and inseparable from the whole.

The same dynamic was present in much of pre-timba Latin dance music – it's often difficult to know what song you're hearing if all you have to go on are the piano, bass and percussion parts. The themes and the "hooks" are primarily contained in the voices and horns. Of course, almost five decades before timba, Arsenio Rodríguez had pioneered the idea song-specific bass tumbaos and other examples can be found sprinkled through all the pre-timba genres. It wasn't so much that the timberos *started* the practice of using song-specific accompaniments – it was that they *stopped* the practice of *not* using them, raising the creative bar for their competitors and public. Timba pianists like Juan Carlos González, Melón Lewis, Tony Pérez, Sergio Noroña and Tirso Duarte weren't content to simply arpeggiate the chord progression of each new coro – they felt compelled to invent a piano tumbao that announced the identity of the song as soon as they started playing it – a piano tumbao that on the strength of its own catchiness and originality gave their fans a reason to buy the record. As Duarte puts it, they strove to turn *tumbaos soneados* into *tumbaos mágicos,* i.e., to turn "son-style tumbaos" into "magical tumbaos". By the late 1990s, even congueros like Tomasito Cruz were getting into the act, with conga marchas lasting two or even four claves and carrying within them enough thematic material to identify the song in question.

Rock & Roll provides an even better analogy than Papa Haydn because, like timba, rock is based on the idea of repeating riffs. If you do a survey of 1950s rock, you'll find the same guitar and bass riffs used over and over, providing a solid groove, but relying on the lyrics and melody to make the song a recognizable hit. But by the 1960s, guitar riffs like those of *Satisfaction, Day Tripper, Beat It,* and *Whole Lotta Love* were as important as the vocals to the success and identity of a song. Their timba counterparts include *No me mires a los ojos, Nube pasajera, El bla bla bla* and *No te lo creas.*

Salsa, Timba, Gears and Dancing

Probably the most important and far-reaching timba innovation is what we call "rhythm section gears". These are covered in expansive detail in the other *Beyond Salsa* volumes, but for this book, we need to separate the forest from the trees – to understand the general concept and how it relates to dancing without getting bogged down in the details. For this Listening Tour, you don't need to know the names of the gears, which gear you're in, or which gear you're going to – only that you feel *something* when the rhythm section shifts gears.

When timba first started to be heard outside Cuba, salsa dancers we sometimes heard to complain: *"I can't dance to this crazy timba! The rhythms keep changing and throwing me off! This music isn't meant for dancing!".*

I direct these critics to a telling line from that old New York slot-dancing standard, *Ballad of a Thin Man,* by Bob Dylan: *"There's something going on here, and you don't know what it is … ".* For this listening tour, you don't even need to know what "it" is – all you need to know is that there is indeed "something going on". When the gear changes, just think to yourself *"oh yeah, I felt that – something changed somewhere in the rhythm section"*. That's all it takes. Dancers used to hearing a homogenous groove can get caught off-guard and lose the beat when the gear changes.

Many dancers – even in Cuba, and especially when dancing *rueda* – will dance right through the gear changes as if nothing happened. This is perfectly fine, but you should also be aware that some dancers change their dancing when the rhythm section changes its gear. In fact, this is exactly how timba gears came about in the first place. Far from being some kind of self-indulgent, geeky creation of musicians, gear changes were inspired by dancers, requested by dancers, and are constantly tweaked to adjust to changing dance styles. The idea of having changes in dance steps that go along with changes in the drums is something that goes all the way back to danzón, and before that, all the way back to Africa.

To give you a very basic example, think how often you've heard a timba singer shout *"manos pa' arriba!"* *("hands in the air!")* during a concert. It often happens several times per song. Now, imagine yourself dancing salsa, your arms wrapped around your partner. If you both throw your arms in the air, and stop doing your basic step, you're freer to dance with your hips and shoulders, and the changes in the rhythm (such as the bass tumbao, bells, and congas dropping out) make this feel much more natural (and make dancing with your feet seem *less* natural). This is exactly the point where salsa dancers start complaining. They're right when they say that it's harder to keep dancing with their *feet* when the bass, bells and congas stop. What they don't realize is that they're *supposed* to stop dancing with their feet, and that all these changes in the music make it easier and more natural to throw their hands up in the air and undulate with the groove. After this has happened for a short, predictable period of time (four or eight basic steps), the drummer plays a fill alerting you that the bass, bells and congas are about to come back. You grab your partner and just as the original groove returns you strut into your basic step. The feeling of returning to the normal dance step is just as exhilarating as the feeling of letting go and throwing your arms up. Once you get the hang of this, you'll start to miss it when you're dancing to salsa. Furthermore, once you get used to hearing the bass drop out and return, you *can* continue dancing normally (if you feel like it) and not get thrown off. There's also an even more intense and climactic *bomba* gear where the bass starts thumping and sliding, calling for more intense hip and shoulder movement, and giving you a chance (if you feel like it) to really let loose and strut your stuff. Again, you don't *have* to change your dancing – as long as you're prepared for the changes, you can dance normal salsa if you like.

Now, salsa has gears too – in fact, every kind of music has gears. If two or more members of the rhythm section change their patterns in tandem with each other, that's a gear change. The gears that salsa bands use all have *"marcha"* in their names – *marcha abajo, marcha arriba, marcha de mambo* and so on. What all these gears have in common is that the bass keeps playing a normal tumbao and the dancers keep dancing the basic step in couples. The steady bass tumbao stops in the timba gears *(presión, masacote* and *bomba)* – and the dancers *can* – but don't always – separate, stop their basic step, and dance more with their hips and shoulders.

NG La Banda

La bruja
José Luis Cortés y NG La Banda

highlighted track: *Picadillo de soya* – NG La Banda: *La bruja* – Inspector de la Salsa (1994)
(or *Simplemente lo mejor* – BIS) – singers: El Tosco, Tony Calá

time	tempo	gear	comments
0:00	97	muela	El Tosco raps humorously about cooking a meat dish with soybeans because of the food shortage
0:29	99	presión	piano intro – note Calixto Oviedo's trademark hihat presión style
0:40		marcha arriba	montuno preview (coro 1)
0:53	100	marcha abajo	cuerpo
1:34	102	presión	piano tumbao 1
1:44		marcha arriba	coro 1
2:17	104	marcha de mambo	mambo 1
2:36		marcha arriba	coro 1
2:58		muela	more rapping from El Tosco – now detailing the nutritional benefits of soybeans
3:35		presión/masacote	piano tumbao 2 with extended lead vocal (Tony Calá)
4:24	106	marcha arriba	coro 2
4:34	109	marcha de mambo	mambo 2 (with trumpet solo)
4:56	111	bomba	mambo 2 continues
5:15		marcha de mambo	mambo 2 continues
5:32		presión/masacote	piano tumbao 2 with extended lead vocal (Tony Calá)
6:01	115	marcha arriba	coro 3
6:19		bomba	coro 3 continues
6:35		marcha arriba	mambo 3
7:00	110	muela	more rapping … into coda

Flutist/composer José Luis "El Tosco" Cortés began his career with Los Van Van before moving on to Irakere in the early 1980s, during which time he produced several experimental Latin jazz albums as the leader of a side project he called "Nueva Generación". In 1989 he and others left Irakere to join forces with Tony Calá of Ritmo Oriental and Issac Delgado of Pachito Alonso, turning their focus to popular music, and shortening the name of the group to NG La Banda. Bassist Feliciano Arango and pianist Rodolfo "Peruchín" Argudín were the first important proponents of many of the timba innovations discussed above and NG La Banda was the first group to consistently use gear changes as part of their style. NG was also the first in a series of timba bands to achieve "mania"-level popularity in the suddenly torrid Havana music scene.

NG La Banda's founding drummer was Giraldo Piloto. The rhythm section also included bongó with hand bell, congas and güiro. Piloto had a set of timbales to his left, and mounted a contracampana on his kick drum.

In addition to being one of Cuba's all-time greatest drummers, Piloto is one of its best and most prolific composers. He wrote several songs for NG La Banda and (as a freelancer) for Charanga Habanera before becoming Issac Delgado's musical director in 1991, writing many of Delgado's early hits. Since 1995, Piloto has been the leader, drummer and principal composer of Klímax.

Piloto was replaced in NG La Banda by Calixto Oviedo, the subject of two volumes of the *Beyond Salsa Percussion* series. Calixto also places a set of timbales to the left of his drumset, and also mounts a bell on his kick drum, but in Calixto's case, it's a large campana, and in NG, he didn't use it as his primary bell, because, as always with NG La Banda, the campaneo part (Exercise 3-13) was being played by the bongosero. Calixto also played contracampana (Exercise 3-15), but mounted it on his timbales rig. Calixto played a lot more clave on his jam block than Piloto, and had a very personal hihat sound. It's well worth scouring YouTube for the many live videos of NG La Banda with Piloto and Calixto to compare two of Cuba's greatest drummers dealing with the same situation. Their tenures covered the band's most productive years and best material.

When Oviedo left NG La Banda, he was replaced by yet another truly great drummer, Jimmy Branly, but although you can find clips of one great live 1997 show on YouTube, Branly never recorded with the band, leaving soon after for Los Angeles, where he still lives, playing mostly jazz. The next drummers, Jorge Baglan and José Alán Pérez de Valle, are both excellent and the band still periodically releases new material, but unlike Revé, Los Van Van and Pupy Pedroso, they've slowed down. To hear the innovative classics that make NG La Banda so important in Cuban music history, start with the Piloto and Oviedo eras (1989-1996).

Further Listening Recommendations for NG La Banda – Giraldo Piloto Era

Year	Song	Singer	Source
1989	*La expresiva*	Issac Delgado	*En la calle* – QBADisc
1989	*To'el mundo e' bueno camará*	Tony Calá	*En la calle* – QBADisc
1989	*Qué viva Changó*	Tony Calá	*To'el mundo baila con NG*– Max Music GDN
1990	*Los Sitios entero*	Issac Delgado	*En la calle* – QBADisc
1990	*Por qué tú sufres con lo que yo gozo*	Tony Calá	*En la calle* – QBADisc
1991	*Rap de la muerta*	Tony Calá	re-recorded 2012 – *Mis 22 años* (EGREM)
1991	*Yo soy un hombre*	Mariano "Mena" Pérez	*Llegó NG, Camará* – ARTEX

Giraldo Piloto with Klímax – Toronto – photo by Bohdan Kiszczuk – bwkphotography.com

Further Listening Recommendations for NG La Banda – Calixto Oviedo Era

Year	Song	Singer	Source
1992	*Santa palabra*	Tony Calá	*Simplemente lo mejor de NG La Banda* – BIS
1992	*Échale limón*	El Tosco, Tony Calá	*Simplemente lo mejor de NG La Banda* – BIS
1992	*El trágico*	Tony Calá	*Simplemente lo mejor de NG La Banda* – BIS
1994	*Hice mi papel*	Tony Calá	*La que manda* – Inspector de la Salsa
1994	*Te pongo mal*	Tony Calá	*La bruja* – Inspector de la Salsa
1994	*La bruja*	El Tosco, Tony Calá	*Simplemente lo mejor de NG La Banda* – BIS
1994	*Película del sábado*	Tony Calá	*La bruja* – Inspector de la Salsa
1994	*Un sueño terrible*	Tony Calá	*La bruja* – Inspector de la Salsa
1995	*La apretadora*	Mariano "Mena" Pérez	*En directo del patio de mi casa* – Inspector de la Salsa

Calixto Oviedo with the Afro-Cuban All Stars – Napa, California – photo by Tom Ehrlich

Charanga Habanera

highlighted track: *Nube pasajera – Pa' que se entere la Habana* (1996) – Inspector de la Salsa – singer: Michel Maza

time	tempo	gear	comments
0:00	105	presión	piano tumbao and montuno preview
0:23	102	marcha abajo	horn intro
0:42	89		cuerpo (keyboards and horns only – no percussion)
0:53	92	marcha abajo	cuerpo continued
1:41	98	marcha media	coro 1 (timbalero goes to cha bell – bongosero stays on bongó)
2:02	101	marcha arriba	coro 1 continued (timbalero and bongosero go to their normal bells)
2:31			short horn transition
2:35		presión/masacote	coro 2a song-specific motivo figure (piano doubles bass instead of tumbao)
3:04	106	marcha arriba	coro 2a
3:26		masacote	mambo 1
3:45		marcha arriba	coro 2b
4:11		presión	rapped intro for coro 3
4:20		masacote	coro 3a
4:43		marcha arriba	coro 3b (great efectos at 4:47)
5:01	107	presión	coro 3b continues ... horns enter ... fade

The second timba band to take Havana by storm was David Calzado's La Charanga Habanera. Its sound and stage show differed drastically from NG La Banda. Each used gears and song-specific tumbaos, but in very different ways. The band has remained consistently popular ever since, with three distinct style periods. The first group featured the visionary musical director and pianist Juan Carlos González and a string of brilliant and iconic singers: Leo Vera, Mario "Sombrilla" Jiménez, Michel Maza and Dany Lozada. They recorded four classic albums between 1992 and 1997, each described in meticulous, book-length, song-by-song detail with multiple audio clips on timba.com. The band's colorful and extremely controversial history is also recounted in minute detail.

Charanga Habanera had an extraordinarily melodic bassist in Pedro Pablo and an extremely innovative founding timbalero in Eduardo Lazaga, the son of Enrique Lazaga, the leader of Ritmo Oriental, where David Calzado got his start. Lazaga was briefly followed by Gilbertón Moreaux.

Only Calzado himself (and briefly Michel Maza) connect this band to the second great incarnation of Charanga Habanera, featuring another visionary, Tirso Duarte, as musical director, pianist and vocalist, and Calixto Oviedo's child prodigy son, Yulién Oviedo, on timbales. Finally, we have the current "boy band" version, with timbalero/vocalist Randy Martínez serving as Calzado's principal creative collaborator. The new group is as successful and prolific as ever, and has lots of excellent material, but it's not as interesting from a percussion point of view – having dropped the bongosero and sometimes going so far as to use sequenced tracks. This is particularly ironic because the other two Charanga Habanera bands were famous for their skillful manipulation of tempo and "live-in-the-studio" groove, both of which are completely negated by the use of sequencers. Remember that Calzado got his start with Ritmo Oriental, the all time masters of tempo manipulation. The *Nube pasajera* tempo map will allow you to experience La Charanga's brilliant use of tempo. But don't get me started! I've already used my "soapbox sidebar" for this volume (it's coming in the Rhythm Exercises 3 section, on the dreaded subject of terminology).

The rhythm section approach of the first two incarnations of Charanga Habanera (and to some extent the current one) could scarcely have been more different from that of NG La Banda. Instead of having a drumset player, they used the standard salsa triumvirate of congas, bongó and timbales, with the timbalero playing kick drum (and occasionally snare) from a standing position. Their use of kick and clave were also drastically different – not only from NG, but from most other timba bands.

The Clave Instrument in Timba

The original NG La Banda, with Giraldo Piloto on drums, rarely used the clave pattern itself. The bells, bass, horns and vocals expressed the feel and direction of the clave with force and clarity, but the group's artistic choice was to refrain from playing the actual clave cell. Calixto Oviedo played clave more often than Piloto. On *Santa palabra,* for example, you can hear it quite clearly. Like Los Van Van's Samuel Formell, or the various timbaleros of Issac Delgado, Calixto played a loose and flexible mix of rumba clave (Exercise 3-9) and son clave (Exercise 3-7) – with son more common in cuerpos and mellower coros, and rumba more common in the more hardcore timba passages. If you listen to the first half of *Santa palabra,* however, he uses son and rumba patterns interchangeably.

Charanga Habanera uses a very different approach from either NG La Banda drummer. With La Charanga (a common nickname for Charanga Habanera), the clave never stops – you can hear it on the jam block throughout almost every track from beginning to end. And whether it's during the cuerpo or the montuno section, it's always rumba clave. This, again, is a strictly aesthetic choice – part of Charanga Habanera's *sello*, or trademark style.

There is actually one Charanga Habanera CD, *Live in the USA,* where you'll hear rumba clave in the montunos and son clave in the cuerpos and there's an interesting story behind this. The album was recorded at a concert and the instrument rental company failed to bring a jam block for timbalero Yulién Oviedo. When it was decided that the concert would be released, the producers considered the jam block clave to be so essential to the band's style that they decided to overdub it (and also a güiro part). The band, however, had already returned to Cuba, so Ángel "Pututi II" Arce, a world-class timbalero who had played for years with Manolín, el Médico de la Salsa, was brought in, and it was he who played son clave on the cuerpos.

So let's review the clave choices of four of the greatest Cuban drummers with two of the greatest Cuban groups. Piloto chose not to play clave with NG but to express it in other ways. Calixto used it some of the time, and when he did, felt free to switch between son and rumba. Calixto's son Yulién played rumba clave constantly and exclusively, and Angel "Pututi II" Arce also played clave constantly, but chose to use son for the cuerpos and rumba for the montunos. It's like four master chefs – each with access to the same spice rack, and each preparing a different savory dish. What all four have in common, of course, is aligning the 2-side and 3-side correctly with the bass, bells and vocals. All four approaches worked brilliantly, so the moral of the story is to listen and be flexible.

As an epilogue to this clave tangent, I once had the opportunity to do a MIDI session with the aforementioned Yulién Oviedo. When we got through with the Charanga Habanera material, I asked him to record some tracks along with MIDI arrangements I had of songs by Los Van Van, Paulito FG and Issac Delgado. In each case, he used a completely different – and band-appropriate – approach to the clave.

Another unique element of Charanga Habanera's rhythm section style has to do with the kick drum. Charanga Habanera uses the patterns taught in Exercises 3-29 and 3-30 for breakdowns, but for their main marcha gear they don't use the standard pattern taught in Exercises 3-27 and 3-28. Instead, they have a special kick drum pattern that aligns with the strokes of the clave instead of conversing with them as most other bands do (X○X○ X○○○ ○○○X X○○○ in 2-3 clave).

Further Listening Recommendations for Charanga Habanera – Juan Carlos González Era

Year	Song	Singer	Source
1993	*Extraños ateos*	*Mario "Sombrilla" Jiménez*	*Love Fever (Me sube la fiebre)* –Milan Latino
1994	*Quítate el disfraz*	*Mario "Sombrilla" Jiménez*	*Hey You Loca* – Magic Music
1994	*Hey You Loca*	*Mario "Sombrilla" Jiménez*	*Hey You Loca* – Magic Music
1994	*Mi estrella*	*Leo Vera*	*Hey You Loca* – Magic Music
1994	*Para el llanto*	*Leo Vera*	*Hey You Loca* – Magic Music
1996	*Que te lleve otro*	*Michel Maza*	*Pa' que se entere la Habana* – Magic Music
1996	*El temba*	*Michel Maza*	*Pa' que se entere la Habana* – Magic Music
1996	*Yuya la Charanguera*	*Mario "Sombrilla" Jiménez*	*Pa' que se entere la Habana* – Magic Music
1997	*Charanguéate*	*Dany Lozada*	*Tremendo delirio* – Magic Music
1997	*Usa condón*	*Dany Lozada*	*Tremendo delirio* – Magic Music
1997	*Hagamos un chen*	*Michel Maza*	*Tremendo delirio* – Magic Music
1997	*Lola Lola*	*Michel Maza*	*Tremendo delirio* – Magic Music

Further Listening Recommendations for Charanga Habanera – Tirso Duarte Era

Year	Song	Singer	Source
1999	*Charanguero mayor*	*all (cuerpo) Tirso Duarte (guías)*	*Charanguero mayor* – Ciocan Music
1999	*El bla bla bla*	*Aned Mota*	*Charanguero mayor* – Ciocan Music
1999	*Sube y baja*	*Aned Mota*	*Charanguero mayor* – Ciocan Music
1999	*Tema introducción*	*Aned Mota*	*Charanguero mayor* – Ciocan Music
1999	*Pa' que me importa a mí*	*Tirso Duarte*	*Charanguero mayor* – Ciocan Music
2000	*Pila cerrá*	*Dantes "Riki Ricón" Cardosa*	*Live in the USA* – Ciocan Music
2001	*Gozando a lo cubano*	*Leonid Torres*	*Chan Chan Charanga* – Ciocan Music
2001	*Ella es como es*	*Tirso Duarte*	*Chan Chan Charanga* – Ciocan Music

Further Listening Recommendations for Charanga Habanera – Current Era (as of 2012)

Year	Song	Singer	Source
2003	*Soy cubano soy popular*	*Leonid Torres*	*Soy cubano soy popular* – EGREM
2009	*Gozando en Miami*	*Randy Martínez*	*No mires la carátula* – EGREM
2011	*La suerte*	*Randy Martínez*	*La suerte* – EGREM

Sidebar: Comparing Issac Delgado and Paulito FG

Issac Delgado and Paulito FG are quite different in terms of vocal timbre, personality and choice of repertoire, but when discussing the deeper musical aspects of timba, it's hard to mention one without mentioning the other. In my opinion, these are far the two best *live* timba bands. I say this because each has the ability to play the same song very differently from concert to concert through the use of "controlled improvisation" and "gear changes", two topics covered extensively in the more technical volumes of the *Beyond Salsa* series. Just as interesting is the fact that Issac and Paulito use such drastically different approaches to achieving the coveted state of "improvisation of form" that for me, as a diehard timba connoisseur, is the ultimate holy grail.

Gear changes are a complex topic best left for our later *volumes (Beyond Salsa Piano, Vol. 5, Beyond Salsa Percussion, Vol. 3, and Beyond Salsa for Ensemble, Vol. 2)* but you don't have to understand them to experience the euphoric rush that they produce in a live concert setting. Every timba band is built from the ground up to produce this rush, but Issac and Paulito – more often than others – have been able to produce it spontaneously by using rhythm section schemes that allow them to alter the form of an arrangement to fit the flow of each performance.

A more practical reason for grouping Issac and Paulito together is that they used so many of the same musicians. The list of musicians who played with, and/or, arranged for both bands reads like a "who's who" of timba masters – among them, Yoel Páez, Joel Domínguez, Frank Rubio, Rolando Luna, Joaquín Betancourt, Juan Ceruto, Alexander Abreu, Yaniel "El Majá" Matos, Pepe Rivero, and Roberto "Cucurucho" Valdés.

Issac Delgado

highlighted track: *Se te fue la mano – Exclusivo para Cuba* (1997) – Geminis (or RMM, or Ciocan)
(The RMM version is entitled *Forbidden Cuba: Rarities*)

time	tempo	gear	comments
0:00	90	piano/bongó	piano intro
0:11		marcha abajo	horn intro
0:21		marcha arriba	(horn intro continues)
0:32		piano/bongó	cuerpo
0:54		marcha arriba	horn interlude
1:05		marcha abajo	cuerpo continues
1:28		marcha arriba	coro
1:46		marcha abajo	horn bridge
2:00		marcha abajo	coro 1
2:15		marcha arriba	(coro 1 continues)
2:40		marcha abajo	mambo 1 (champola)
3:02		marcha arriba	(mambo 1 continues)
3:23		presión	piano tumbao
3:34		marcha arriba	coro 2
4:16		marcha de mambo	mambo 2
4:37		marcha media	piano tumbao/horn interlude
4:47	92	marcha arriba	coro 3
5:18		presión	coro 4
5:30		bomba	(coro 4 continues)
5:40		marcha arriba	mambo 3 (with coro 4) ... fade

After starting his career with Pachito Alonso, Gonzalo Rubalcaba and others, Issac Delgado became a superstar with NG La Banda in 1989, and the leader of his own band in 1991. Delgado is one of timba's best composers and most melodic improvisers, often taking off on flights of fancy in concert where he improvises words and melody for several minutes at a time. This, combined with his group's flexible gear system make it imperative to hear him live to get a complete sense of his music. Fortunately, YouTube is well-stocked with live performances from each of the major Delgado groups.

Perhaps inspired by his work with Rubalcaba and the virtuosos of NG La Banda, Delgado has tended to stock his band with the most sophisticated jazz musicians available and to give them an exceptional amount of creative freedom. The result has been a long string of unique and fascinating groups. It's almost easier to list the great Cuban pianists who *haven't* played in Delgado's band, but here's a partial list of those who have: Tony Pérez, Javier "Caramelo" Massó, Iván "Melón" Lewis, Pepe Rivero, Yaniel "El Majá" Matos, Roberto Carlos "Cucurucho" Valdés, Rolando Luna, Tony Rodríguez and Issacito Delgado.

The list of bassists is equally impressive: Arnaldo Jiménez, Charles Flores, Alain Pérez, Joel Domínguez, Frank Rubio, Alfredo Hecchavarría and Avis Tobías. When Delgado teamed Melón Lewis with Alain Pérez between 1996 and 1998, the result was perhaps the best piano-bass tandem in Cuban popular music history.

The first great Delgado group featured the drumming, writing and arranging of another NG La Banda alumnus, Giraldo Piloto. For their rhythm section, they pioneered a new approach. Instead of a bongosero who doubled on hand bell, they had a timbalero, Yonder Peña, who mounted the hand bell so he could play it with one hand while playing clave and timbales. Piloto retained his own set of timbales and continued to play contracampana mounted on his kick drum. When Piloto left to start his own band, Klímax, he took Yonder with him. Issac replaced Yonder with José Miguel and Piloto with the aforementioned Jimmy Branly. When José Miguel went to Irakere and Branly to NG la Banda, Issac brought in Andrés Cuayo on timbales and Georvis Pico on drums.

This was the famous 1996-1998 group with Alain Pérez on bass and Melón Lewis on piano, who account for eight volumes of *Beyond Salsa* between them. When this entire rhythm section moved to Spain, Issac added Antonio "Pachá" Portuondo on timbales and Denis "Papacho" Savón on congas, while convincing drummer Yoel Páez, bassist Joel Domínguez and pianist Yaniel Matos to come over from Paulito's band, creating the second of his three greatest bands from the "gears" point of view.

When Yoel and Joel (aka, "los Yoeles") left for Spain and el Majá moved to Brazil, Issac had yet another miracle up his sleeve, creating a short-lived band that never recorded in the studio, but had more efectos and gear changes than even their illustrious predecessors. This time it was Bombón Reyes (now with Los Que Son Son) on drums, Frank Rubio (formerly with Paulito FG, Chucho Valdés and Bamboleo) on bass and Cucurucho (who would go on to Paulito and then to Van Van) on piano. Have you got all of that?

Each of these rhythm sections was brilliant and each very different from the others. The basic distribution of roles followed Issac's original *sello* – the drummer played contracampana and the standing timbalero played campana and clave. The way the bands differed (and they differed dramatically) had to do with the ways they handled gears and efectos and the way they distributed the "controlled improvisation" responsibilities. For example, in the 1997 band, the percussionists were more conservative in order to allow maximum freedom for Alain and Melón – the two most creative improvisers on their instruments. The next two bands put more emphasis on percussion, efectos and gear systems.

Issac Delgado moved to the United States in 2007, where he's recorded several albums, some with the participation of Alain Pérez, and participated in all sorts of special projects with José Lugo, Spanish Harlem Orchestra, Freddy Cole (on *L.O.V.E.,* a tribute to Nat King Cole), and many others.

Further Listening Recommendations for Issac Delgado

Year	Song	Source
1996-2000	live recordings on Youtube	Use the studio tracks to familiarize yourself with each song, then seek out multiple live versions to experience the full magic of this group.
1993	*Dime tú lo que sabes*	*Con ganas* – QBADisc
1995	*No me mires a los ojos*	*El año que viene* – RMM
1994	*La vida sin esperanza*	*El año que viene* – RMM
1994	*Por qué paró*	*El año que viene* – RMM
1996	*Deja que Roberto te toque*	*Otra idea* – RMM
1996	*Luz viajera*	*Otra idea* – RMM
1997	*Con la punta del pie*	*Exclusivo para Cuba* – Geminis, RMM, Ciocan
1997	*Tú tranquilo*	*Exclusivo para Cuba* – Geminis, RMM, Ciocan
1997	*Pa' que te salves (La soga)*	*Exclusivo para Cuba* – Geminis, RMM, Ciocan
1997	*La temática*	(live only)
1998	*La sandunguita*	*La primera noche* – RMM
1998	*Mi romántica*	*La primera noche* – RMM
1998	*Amigo Juan*	*La primera noche* – RMM
1998	*Que me disculpen*	*La primera noche* – RMM
2001	*La fórmula*	*La fórmula* – Ahí Namá
2001	*Amor sin ética*	*La fórmula* – Ahí Namá
2001	*Malecón*	*La fórmula* – Ahí Namá
2001	*Solar de la California*	*La fórmula* – Ahí Namá
2002	*Vamos a andar*	*Versos en el cielo* – BIS
2004	*Dime cuál es*	*Prohibido* – BIS
2008	*No vale la pena*	*Así soy yo* – Universal-Machete
2011	*Salsa, timba y amor*	*Supercubano* – Planet Records

Paulito FG y su Élite

highlighted track: *Enredadera de amor – Una vez más … por amor* (2000) – PROMUSIC

time	tempo	gear	comments
0:00	102	marcha arriba	horn introduction
0:19		marcha abajo	cuerpo
0:48		marcha de cumbia	horn interlude
0:57		marcha abajo	cuerpo
1:07		presión (aka pedal)	piano tumbao, then coro 1 with efectos
1:26		marcha arriba	coro 1
1:44		marcha de mambo	mambo 1
2:04		songo con efectos	(songo con efectos is Paulito's *masacote* gear)
2:13		marcha de mambo	
2:22		presión	coro 2
2:32		marcha arriba	
2:50		muela	guitar solo and vocal banter
3:30		marcha arriba	guitar solo builds with horns
3:47		presión	coro 3
4:05		bomba	
4:24		marcha arriba	coro 4
4:43		songo con efectos	
5:02		marcha de mambo	mambo 2

With his razor sharp ability to improvise and think on his feet, Paulito Fernández Gallo (aka, Paulito FG, Paulo FG, Pablo FG) is one of the great "field generals" of music, using a dizzying array of hand signals to put his world-class rhythm section through its paces like a Lamborghini, all the while dancing, interacting with the crowd, improvising and rephrasing his own vocal lines – often inventing new coros on the spot based on guest artists or interaction with the crowd.

When you see Paulito live, keep in mind that many of the things he does that appear to be dance moves are actually signals to his rhythm section for gear changes. By the time you get to the last half of a live song, he's literally changing the gear nearly every eight claves or basic dance steps. Some bands rehearse all their gear changes in advance, while others have a single signal that instigates a series of gears, but Paulito calls them one by one, maximizing the permutations and the unpredictable nature of each performance.

After beginning his career with Adalberto Álvarez and Dan Den, Paulito joined Opus 13, a virtuosic band of all-star musicians built around the exceptional arranging talents of Joaquín Betancourt and Juan Manuel Ceruto. We covered Opus 13's seminal 1980s period in Listening Tour 2. In the early 1990s, Paulito took over the band and changed the name, developing an extraordinary chemistry with Ceruto that produced many of timba's greatest classics.

As you begin searching YouTube for live timba masterpieces, keep in mind that with bands that place such an emphasis on the creativity of individual live performances – the standouts being those of Paulito and Issac Delgado – each personnel and repertoire change makes a difference in the chemistry. Each incarnation of the band is like a different vintage of a fine wine. In the case of Delgado, I'd suggest beginning your search with three such vintages: the 1996-1998 band, with Alain Pérez and Melón Lewis; the 1999 band with Joel Domínguez, Yoel Páez and Yaniel "El Majá" Matos (all of whom came over from the Paulito band discussed below); and the phenomenal and vastly under-rated early-2000 band with Bombón Reyes, Cucurucho Valdés and Frank Rubio. With Paulito FG y su Élite, there was one rhythm section that stands out above all others (although it cycled through a string of great pianists). Paulito and Ceruto already had a world-class band at the beginning of 1997, with the percussion section of Tomasito Cruz, Yoel Páez and Coqui Chacón already established. When bassist Frank Rubio left to join the first incarnation of the Chucho Valdés Quartet and Emilio Morales left to replace Peruchín in NG La Banda, their brilliant young replacements, Joel Domínguez and Sergio Noroña, were greeted by a windfall of the greatest collaborations of Paulito's songwriting and Ceruto's arranging. The album that resulted, *Con la conciencia tranquila,* is considered Paulito's greatest, and one of the greatest of the entire era, but from the point of view of live performance, the fireworks were just beginning. By early 1998, a third timba gear – a type of masacote called *songo con efectos* – had been added to counter-balance Paulito's dramatic *pedal* approach to presión and the furious bombas that he'd ridden to the highest echelon of popularity among the hardcore timba dancers.

"Songo con efectos" is actually a term introduced in hindsight by Tomás Cruz. The band didn't have a name for this masacote-style gear – it was invoked by a hand-and-body signal from Paulito. If this seems odd, permit me one last classical music analogy. Every book and course on the music of Haydn, Mozart and Beethoven focuses heavily on the idea of "sonata allegro form". It's a wonderful and complex system, with multiple subsections, great dramatic potential, hair-raising twists and turns, and pages upon pages of rules, guidelines and exceptions. In your first semester, you'll spend hours on terms like *exposition, development, secondary theme, retransition, coda* and so on. You'll marvel at the ways each composer cleverly manipulated the rules to further his own artistic designs and be scandalized when you encounter some particularly reckless example of blatant disregard for the regulations you've worked so hard to learn. But consider this: all of these rules and terms were invented and catalogued well after the death of Beethoven. The beloved sonata allegro form that these powdered wigged early timberos took such delight in had no name and no articulated rules at the time that they were actually creating the music that's resulted in us the form at such length.

Paulito FG at Yoshi's Oakland – 2010 – photos by Tom Ehrlich

In any case, all hell broke loose with the addition of Paulito's songo con efectos gear. At this point the Havana music was like the rock scene in June, 1967 when Sgt. Pepper's was released. Every group seemed to be peaking at the same time. Paulito and Ceruto added two more amazing charts: *Laura* (never recorded in the studio but available live on YouTube), and *La última bala* (eventually recorded in 2000 under the title *Por amor).* By mid-2000, four key rhythm section members had left and Ceruto himself left halfway through the recording of *Una vez más por amor,* from which our highlighted track, *Enredadera de amor* (a Ceruto arrangement), is drawn.

Although the late 90s period is the clear starting point in understanding Paulito and Issac (and timba in general), both of these artists are still active. Issac is in the United States engaging in a wide range of eclectic collaborations while Paulito never left Cuba and still has a very aggressive live band that uses the same types of gear schemes and hand signals that were used in the late 90s. The years leading up to the late-90s peak were also very productive for both groups.

Paulito's Rhythm Section Format

La Élite used the same configuration as NG La Banda – a drumset player with timbales, responsible for the contracampana, and a bongosero with a hand bell. The founding drummer, Héctor Salazar, was replaced in about 1995 by Yoel Páez, another of the all-time great drummers and a master of orchestration and controlled improvisation. Páez later played with Issac Delgado and Manolín before moving to Spain. He's written one excellent book on adapting folkloric rhythms to the drumset and has been promising to write a timba book for years. It should be well worth the wait.

Páez was followed by a long list of drummers, including Mauricio Herrera, now in New York, and Armando "Pututi III" Arce, now in Miami with Tiempo Libre. And just in case you were wondering, all of the Pututis (there are 6 counting the father) have first names that begin with the letter A.

Paulito's famous "pa'l piso" dance move (left) – Yoshi's Oakland – 2010 – photos by Tom Ehrlich

Paulito FG y su Élite: Tempo and Gears – Studio and Live

Our highlighted track, *Enredadera de amor,* was recorded with a click, but this is the only studio track using all of Paulito's timba gears. The previous album, *Con la conciencia tranquila* (also recorded with a click), dates from the period before Paulito's *songo con efectos,* or *masacote* gear was added. Click or no click, *Con la conciencia* is easily Paulito's best album and a candidate for the best timba album in general. It has extensive and very creative use of presión gear (Paulito calls his version *pedal)* and bomba on nearly every track. As with Issac Delgado, you should use the studio albums to familiarize yourself with the starting points for the incredible late-90s live performances that can be found on YouTube. Almost every song on *Con la conciencia* can be found in multiple live versions, each exquisitely different from the other performances. And don't forget to track down the live-only masterpiece *Laura,* one of Paulito and Ceruto's greatest collaborations.

Further Listening Recommendations for Paulito FG

Year	Song	Source
1994	*Amiga no*	*Sofocándote* – QBADisc
1996	El vuelo	*El bueno soy yo* – EGREM
1996	*Como una postal*	*El bueno soy yo* – EGREM
1996	Exclusivamente exclusivo	*El bueno soy yo* – EGREM
1997	*Con la conciencia tranquila*	*Con la conciencia tranquila* – Nueva Fania
1997	Y ahora qué	*Con la conciencia tranquila* – Nueva Fania
1997	*Y San Toma qué*	*Con la conciencia tranquila* – Nueva Fania
1997	No te lo creas	*Con la conciencia tranquila* – Nueva Fania
1997	*De la Habana*	*Con la conciencia tranquila* – Nueva Fania
1997	Laura	radio demo (search on YouTube)
2000	*Por amor (La última bala)*	*Una vez más por amor* – PROMUSIC

Manolín, el Médico de la Salsa

highlighted track: *Pegaíto pegaíto – De buena fe* (1997) – Metro Blue (Caribe)

time	tempo	gear	comments
0:00	97	marcha abajo	montuno preview – piano tumbao
0:10	94	marcha abajo	horn introduction
0:20	95	guaguancó	cuerpo
0:37		marcha abajo	
1:14	98	presión	piano tumbao with rapped intro to coro 1
1:25		marcha arriba	coro 1
2:04		marcha de mambo	mambo 1
2:23	99	presión	piano tumbao with rapped intro to coro 2
2:33		marcha arriba	coro 2 (guías: Manolín, Robertón of Van Van, Mayito of Van Van)
3:32		marcha de mambo	mambo 2
3:52		presión	piano tumbao with rapped intro to coro 3
4:01		marcha arriba	coro 3 (coristas: Haila & Vania of Bamboleo)
4:34	100	presión	piano tumbao with rapped intro to coro 4
4:44		masacote	
4:54		marcha arriba	coro 4
5:18		masacote	coro 4 with mambo 2
5:37		marcha de mambo	
5:48	101	bomba	
6:06		marcha de mambo	
6:16	97	marcha abajo	coda

Manuel "Manolín, el Médico de la Salsa" González wasn't trained as a musician or singer, but had an unsurpassed genius for mixing rhythms, syllables and slang – or to put it more simply, for writing coros. He used this gift, and his tightly knit team of world-class arrangers and rhythm section players, to field – for a period of about 3 years – the most popular band in Cuban music history, filling 90,000-seat soccer stadiums and churning out mega-hits such as *La bola*, which stayed at #1 for over 50 weeks. The psychological impact of Manolín-mania on his competitors was perhaps even more important to the timba explosion that his actual musical output. Evaluating the 1990s with the benefit of hindsight, the adrenaline that Manolín's popularity injected into the timba scene cannot be overestimated.

"El Médico" (he was actually a psychology student when NG La Banda's El Tosco gave him that nickname) made so much money (by Cuban standards) that he was able to use an unprecedented five-man percussion section: conguero, bongosero with hand bell, standing timbalero, drummer with timbales, and güirero. When the band hit its stride it featured Alexis "Pututi I" Arce on drums and Ángel "Pututi II" Arce on timbales, along with the highly innovative Alexis "Mipa" Cuesta on congas. Pututi II played contracampana and clave, and since the other bell was played by the bongosero, José Miguel Velázquez, Pututi I was free to devote all of his considerable talent to the drumset. Los Pututi were the first members to move to Miami and were replaced by Raymer Olalde on timbales and the electrifying (and I do mean *electrifying)* Reinier Guerra on drums.

Armando Gola (bass), Manolín, Reinier Guerra (drums), Hamed Barroso (guitar), Joaquín "El Kid" Díaz (coro)
SF Jazz Festival – 2001 – photo: Peter Maiden

When Manolín and his entire group moved to Miami, Manolín made so little money (by North American standards) that he switched to a two-man rhythm section. Fortunately, those two were Reinier Guerra on drums and Tomasito Cruz on congas, and it was this combination that recorded the stupendous live double album *El puente*. The two-man approach is now by far the most common configuration for United States timba bands, including Tiempo Libre, El Pikete (led by the aforementioned Mipa Cuesta), Havana NRG, and many others. It requires a monstrously good drummer but there are plenty to go around because so many great Cuban musicians have emigrated to Miami (not so affectionately referred to as "the timba graveyard" because of its excess of talent and scarcity of musical employment).

If I sound a bit cynical it's because I experienced timba in Cuba in the late 1990s at the very crest of the wave. It's quite rare in human history that all of the necessary factors come together to produce this kind of explosion. It takes a very special alignment of social, cultural, economic and political circumstances, a concentration of fiercely competitive talent and a fanatically responsive public. Most of humanity's great music has been produced in clusters in the midst of one of these wonderful but short-lived creative frenzies. Cuba has played host to far more than its fair per capita share of historic "scenes" – highlighted by the son explosion of the late 20s, the whole period from the mid-40s to the late 50s, and the 90s.

For more on the Manolín phenomenon, see my two-part online essay written when *El puente* was first released. There are multiple embedded audio files to help you get up to speed on this amazing group: (www.timba.com/artist_pages/311).

Further Listening Recommendations for Manolín, el Médico de la Salsa

Year	Song	Source
1994	*A pagar allá*	*Aventura loca* – Caribe
1996	*La bola*	*Para mi gente* – Ahí Namá
1996	*Ella no vale nada*	*Para mi gente* – Ahí Namá
1996	*Voy a mí*	*Para mi gente* – Ahí Namá
1996	*Me pasé de copas*	*Para mi gente* – Ahí Namá
1996	*Te conozco mascarita*	*Para mi gente* – Ahí Namá
1997	*Somos lo que hay*	*De buena fe* – Metro Blue (Caribe)
1997	*No lo comentes*	*De buena fe* – Metro Blue (Caribe)
1997	*Romeo y Julieta*	*De buena fe* – Metro Blue (Caribe)
1997	*Que le llegue la mano*	*De buena fe* – Metro Blue (Caribe)
1997	*Tengo mi mecánica*	*De buena fe* – Metro Blue (Caribe)
1997	*Que el que esté que tumbe*	*De buena fe* – Metro Blue (Caribe)
1998	*Y ahora baila*	*Jaque mate* – Inspector de la Salsa (Caribe)
1998	*La hiciste buena*	*Jaque mate* – Inspector de la Salsa (Caribe)
1998	*Jaque mate*	*Jaque mate* – Inspector de la Salsa (Caribe)
2000	*Dios sabe*	*El puente* – Ciocan
2005	*De tarea pa' la casa*	demo, *Tiene que ser Manolín* (2012) – Xplosion
2006	*Me falta La Habana*	demo (search YouTube)

Manolito y su Trabuco

highlighted track: *Hablando en serio – Hablando en serio* (2007) – EGREM – singer: Ricardo Amaray

time	tempo	gear	comments
0:00			rubato sax and keyboard intro
0:19	102	(funk drums)	keyboard intro
0:29		(add bell, congas, güiro)	
0:36		marcha arriba	horn intro
0:57		marcha abajo	cuerpo
1:35		marcha media	
1:44		marcha arriba	horn interlude
2:03		marcha abajo	cuerpo bridge
2:26		presión	piano tumbao with efectos
2:38		masacote	(masacote refers to entrance of the congas and bell)
2:47		marcha arriba	montuno – coro 1 (efecto is efecto 6 from Beyond Salsa for Ens.)
3:06		marcha de mambo	mambo 1
3:25		marcha arriba	appears to return to coro/guía but goes to efecto (brilliant touch)
3:30		presión	stunning transition to piano tumbao with efectos to coro 2
3:46		marcha arriba	coro 2 (great series of paraphrases from singer Amaray)
4:14		marcha de mambo	mambo 2
4:25		masacote	bass tumbao stops, efectos added, mambo 2 continues
4:43		marcha de mambo	conclusion of mambo 2
4:52		marcha arriba	coro 2
5:06		marcha de mambo	bloque into mambo 3
5:30		masacote	bass tumbao stops, efectos added, mambo 3 continues
5:52			coda

Pianist Manolito Simonet spent most of the 1980s as the musical director of Maravilla de Florida, a modernized charanga with flute and violins that we covered in Listening Tour 2. When he formed his Trabuco in 1993, Simonet wanted maximum resources for his exceptional arranging and orchestration talents, so he created a charangón on steroids, with violin, cello, flute, two trumpets, two trombones and a synth player responsible for a wide range of timbres, including tres.

The original Trabuco used güiro, congas and a standing timbalero with kick drum, Carlos Rodríguez, who had come over from Maravilla de Florida. By the time of the famous 1997 Concierto Eurotropical concert, Rodríguez had been replaced by a fiery young drumset player with a hardcore timba feel named Yuri Nogueira. After recording on Manolito's breakthrough album, *Marcando la distancia,* Yuri moved to Madrid in 1998 where he played and recorded briefly with Issac Delgado. Fortunately, Manolito was able to replace him with one of the great powerhouse drummers of the timba era, Roicel Riverón, still with the group as of 2012.

On paper, El Trabuco's approach is like Los Van Van– güiro, congas and one player handling drums and timbales – but Riverón has a markedly different style from Samuel Formell. Like Piloto and Oviedo with NG La Banda, Formell and Riverón make for a great comparison of two master drummers handling the same situation in different ways. Trabuco also has one of the most creative congueros in timba, Evelio Ramos, and an explosive güirero, Jorge Luis Guerra.

On some albums, Manolito has adopted the unusual approach of using a different rhythm section configuration than he uses in concert. Riverón plays his part without the large bell, freeing himself to play more a more detailed timbales part, and then overdubs bongó and campana separately.

Further Listening Recommendations for Manolito y su Trabuco

Year	Song	Singer	Source
1993	*Después de ti*	Rosendo "El Gallo" Díaz	*Directo al corazón* – Bembe Records
1996	*El águila*	Rosendo "El Gallo" Díaz	*Contra todos los prognósticos* – Eurotropical
1996	*Caballo grande*	Alex Fernández	*Concierto Eurotropical I* – Eurotropical
1997	*Marcando la distancia*	Sixto "El Indio" Llorente	*Marcando la distancia* – Eurotropical
1997	*Llegó la música cubana*	Sixto "El Indio" Llorente	*Marcando la distancia* – Eurotropical
2000	*Para que baile Cuba*	Sixto "El Indio" Llorente	*Para que baile Cuba* – Eurotropical
2000	*La boda de Belén*	Rosendo "El Gallo" Díaz	*Para que baile Cuba* – Eurotropical
2000	*Ven ven Siroco ven*	Sixto "El Indio" Llorente	*Para que baile Cuba* – Eurotropical
2000	*Saliditas contigo*	Ricardo Amaray	*Para que baile Cuba* –Eurotropical
2002	*Linda melodía*	Carlos Kalunga	*Se rompieron los termómetros* – Eurotropical
2002	*Tú me dijiste mentiras*	Ricardo Amaray	*Se rompieron los termómetros* – Eurotropical
2002	*Güiro, calabaza y miel*	Ricardo Amaray	*Se rompieron los termómetros* – Eurotropical
2006	*Comunícate*	Ricardo Amaray	*Hablando en serio* – EGREM
2006	*La raspadura*	Lázaro "Mayami" Díaz	*Hablando en serio* – EGREM
2006	*El cantor*	all	*Hablando en serio* – EGREM
2006	*Sacude la mata*	Lázaro "Mayami" Díaz	*Hablando en serio* – EGREM

Klímax

highlighted track: *Consejo a una amiga* – *Concierto Eurotropical I* (1997) – Eurotropical
singers: Manuel Denis, Carlos Kalunga, Ernesto Manuitt

time	tempo	gear	comments
0:00			spoken intro, clave with crowd
0:17	103	masacote	montuno preview – coro 1
0:55		marcha de mambo	horn introduction
1:13		presión/masacote	a cappella coro, efecto
1:34		marcha abajo	cuerpo verse 1 (Manuel Denis)
1:53		marcha arriba	coro (used as chorus of cuerpo)
2:02		marcha abajo	cuerpo verse 2 (Kalunga)
2:21		marcha arriba	coro (used as chorus of cuerpo)
2:30		marcha abajo	cuerpo bridge (Ernesto with harmonization)
2:49		masacote	montuno – breakdown with coro and efectos
3:07		marcha arriba	coro 1 (singers alternate guías)
3:55		marcha de mambo	mambo 1
4:14		masacote	coro 2
4:32		marcha arriba	
4:42		marcha de mambo	mambo 2
4:51		bomba	
5:00		masacote	coro 3 (with efectos)
5:28		marcha arriba	
5:37		marcha de mambo	mambo 3
5:48		bomba	
5:56		masacote	coro 4
6:15		marcha arriba	
6:24		marcha de mambo	mambo 4
6:43		bomba	
6:51		muela	motivo (keyboards double bass) while singer talks to crowd and sets up coro 5

7:41		masacote	coro 5 (rapped with just percussion)
8:09		marcha de mambo	mambo 5 with coro 5b
8:27		marcha arriba	coro 5b
8:46		muela	softer tumbaos while singer talks to crowd and sets up coro 6
9:36		masacote	coro 6
10:03		marcha de mambo	mambo 6 with coro 6
10:20		muela	softer tumbaos while singer sets up coro 7
10:40		masacote	coro 7 (with just percussion, then with crowd)
11:07		marcha de mambo	mambo 7
11:26			coda

From a harmonic and songwriting standpoint, Klímax is by far the most sophisticated and original of the timba bands. Rhythmically speaking, Piloto has kept the same basic scheme he used with Issac – himself on drums and timbales, with the contracampana mounted on the kick drum, and a "utility man" timbalero playing clave, mounted bongó bell, a mounted güiro and a mounted bongó, played with sticks, the latter a unique and wonderful element of the Klímax *sello*.

Piloto's primary creative collaborator is tecladista Yusef Díaz. Great arrangements have also been provided by founding pianist Tony Pérez and bassist Roberto Riverón (brother of Roicel, drummer of Manolito y su Trabuco). The soaring tenor Carlos Kalunga was the group's most iconic singer.

The founding timbalero, Yonder Peña, also from Issac's band, recorded the first three albums before moving to México. Next came Pepe Espinosa, then Jean Roberto San Cristóbal who remains with the group as of 2012. Another standout was founding conguero Jorge Luis "Papiosco" Torres.

Further Listening Recommendations for Klímax

Year	Song	Singers	Source
1995	*Mira si te gusta*	*Manuel Denis*	*Mira si te gusta* – Eurotropical
1995	*Una corazonada*	*Manuel Denis*	*Mira si te gusta* – Eurotropical
1995	*Lo que me falta por hacerte*	*Ernesto Manuitt*	*Mira si te gusta* – Eurotropical
1997	*Catarro chino*	*Carlos Kalunga*	*Concierto Eurotropical I* – Eurotropical
1997	*Aún así*	*Carlos Kalunga*	*Juego de manos* – Eurotropical
1997	*Juego de manos*	*Carlos Kalunga*	*Juego de manos* – Eurotropical
1997	*El cocinero*	*Kalunga, Denis, Manuitt*	*Juego de manos* – Eurotropical
1998	*El ventilador*	*Manuel Denis*	*Concierto Eurotropical II* – Eurotropical
1999	*Regalo de amor*	*Carlos Kalunga*	*Oye como va* – Eurotropical
1999	*Yo no quiero que mi novia sea religiosa*	*Leo Vera, J.C. Hechevarría*	*Oye como va* – Eurotropical
2008	*Dale cuatro malas*	*Juan Carlos Hechevarría*	*Sólo tú y yo* – BIS
2008	*La tentación*	*Luis Fernando (of Guaco)*	*Sólo tú y yo* – BIS

Bamboleo

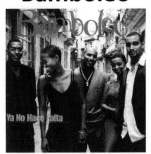

highlighted track: *Ya no hace falta – Ya no hace falta* (1999) – Ahí Namá – singer: Vania Borges

time	tempo	gear	comments
0:00	84	marcha abajo	horn intro
0:44		marcha abajo	cuerpo
2:10	87	motivo	transition
2:33	91	marcha arriba	montuno – coro 1
3:04	94	marcha de mambo	mambo 1
3:25		presión	coro 2 – *Efectos within presión can be called with separate signals - the presión begins with a 2+2+1 efecto. Next come the two "call-able" efectos – in this case, 2 hits, then 2 hits again. Finally a flourish of steady subdivisions in the congas leads to bomba.*
3:35		bomba	
3:45	95	presión	mambo 2 (efectos: 2 hits, 3 hits)
3:55	97	bomba	*(Another pre-determined efectos leads from bomba back to marcha)*
4:05		marcha de mambo	*(Another efecto occurs after the marcha section is in progress)*
4:15		presión	coro 3 (efectos: 2 hits, 2 hits)
4:25	99	bomba	
4:35		presión	mambo 2 (efectos: 2 hits, 3 hits)
4:44		bomba	
4:54		marcha de mambo	
5:04		presión	coro 4 (efectos: 2 hits, 2 hits)
5:13	101	bomba	
5:22		marcha de mambo	mambo 3
5:41		presión	(efectos: 1 hit, 1 hit)
5:50		bomba	
6:00	102	marcha de mambo	… fade

Bamboleo was able to break into the incredibly competitive mid-90s scene on the strength of Leonel Limonta's songwriting, Lazarito Valdés' lean, dark, polyrhythmic, R&B-laced arranging, a striking front line that included two gorgeous mulata singers with completely shaved heads, and, perhaps above all, a truly vicious rhythm section groove that left me buzzing each of the 40 times I heard them live in the late 90s. If their gear system wasn't quite as flexible as those of Paulito and Issac, it had plenty of interesting and unique aspects, including elaborate hand signals whereby the individual efectos could be altered within each presión section.

The 1996-1998 rhythm section was set up like Paulito's – a bongosero with a hand bell (Ulises Texidor) and a drummer, the amazing Ludwig Núñez, who combined contracampana and clave on timbales with lots of explosive drumset work.

In the spring of 1998 one of the divas, Haila Mompié, broke off to form Azúcar Negra with the main songwriter (Leonel Limonta), bassist/co-arranger (Rafael Vargas) and others. Bamboleo never missed a beat, producing another brilliant album the next year. The bongosero was replaced with a timbalero who played mounted campana and clave, but, in an interesting twist, Ludwig Núñez abandoned his timbales and played pure drumset with no bells at all, resulting in the only timba band to use only one bell. In that respect they were like an old-school conjunto, but that's where the comparison ended. Bamboleo's sound became even more modern, stark and aggressive.

Bamboleo, like many bands, became less focused and productive in the first decade of the 2000s, but – also like many bands – they're experiencing a resurgence here in the second decade. They now use the Van Van rhythm section formula: congas, güiro and a combination drummer/timbalero.

Further Listening Recommendations for Bamboleo

Year	Song	Singers	Source
1996	Circúlame	Osvaldo Chacón	Te gusto o te caigo bien – Ahí Namá
1997	Opening estudio	(instrumental and coro)	Yo no me parezco a nadie – Ahí Namá
1997	Yo no me parezco a nadie	Haila Mompié	Yo no me parezco a nadie – Ahí Namá
1997	Si no hablaras tanto	Vania Borges	Yo no me parezco a nadie – Ahí Namá
1997	Amor sin traspaso	Rafael Labarrera	Yo no me parezco a nadie – Ahí Namá
1997	Tú y yo, somos una misma cosa	Vania Borges	Yo no me parezco a nadie – Ahí Namá
1997	Película vieja	Rafael Labarrera	Yo no me parezco a nadie – Ahí Namá
1997	Con un canto en el pecho	Haila Mompié	Yo no me parezco a nadie – Ahí Namá
1999	Opening	(instrumental and coro)	Ya no hace falta – Ahí Namá
1999	Candil de nieve	Vania Borges, Jorge D. Rodríguez	Ya no hace falta – Ahí Namá
1999	Recapacita	Yordamis Megret	Ya no hace falta – Ahí Namá
1999	La tremenda	Alejandro Borrero	Ya no hace falta – Ahí Namá
1999	El protagonista	Vania Borges	Ya no hace falta – Ahí Namá
2001	El maíz	Yordamis Megret	various bootlegs
2001	El virus	Vania Borges	various bootlegs
2001	No puedo estar sin él	Yordamis Megret	various bootlegs

Azúcar Negra

highlighted track: *Te traicionó el subconciente* (1998) – MP3.com – singer: Haila Mompié

The album pictured, *Andar andando,* on the BIS label, is the only Azúcar Negra album with Haila Mompié that's easy to find and it's excellent, but even better was their initial 1998 Havana recording session – released on MP3.com, but no longer in print. Our track map below refers to this first version. Also note that YouTube has some great live Cuban television performances by the original band playing *Tratado de timba y salsa, Vengo de estreno* and others. *Vengo de estreno* and *Te traicionó* were also re-recorded in the 2000s with other singers and rhythm sections. The most important track to hunt down is the deliciously great *Almas disfrazadas,* only released on the MP3.com album.

time	tempo	gear	comments
0:00	97	marcha abajo	horn intro
0:19			percussion break
0:24		marcha abajo	cuerpo
1:22		marcha media	horn bridge to montuno
1:31		presión	montuno – coro 1
1:50		marcha arriba	
2:36		marcha de mambo	mambo 1
2:55		marcha arriba	coro 2
3:31		marcha de mambo	mambo 2
3:56		motivo	
4:07			coro 3
4:25		marcha de mambo	mambo 3 (note interesting 2-clave conga marcha)
4:43			add coro 3b
5:00		presión	note trademark folkloric triplet efectos
5:18		masacote	
5:36		marcha arriba	note after-efecto returning to marcha
5:44			coro 4
6:04			mambo 4
6:19		presión	
6:36		masacote/bomba	
6:54		marcha arriba	

Azúcar Negra broke off from Bamboleo in 1998 and featured Leonel Limonta's brilliant songwriting, Haila Mompié's iconic vocals, pianists Rey Ceballo, Roberto Linares, and Aisar Simón, and bassists Rafael Vargas and Adalberto "El Bamba" Domínguez. Later singers including Mónica Mesa and Tanja

Pantoja. Pepito Gómez, who got his start with Azúcar Negra, later became famous with Los Que Son Son and José Lugo.

The original Azúcar Negra had a very creative and throbbingly hot rhythm section with a unique approach. Pepe Espinosa played timbales, covering the jam block, contracampana, and doing all sorts of interesting things with his cha bell during breakdowns. The large campana was played by the drumset player, Pavel Rodríguez, who would later play timbales with Charanga Habanera. This is the only example in timba of a drumset player playing campaneo (Exercise 3-13) without also playing contracampaneo (Exercise 3-15), a combination that would work well for local bands seeking to achieve a timba groove without access to a virtuoso drummer. After the departure of Espinosa, Azúcar Negra switched to the Los Van Van approach of güiro, congas and a drumset player, Maikel Zamora, playing both bells.

Further Listening Recommendations for Azúcar Negra

Year	Song	Singers	Source
1998	*Vengo de estreno*	*Haila Mompié*	*Azúcar Negra* – MP3.com
1998	*Tratado de timba y salsa*	*Haila Mompié*	*Azúcar Negra* – MP3.com
1998	*Almas disfrazadas*	*Haila Mompié*	*Azúcar Negra* – MP3.com
2001	*Tíralo pa'l agua (Pelota)*	*Alexander Lara*	*Andar andando* – BIS
2001	*Frente frío*	*Mónica Mesa*	*Andar andando* – BIS
2001	*Eres como yo*	*Alexander Lara*	*Andar andando* – BIS
2001	*Se acabó la rabia*	*Haila Mompié*	*Andar andando* – BIS

Leonel Limonta – photo by Tom Bauer

Leonel Limonta is one of Cuba's great songwriters. Among his compositions are four of Charanga Habanera's greatest hits: *Extraños ateos, Quítate el disfraz, Nube pasajera* and *El avión;* most of Bamboleo's *Yo no me parezco a nadie* album, *24 días* for Issac Delgado, and almost all of Azúcar Negra's songs.

Los Van Van (timba era)

highlighted track: *Te pone la cabeza mala* (1997) – Caribe – singer: Robertón Hernández

The original version of this epic timba anthem, on the album of the same name, is broken into two tracks, the first and last of the album, fading out and fading back in, in "bookend" fashion. It works brilliantly for the flow of the album – in my opinion the greatest single Los Van Van album (many would argue strenuously for any of about six others). In any case, the two edits were rejoined and nicely remastered for the "Thirty Years" box set on the Aché label and our roadmap refers to the timings of this rejoined version.

time	tempo	gear	comments
0:00	103	marcha arriba	horn intro
0:14			cuerpo A (repeated twice)
0:42		motivo	cuerpo B (conga marcha, repeating figure in toms)
0:56		motivo	cuerpo C (bota)
1:20		marcha arriba	montuno: coro 1
2:06		motivo	transition (similar to cuerpo B)
2:12		marcha arriba	coro 2
2:40			mambo 1
3:00			coro 2
3:26		masacote	(bass drops out)
3:45		marcha arriba	mambo 2 with coro 2
4:04		masacote	mambo 3 (flute and synth)
4:23		marcha arriba	mambo 2 with coro 2
4:42			coro 2
5:14		masacote	vocal rap without coro
5:37		marcha arriba	mambo 2 with coro 2

Los Van Van could have laid claim to immortality based on what they did in the 70s, *or* what they did in the 80s, but it was in the 90s that Juan Formell and Pupy Pedroso, well into middle age, reached a new musical maturity that transcended the ephemeral trends of style and genre. NG La Banda had been the first beneficiary of a "mania" level of popularity in Havana. Charanga Habanera hit with even greater force, and as explained above, Manolín's brief period at the top was analogous – within Cuba – to the Beatles in the 60s or Michael Jackson in the 80s in the English-speaking world. Formell, Pupy & Co. had a choice – they could either throw in the towel and settle into a nice, comfortable career as a well-loved heritage act, playing *Sandunguera* and *Chirrín Chirrán,* or they could try to out-timba the testosterone-crazed timberos at their own game. They opted for the latter, and succeeded brilliantly – driven by genius songwriting, an uncanny feel for the public pulse, the powerhouse drumming of Samuel Formell, and two incredible young singers – Mayito Rivera and Robertón Hernández. They churned out one classic hit after another – *Voy a publicar tu foto, Pura vestimenta, Te pone la cabeza mala, Ni bombones ni caramelos* and their quintessential masterpiece, *Soy todo,* a breathtaking summation of the entire Cuban experience, certain to bring tears to the eyes and send chills down the spine of any red-blooded Cuban music lover. Then came the Grammy-winning *Llegó Van Van* album and the historic 1999 Miami tour.

Samuel Formell – photo by Tom Bauer

Samuel Formell is the prototype for the two-man monster drummer format so popular in the United States. Of course, Los Van Van could have afforded a whole drum corps, but they opted for a rock solid güirero and conguero and Samuel's pyrotechnics to produce the groove that earned them the *apodo* (nickname) *el tren* (the train). Samuel plays cáscara (Ex.3-19) and clave on cuerpos and, in the montuno sections, his trademark combination of three patterns we'll learn in the Rhythm Exercises 3 section: the "standard timba kick pattern" (Ex. 3-27), campaneo (Ex. 3-13), and contracampaneo 2 (Ex. 3-17), laced with wicked fills and alternating with song-specific interludes and special grooves.

Van Van's conquest of the 1990s was amazing, but when Pupy Pedroso left in 2001, that really should have been the end of it. It wasn't – not by a longshot. Pupy reunited with Changuito, who created an entirely new rhythm section scheme and assembled a group of his best protégées, including Bombón Reyes (who had by now finished his stint with Delgado). Van Van recovered by replacing Pupy with the well-traveled master timba pianist, Roberto Carlos Valdés, aka "Cucurucho", who had played with Bombón in the great 2000 Issac Delgado band. Due to problems with health and record companies, Van Van has not been as prolific as Pupy in the 2000s, but they've produced several strong albums and continue to tour the world and sound just as much like a runaway diesel locomotive as ever.

Further Listening Recommendations for Los Van Van (timba era)

Year	Song	Singers	Source
1992	Disco Azúcar	Ángel Bonne	Disco Azúcar – Xenophile
1992	Tú no colabores	Ángel Bonne	Disco Azúcar – Xenophile
1992	Que le den candela	Pedrito Calvo	Disco Azúcar – Xenophile
1992	La historia de Tania y Juan	Ángel Bonne	Disco Azúcar – Xenophile
1994	Qué tiene Van Van	Rivera, Bonne, Calvo	Lo último en vivo – QBADisc
1994	La sorpresa (Voy a publicar tu foto)	Mayito Rivera	Lo último en vivo – QBADisc
1994	Pura vestimenta	Ángel Bonne	Lo último en vivo – QBADisc
1994	Mándalo y ven	Mayito Rivera	Lo último en vivo – QBADisc
1996	Soy todo	Mayito Rivera	Ay Diós, ampárame – BIS
1996	Camina pa' que te conozcan	Robertón Hernández	Ay Diós, ampárame – BIS
1996	La fruta	Pedrito Calvo	Ay Diós, ampárame – BIS
1996	Empezó la fiesta	Mayito, Robertón, Pedrito	Ay Diós, ampárame – BIS
1997	Barriste con el	Mayito Rivera	Te pone la cabeza mala – Caribe
1997	Llévala a tu vacilón	Mayito Rivera	Te pone la cabeza mala – Caribe
1997	El tren se va	Mayito Rivera	Te pone la cabeza mala – Caribe
1997	Ni bombones ni caramelos	Robertón Hernández	Te pone la cabeza mala – Caribe
1997	Qué pasa con ella	Robertón Hernández	Te pone la cabeza mala – Caribe
1999	El negro está cocinando	Pedrito Calvo	Llegó Van Van – Caribe
1999	Mi chocolate	Pedrito Calvo	Llegó Van Van – Caribe
1999	La bomba soy yo	Mayito Rivera	Llegó Van Van – Caribe
2004	Quién no ha dicho una mentira	Robertón Hernández	Llegó Van Van – Caribe
2004	Permiso que llegó Van Van	Robertón Hernández	Llegó Van Van – Caribe
2004	Chapeando	Robertón Hernández	Chapeando – Unicornio
2004	Anda ven y quiéreme	Lele Rasalps	Chapeando – Unicornio
2004	Agua	Mayito Rivera	Chapeando – Unicornio
2004	Después de todo	Yeni Valdés	Chapeando – Unicornio
2009	Me mantengo	Lele Rasalps	Arrasando – Planet Records

Pupy Pedroso and Los Que Son Son

highlighted track: *De la Timba a Pogolotti* (2004) – *Mi timba cerrá* – EGREM – singer: Mandy Cantero

time	tempo	gear	comments
0:00	109	masacote	synth and percussion intro
0:09		marcha de songo	piano and bass enter
0:18			horn intro
0:27			cuerpo A1
0:44		marcha arriba	cuerpo B (coro)
1:02			horn interlude
1:20		marcha de songo	cuerpo A2
1:37		marcha arriba	montuno: coro 1 (same coro as in cuerpo)
2:30	110	marcha de mambo	mambo 1
2:47		marcha arriba	coro 2
3:31		presión with efectos	coro 2b
3:49		marcha de mambo	mambo 2
4:05	111	marcha arriba	coro 3
4:23		masacote	
4:32		marcha de songo	
4:47		marcha de mambo	mambo 3
5:25	112	masacote	... fade

César "Pupy" Pedroso was Formell's musical soulmate in Van Van for 32 years, but when he left, he never looked back – and never missed a beat. Within a year of leaving Van Van he had an album, *Qué cosas tiene la vida,* that was the talk of the timba world, and of 2012, he now has five albums of consistent brilliance.

The Los Que Son Son rhythm section, masterminded by Changuito, is one of the most innovative of the 2000s, with Bombón Reyes on drums, now also an arranger, conguero Duniesky Barreto and a changing, but consistently brilliant cast of bassists (Rafael Paceiro, Reinier "Negrón" Elizarde, Daymar Guerra) and timbaleros (René Suárez, Miguelito Escurriola, Albertico Ramos).

The initial lineup of singers was historic: Tirso Duarte, from Charanga Habanera (now a bandleader), Pepito Gómez, now in Puerto Rico recording with José Lugo, and Mandy Cantero, who also began with Charanga Habanera and has now replaced Mayito Rivera in Los Van Van.

Pupy's rhythmic scheme is unique. The timbalero plays special patterns using all three bells and the jam block. The drummer, Bombón, has no timbales and no bells, playing an incredibly improvisational and funky combination of hihat with his left hand and ghost snare and toms with his right. Changuito's formula called for a loud snare on the frontbeat of the 2-side (Exercise 3-33). At first this seems completely counterintuitive. Timba is closely related to funk and R&B, in which the snare is on the backbeat. In a clave setting, it makes perfect sense to play the snare on the 2-side backbeat, but on the frontbeat? Closer examination reveals that the snare is actually replacing the kick drum stroke in the standard timba kick pattern (Exercise 3-27). Maybe that's the explanation – maybe not – but Pupy's band has a truly torrid groove that no one can resist and no one ever gets tired of. For more on Changuito's long history of backbeat-related brilliance, see *Roots of Timba*.

Best of all, Los Que Son Son's entire run of brilliance has occurred *after 2001*. In other words, they've done it without feeling the urgency and extra inspiration of the mania-level popularity of Manolín & NG La Banda bearing down on them.

Further Listening Recommendations for Los Que Son Son

Year	Song	Singers	Source
2000	*La voluminosa*	Tirso Duarte	*Timba: The New Generation* – Termidor
2000	*Vamos a gozar hasta afuera*	various	*Timba: The New Generation* – Termidor
2002	*Qué cosas tiene la vida*	Mandy Cantero	*Qué cosas tiene la vida* – EGREM
2002	*El pregonero*	Mandy Cantero	*Qué cosas tiene la vida* – EGREM
2002	*Ay papá*	Pepito Gómez	*Qué cosas tiene la vida* – EGREM
2002	*Juégala*	Pepito Gómez	*Qué cosas tiene la vida* – EGREM
2002	*Te molesta que sea feliz*	Tirso Duarte	*Qué cosas tiene la vida* – EGREM
2005	*El buenagente*	Pepito Gómez	*El buenagente* – Pimienta
2005	*Dicen que dicen*	Pepito Gómez	*El buenagente* – Pimienta
2005	*Los tres gordos*	Mandy Cantero	*El buenagente* – Pimienta
2005	*La borrachera*	Pepito Gómez	*Mi timba cerrá* – EGREM
2005	*Cuéntamelo todo*	Pepito Gómez	*Mi timba cerrá* – EGREM
2008	*Si me quieres conocer*	Mandy Cantero	*Tranquilo que yo controlo* – EGREM
2008	*Se parece a aquel*	Pepito Gómez	*Tranquilo que yo controlo* – EGREM
2008	*Un poquito al revés*	Pepito Gómez	*Tranquilo que yo controlo* – EGREM
2008	*Baílalo hasta fuera (Machucadera)*	Machucadera	*Tranquilo que yo controlo* – EGREM
2008	*Nadie puede contra eso*	Mandy Cantero	*Tranquilo que yo controlo* – EGREM
2012	*Un loco con una mota*	Norisley "El Noro" Valladares	*Siempre Pupy* – EGREM
2012	*No te dejé por mala*	Norisley "El Noro" Valladares	*Siempre Pupy* – EGREM

Elito Revé y su Charangón

highlighted track: *Dale agua al dominó– Se sigue comentando* **(2005) – BIS – singer: Dagoberto Vásquez**

time	tempo	gear	comments
0:00	101	marcha abajo (changüí)	horn intro *(bongosero on bongó – timbalero plays special Revé changüí part, featuring cha bell and timbales)*
0:10			cuerpo A1
0:34		motivo	cuerpo A2 *(bongosero plays masacote style bell)*
0:52		marcha abajo (changüí)	cuerpo B (coro)
1:02	102		horn bridge
1:10		presión	montuno: introduction to coro 1
1:33	103	marcha arriba (changüí)	coro 1
1:52		presión	mambo 1
1:55	104	masacote	(folkloric efectos)
2:11		marcha arriba (changüí)	free-standing efecto at 2:29 *(efecto 4 from Beyond Salsa for Ens.)*
2:43	106	muela	Elito Revé's trademark vocal cameo
2:55		presión	coro 2 – mambo 2
2:58		masacote	
3:14	107	marcha arriba (changüí)	(another free-standing efecto at 3:23)
3:33			coro 2
3:46		presión	coro 2 – mambo 2
3:49		masacote	
3:55		marcha arriba (changüí)	... fade

Revé again? The same Revé that traveled from Guantánamo in 1956 to take Havana by storm with their rustic changüí-flavored chachachás? Yes, that's the one. In spite of having 56 years on the old odometer, Elito Revé y su Charangón is anything but a "heritage act". The group's last three albums have been as good as, or better than, anything they've ever done. Even if you ignore their illustrious history, *Se sigue comentando, Fresquecito* and *De qué estamos hablando* are among the most exciting new releases of the 2000s. Their key arrangers have been bassists Giovanni Cofiño and Aisar Hernández.

Andy Fornet – 2010 – Yoshi's San Francisco – photo by Tom Ehrlich

On paper, the current group uses the same rhythm section configuration as Charanga Habanera – a bongosero with hand bell, güiro, congas, and a standing timbalero with a kick drum. The timbal style, however, is completely different and unique to Revé. Elio Revé, Sr., who passed away in 1997, was the architect of the style, using a cha bell instead of a contracampana and playing patterns derived from the changüí bongó del monte on the open low timbal. Revé had a quirky technique with all sorts of unusual abanicos, rolls and other figures. The current timbalero, Andy Fornet, is an amazing musician. He's mastered Revé's rustic style and mixes it brilliantly with his own polished and sophisticated technique. Revé's gear scheme is also quite unique.

Further Listening Recommendations for Elito Revé y su Charangón

Year	Song	Singers	Source
2003	*Así es él*	Rosendo "El Gallo" Díaz	*45 Años* – TUMI
2005	*1999*	Dagoberto Vásquez	*Se sigue comentando* – BIS
2005	*MI vecina*	Alexei "El Nene" Sánchez	*Se sigue comentando* – BIS
2005	*Tu zorreo*	Alexei "El Nene" Sánchez	*Se sigue comentando* – BIS
2005	*Se sigue comentando*	Dagoberto Vásquez	*Se sigue comentando* – BIS
2007	*Fresquecito*	Dagoberto Vásquez	*Fresquecito* – BIS
2007	*El teléfono*	Lázaro Cuesta	*Fresquecito* – BIS
2007	*Ya no te doy más na'*	Eric Broche	*Fresquecito* – BIS
2007	*El jonrón*	Robertón Hernandez/ Dagoberto Vásquez	*Fresquecito* – BIS
2007	*La madrugada*	Lázaro Cuesta	*Fresquecito* – BIS
2010	*De qué estamos hablando*	Dagoberto Vásquez	*De qué estamos hablando* – BIS
2010	*Agua pa' Yemayá*	Emilio "El Niño" Frías	*De qué estamos hablando* – BIS

Havana d'Primera

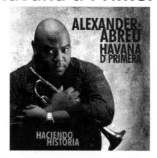

highlighted track: *Cosas de un amigo – Haciendo historia* (2009) – Ahí Namá – singer: Alexander Abreu

time	tempo	gear	comments
0:00	112	motivo	intro played in unison by all
0:05		marcha arriba	horn intro (interesting conga marcha)
0:13			cuerpo A1 and A2
0:39		marcha abajo	cuerpo B
0:48		marcha media	cuerpo C (bomba sicá feel)
1:06		marcha arriba	cuerpo A3
1:24		marcha arriba	montuno: coro 1 (after efecto at 1:32)
2:15		marcha de mambo	mambo 1
2:49		marcha arriba	coro 2
3:15		marcha de mambo	mambo 2 with coro 2b
3:24		masacote	
3:34		marcha arriba	coro 2b
3:45			coro 3
3:50		masacote	
4:07		marcha de mambo	mambo 3 with coro 3b
4:24		marcha arriba	coro 4
4:41		masacote w/batás	
4:57		marcha arriba	trumpet solo with coro 4 ... fade

Havana d'Primera is the most exciting new timba band since Pupy y Los Que Son Son. Their leader and lead singer, Alexander Abreu, had already established himself as the best trumpeter on the island playing with Paulito FG y su Élite in their glory years, with Issac Delgado, and then spending several years as a freelancer, recording on dozens of albums. Then, incredibly, he transformed himself into a brilliant songwriter, dynamic front man and powerful lead singer. Havana d'Primera was formed by a team of "musicians' musicians", many of whom had played with Opus 13 and/or Paulito FG y su Élite. The band had two stated goals – to rekindle the brilliance of late-1990s timba, and to be a more democratic band where sidemen are treated with respect and given the opportunity to do side projects. In spite of their serious, seemingly less-commercial approach, the band has caught fire in Cuba, South America and Europe, in great part due to Abreu's soulful melodies, lyrics and vocal delivery. *Carita de pasaporte,* from 2012, has become an international hit.

Havana d'Primera ("HdP") has an interesting rhythm section approach that no band has ever used. They have three percussionists, but they set up four percussion "stations" – bongó, congas, timbales with kick, and drumset. When the bassist plays "baby bass" (upright electric), the percussionists play timbales, congas and bongó and when the bassist plays electric, they switch to drums, timbales and congas, with the timbalero playing both bells and the drummer grooving heavily on the hihat.

In order to allow members more freedom to do side projects, the band has two well-rehearsed drummers Rodney Barreto and Keisel Jiménez (an extremely melodic soloist), while Güillermo del Toro switches between timbales and congas.

Further Listening Recommendations for Havana d'Primera

Year	Song	Singers	Source
2007	*Cuando suena el río*	Alexander Abreu	*Haciendo historia* – Ahí Namá
2007	*Mi música*	Alexander Abreu	*Haciendo historia* – Ahí Namá
2007	*Resumen de los 90*	Alexander Abreu	*Haciendo historia* – Ahí Namá
2012	*Carita de pasaporte*	Alexander Abreu	*Pasaporte* – Ahí Namá
2012	*Se te olvida quien soy*	Alexander Abreu	*Pasaporte* – Ahí Namá
2012	*El que sabe está calla'o*	Alexander Abreu	*Pasaporte* – Ahí Namá

Alexander Abreu – 2010 – photo by Patrick Bonnard – patrickbonnard.com

Other Recommended Timba Artists

Dany Lozada was one of the lead singers and composers on Charanga Habanera's epic fourth album, *Tremendo delirio,* writing or co-writing *Usa condón, Lo siento por ti* and *Qué quieres de mí.* He and arranger/pianist Juan Carlos González left together in 1997 to form the brilliant but short-lived Dany Lozada y su Timba Cubana, recording *Tanto le pedí,* one of the great undiscovered treasures of the timba era. Every measure is packed with subtle, witty and uniquely funky musical nuances. After moving to the United States, Lozada has had the familiar problem of not being able to form a steady group capable of doing justice to his intricate arrangements or creating new ones. *Tanto le pedí's* drummer, Raúl Hernández, often played an unusual six-stroke kick pattern, covered in *Beyond Salsa Percussion, Volume 1.* **Suggested starting point:** *Tanto le pedí.*

Like Lozada, **Ángel Bonne** was a singer/songwriter in one of Cuba's top bands (in this case Los Van Van) who set out on his own as a leader. Unlike Lozada, however, Bonne, the son of Enrique Bonne (see Listening Tour 2) stayed in Cuba and produced five strong CDs and a long list of soulful and harmonically gorgeous songs. **Suggested starting points:** *Bonne & Bonne Co.* and *Circunstancias.*

Edel Herrera, Andrés "El Negrón" Miranda of Wil Campa y su Gran Unión – Yoshi's SF – 2012 – photo by Tom Ehrlich

Wil Campa y su Gran Unión is a Havana band that's had very few personnel changes in the last six years, resulting in a degree of tightness and precision unmatched by even their most famous and well-established competitors. Their rhythm section uses the two-man approach, with drummer Edel Herrera and the legendary conguero Andrés "Negrón" Miranda, previously of Issac Delgado and Irakere. **Suggested starting point:** the Cubadisco-nominated *Todo es posible.*

Envidia Studio Bands – In the early 2000s, the label Envidia produced about 30 timba albums using studio bands that seldom played live or toured, and working bands with better sidemen than they could afford to use live in the less lucrative first few years of the new century. These "house band" musicians became quite accustomed to working with each other and were among the best in Cuba (to name a few, bassist Pedro Pablo, conguero Jorge Luis "Papiosco" Torres, pianist Sergio Noroña and three great singers, Tirso Duarte, Mandy Cantero and Michel Maza). From a percussion point of view, the most interesting highlight is Papiosco's conga work on *Ases de la timba* and the two Michel Maza albums. **Suggested starting points:** Los Ases de la Timba, Michel Maza, Tirso Duarte, Arnaldo y su Cosmopólita, Charanga Forever, and Rebambaramba. Charanga Forever's earlier pre-Envidia albums, especially *Fantástica presenta* (with Juan Carlos González) are also excellent.

Salsa Mayor is one of the most popular current bands in Cuba, featuring a tightly rehearsed stage show reminiscent of Charanga Habanera and a rhythm section approach heavily modeled on Los Van Van and Los Que Son Son. **Suggested starting point:** *Anda y pégate.*

Maintaining a well-rehearsed timba band with a continuous stream of new creative material is next to impossible in the **United States** but several have succeeded against long odds. **Tiempo Libre** has had three Grammy-nominated albums and has managed to tour continuously by plugging into the classical music, university and festival circuits. They also use a two-man rhythm section with a conguero and a drummer/timbalero. **Suggested starting point:** *Secret Radio,* featuring the current drummer, Armando "Pututi III" Arce and founding conguero Leandro González.

With hundreds of the world's best Cuban musicians and tragically few gigs, band names and personnel change as often as the weather in the "timba graveyard" of Miami, but three groups have shown staying power and produced repertoires of solid original material.

Timbalive has three drummers from the same family. Leo and Coky García (ex-Opus 13) play timbales and congas, respectively, and their cousin Miguelito was Havana d'Primera's bongosero until 2011. Musical director Bayron Ramos, like his brother Brailly, is among the most creative writers in Miami. **Suggested starting point:** *From Miami a La Habana* (guest pianist Melón Lewis).

Tomasito Cruz is one of the most important congueros in Cuban music history and the subject of my three-volume set, *The Tomás Cruz Conga Method.* His most important innovations were to extend the length of his conga marchas to two or even four claves, and to compose special marchas for each arrangement. He played with Paulito FG in Cuba and Manolín in the US before becoming a band leader. In his own group, singing and composing as well as playing congas, he uses a two-man rhythm section with the great Reinier Guerra on drums. **Suggested Starting point:** *Candela.*

El Pikete is led by one of the other towering congueros of the timba era, Alexis "Mipa" Cuesta. Mipa has a very different approach from Cruz. Instead of composing song-specific marchas, he greatly stretched the envelope for controlled improvisation, especially in his ground-breaking work with Manolín. Like most US-based bands, the cost-effective two-man rhythm section approach is used.

Suggested starting point for El Pikete: *Timba de primera toma.* Other promising Miami-based groups include **Ntaya, Brailly Ramos** and **Palo.**

San Francisco has four timba bands. **Jesús Díaz y su QBA** has two albums of original material. **Fito Reinoso y su Ritmo y Armonía** features a fabulous improvising sonero in the mold of Cándido Fabré. **Rumbaché** has as intricate a gear and efecto scheme as any Cuban band, and the most recent addition, **Team Bahía**, combines stars from each of the other bands and will begin adding original material soon. LA's top bands are **Chalo y su Aché, Rumbanquete** and Edgar Hernández's **Charanga Cubana**. In the north, there are strong Latin scenes in **Seattle, Vancouver** and especially **Toronto.**

Havana NRG is based in Texas and has stayed together for well over a decade with a very tight 7-person lineup using the usual two-man percussion combination. **Suggested starting point:** *Receta perfecta.* Bill Wolfer's **Mamborama**, currently inactive, produced three successful CDs using a variety of top Cuban musicians, garnering two Cubadisco nominations. **Suggested starting point:** *Entre la Habana y el Yuma* with Roicel Riverón and Giraldo Piloto drumming on different tracks. Another interesting recording-only project is drummer Mike Racette's **Soul y Sol**. **Suggested starting point:** *Havana Heavy Hitters,* featuring Michel Maza on vocals.

Perhaps the most successful and certainly the most unique U.S. timba band is **The Pedrito Martínez Group**, which produces powerful and original timba with only four players. It's like a "timba conjunto" – no drums and no timbales. The only bell is the bongosero's hand bell. So, you have a bongosero with hand bell, bass, piano and the leader playing three congas while sitting on (and playing) a large cajón that partially covers the role of the kick drum. All four sing beautifully. Sometimes the band is extended to a septet by adding two horns and third percussionist, the great folkloric master Román Díaz, who responds to the timba gear changes by switching between three batás strapped together and a chékere. Because of this lower density and volume, the group's masacote grooves reveal sublime and otherwise buried nuances of the batás and congas.

Sweden is the unlikely home of several of the world's best timba bands. Most remarkable is **Calle Real**. I've made a game of playing their record for Cuban musicians, challenging them to identify the single Cuban in the group (all the rest are Swedish). So far no one has succeeded (the correct answer is conguero Rickard Valdés, son of Bebo Valdés). This group uses the two-person percussion approach. **Suggested starting point:** *Me lo gané.* Two other great Swedish bands are **La tremenda** (**Suggested starting point:** *La tremenda*) and **Orquesta Pomo**. **Perú** has a torrid timba scene. Keep an eye out for a band called **Mayimbe**. **Suggested starting point:** *De la Habana a Perú.*

Elsewhere in Europe are **Calle Sol**, in Poland, led by Rey Ceballo, the founding pianist of Azúcar Negra, **The Osvaldo Chacón Group**, in England, led by the original male vocalist of Bamboleo, **Contrabando** from Belgium, and the **Cubop City Big Band** with Nils Fischer and Marc Bischoff.

I apologize in advance for leaving out dozens of promising bands in many countries that will make a major impact soon. See timba.com to keep up with the latest developments around the world.

Rhythm Exercises 3: Four-Beat Rhythmic Cells

Among the many four-beat rhythmic cells are the two most important in Latin music: the *clave* rhythm and the *basic dance step,* each of which has several variations. Let's start with dancing.

Dancing Patterns

Ryan Mead and Sidney Weaverling of Rueda con Ritmo
photo by Patrick Hickey – www.idyll.com

On paper, **Exercise 3-1** looks like a two-beat cell, but because dancers alternate left-right-left, right-left-right, it takes four beats to complete one full basic step.

The man usually, but not always, starts on his left foot and the woman on her right. Either way, the pattern takes one full cycle of our four-by-four grid: either left-right-left, right-left-right or right-left-right, left-right-left.

Don't be confused by the way dance teachers count. Their most common counting method, "1-2-3, 5-6-7", is based on eight counts per basic step, but some instructors substitute "4-5-6" for "5-6-7", ignoring the idea of spacing in order to keep the numbers sequential. Don't panic! Once you master the information in this section, you'll be able to "translate" freely between the various "languages" used by different groups of dancers and musicians.

Start by following along with the grid while you listen to **Audio Track 3-1**, then try dancing in place.

Exercise 3-1: basic dance step "on 1" • Audio Tracks 3-1a-d

basic dance step ("on 1")	•		•		•				•		•		•		
footwork (reverse for partner)	L		R		L				R		L		R		
as usually counted by dancers	1		2		3				5		6		7		
emphasized step	>								>						

basic dance step ("on 1")	X○X○	X○○○	X○X○ X○○○
footwork (reverse for partner)	L○R○	L○○○	R○L○ R○○○
as usually counted by dancers	1○2○	3○○○	5○6○ 7○○○
emphasized step	>○○○	○○○○	>○○○ ○○○○

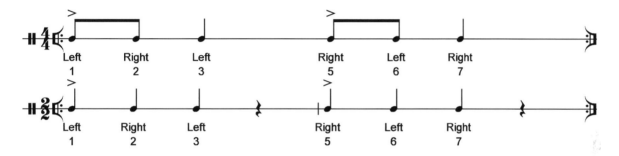

The accent mark (>) indicates the "break" step – the step away from the basic starting position (i.e., feet together side-by-side).

Our method of building the rhythm stroke-by-stroke is a bit trickier with dancing because you'll have to return to the starting position each time. For these exercises, dancing in place should be sufficient. After you master the motion, listen carefully to the maracas to improve your timing.

With help from YouTube, instructional DVDs, and dance instructors in your area, you can learn many different ways to stylize these steps. Some styles require stepping forward with the left foot and back with the right, but a common step in Cuba involves breaking back with both feet.

basic dance step ("on 1")	•		•		•				•		•		•		
		left foot breaks back		shift weight to right foot		replace left foot		(wait, or tap right foot)		right foot breaks back		shift weight to left foot		replace right foot		(wait, or tap left foot)	

The optional "tap", a stylistic flourish executed without shifting weight, is a placeholder, analogous to the *manoteo* of the conguero or the unpitched percussive strokes of a timba bassist – a way for dancers to improve timing by filling the pause after each set of three consecutive steps.

There are several variations on the basic step, some more common than others. **Exercise 3-2** shows a step alternately called *contratiempo,* "on 2", or "Power 2". It's never called "on 4" or "on 8", although, as you can see below, the most accented step comes on these counts and, if you watch good *son* dancers, they also *start* on either 4 or 8 to align with the third stroke of the 3-side of clave. This is the dance step of choice for *son, danzón* and *changüí.* Depending on the song, tempo, region and preferences of the dancers, it's also sometimes used for *salsa* and Cuban *casino* dancing.

Dancing *son* in Havana – 2012 – photo by Richard Robinson

There are two sets of audio files for this particular exercise. Those labeled "prep" (for "preparatory exercise") start on 2, as you'd expect. This will help you understand that the movements of dancing on 2 are identical to those of dancing on 1. Once you're clear on this, abandon the 3-2-prep files, and switch to the normal Exercise 3-2 files, which start on 8, as *son* dancers do.

Exercise 3-2: basic dance step "on 2" • Audio Tracks 3-2a-d and 3-2-prep-a-d

			•		•		•				•		•		•	
basic dance step ("on 2")			•		•		•				•		•		•	
footwork			L		R		L				R		L		R	
as counted by dancers			2		3		4				6		7		8	
emphasized step							>								>	
starting point (non-"prep" tracks)															>	

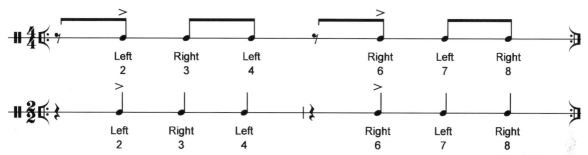

```
basic dance step ("on 2")        ○○X○  X○X○  ○○X○  X○X○
footwork                         ○○L○  R○L○  ○○R○  L○R○
as counted by dancers            ○○2○  3○4○  ○○6○  7○8○
emphasized step                  ○○○○  ○○>○  ○○○○  ○○>○
starting point (non-"prep" tracks) ○○○○  ○○○○  ○○○○  ○○>○
```

Guaguancó – **Members of AfroCuba de Matanzas** – 2012 – photo by Richard Robinson

Dancing "on 3", while seldom discussed, is actually quite common, especially in Cuba.

Exercise 3-3: basic dance step "on 3" • Audio Tracks 3-3a-d

basic dance step ("on 3")	•			•		•		•					•		•	
footwork	R			L		R		L					R		L	
as counted by dancers	1			3		4		5					7		8	
emphasized step				>									>			
alternate emphasized step	>							>								

```
        basic dance step ("on 3")  X○○○  X○X○  X○○○  X○X○
                        footwork   R○○○  L○R○  L○○○  R○L○
             as counted by dancers 1○○○  3○4○  5○○○  7○8○
                  emphasized step  ○○○○  >○○○  ○○○○  >○○○
        alternate emphasized step  >○○○  ○○○○  >○○○  ○○○○
```

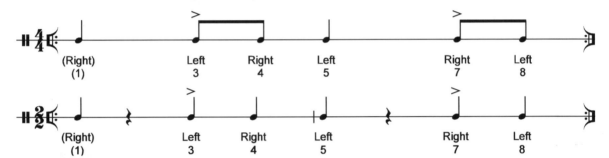

One of many dance workshops at the popular SF SalsaRueda Festival – 2012 – photo by Peter Maiden – maidenfoto.com

Dance congresses are a great way to meet other dancers, learn a lot in a few days, and hear top bands.
SF SalsaRueda (salsavaletodo.com) is probably the best and largest Cuban-style congress in the U.S.

Dancing "on 4" is included for completeness, but seldom used, in spite of the fact that leading out on the *ponche* (dance counts 4 and 8) corresponds to many of the most important parts of the bass and conga patterns.

Exercise 3-4: basic dance step "on 4" • Audio Tracks 3-4a-d

basic dance step ("on 4")	•		•				•		•		•				•	
footwork	L		R				L		R		L				R	
as counted by dancers	1		2				4		5		6				8	
emphasized step							>								>	

basic dance step ("on 4")	X∘X∘	∘∘X∘	X∘X∘	∘∘X∘
footwork	L∘R∘	∘∘L∘	R∘L∘	∘∘R∘
as counted by dancers	1∘2∘	∘∘4∘	5∘6∘	∘∘8∘
emphasized step	∘∘∘∘	∘∘>∘	∘∘∘∘	∘∘>∘

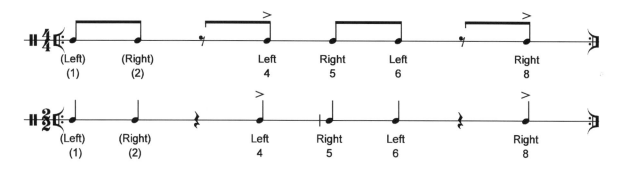

(Left)	(Right)	Left	Right	Left	Right
(1)	(2)	4	5	6	8

Dancing on 1, 3, 5 and 7 simultaneously – Rueda con Ritmo at the 2011 SF SalsaRueda Festival
http://youtu.be/feHsuyDffZc

The many types of dance steps can be mind-numbingly and ankle-twistingly confusing, but can also be used to great artistic effect, as demonstrated in the YouTube clip shown on the previous page, an extraordinary bit of choreography by the Bay Area dance troupe *Rueda con Ritmo,* in which four couples dance on 1, 3, 5 and 7, respectively. At the 3:58 mark, they separate and briefly dance on 1, 2, 3, 4, 5, 6, 7, and 8 simultaneously.

If you're not confused yet, get ready for this next part. There's also "on 2, New York-style" or "ET2" as taught by New York dance instructor Eddie Torres. As you can see from the diagram below, it looks just like "on 1" on paper but the long steps away from the body (the "break" steps), are on 2 and 6. If you invert the L/R pattern, some people call it PR2 instead of ET2.

Variation on Exercise 3-1: basic dance step "New York 2" • (use Audio Track 3-1)

basic dance step ("NY 2")	•		•		•				•		•		•			
footwork	L		R		L				R		L		R			
as counted by dancers	1		2		3				5		6		7			
emphasized step			>								>					

basic dance step ("New York 2")	XoXo	Xooo	XoXo	Xooo
footwork	LoRo	Looo	RoLo	Rooo
as counted by dancers	1o2o	3ooo	5o6o	7ooo
emphasized step	oo>o	oooo	oo>o	oooo

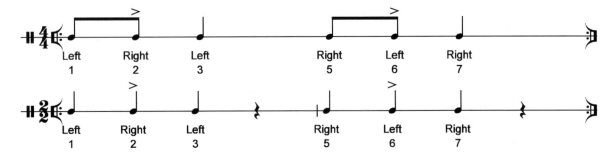

You'll probably never see anyone dancing to the pattern shown below in **Exercise 3-5**, and if you try it on the dance floor, you're likely to end up in a tangled heap of arms, legs and broken stiletto heels. That said, it's a great rhythmic exercise that relates to the son montuno era of the 1940s, one of the most important periods in Cuban music history.

> **Suggested Reading:** The following enigmatic dance step was first written about in David F. García's *Arsenio Rodríguez and the Transnational Flows of Latin Popular Music,* the most important book written about perhaps the most important figure in the history of Cuban music. García reports learning the step from Arsenio's own niece, among other sources. For much more on Arsenio Rodríguez, see Listening Tour 1 above.

This special son montuno step differs from today's dancing practices in three dramatic ways:

1. There are steps on the *offbeats* – the subdivisions *between* the eight numbered steps that dancers usually count.

2. The left-right-left half of the step has a different rhythm from the right-left-right half.

3. The pattern is *clave-aligned.* We'll learn more about this in the next section, but for now, note that the shaded cells coincide with the clave and the third step is an important *clave marker* (see Exercise 3-11).

Exercise 3-5: special son montuno step • Audio Tracks 3-5a-d

			•		•			•				•	•		•	
special son montuno step																
footwork			L		R			L				R	L		R	
as counted by dancers			2		3			&				&	7		8	
emphasized step															>	
2-3 son clave			•		•				•			•			•	

```
basic dance step (special son montuno)   ○○X○  X○○X  ○○○X  X○X○
                              footwork    ○○L○  R○○L  ○○○R  L○R○
                   as counted by dancers  ○○2○  3○○&  ○○○&  7○8○
                        emphasized step   ○○○○  ○○○○  ○○○○  ○○>○
                          2-3 son clave   ○○X○  X○○○  X○○X  ○○X○
```

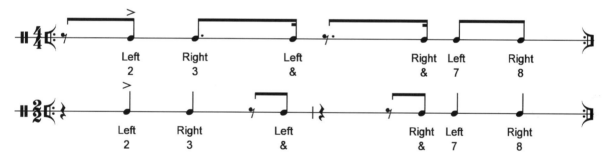

Exercise 3-6, our last dance step, is called *chachachá.*

Enrique Jorrín, a violinist who played with Arcaño and Orquesta América and later led his own group in the 1950s, said he derived the name *chachachá* from the sounds of the dancers' feet shuffling on the dance floor in sync with the güiro (Exercise 2-1). Chachachá must be danced "on 2" for this to happen, unlike the other steps we've learned, where you can dance "on 1" or "on 2".

When chachachá went viral, some dancers unwittingly learned it (and some dance schools taught it) as "one, two, cha-cha-chá" (instead of "two, three, cha-cha-chá") and this way of doing the step can still often be encountered, although most dancers who try it the original Cuban way agree that the dance feels more natural when the steps lock in with the güiro.

Dancing *chachachá* as Cubans do with the güiro

chachachá step	•		•		•		•	•	•		•		•		•	•
güiro pattern	•		•		•		•	•	•		•		•		•	•
(start on >)	cha	>					cha	cha	cha						cha	cha

Exercise 3-6: chachachá • Audio Tracks 3-6a-d

chachachá step	•		•		•		•	•	•		•		•		•	•
footwork	R		L		R		L	R	L		R		L		R	L
as counted by dancers	1		2		3		4	&	5		6		7		8	&
starting point		>														

```
chachachá step        XoXo  XoXX  XoXo  XoXX
footwork              RoLo  RoLR  LoRo  LoRL
as counted by dancers 1o2o  3o4&  5o6o  7o8&
starting point        oo>o  oooo  oooo  oooo
```

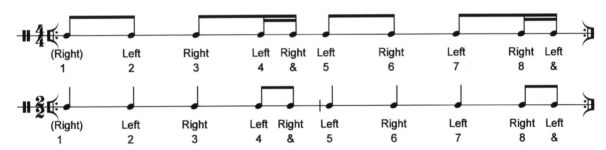

4/4
(Right) Left Right Left Right Left Right Left Right Left
1   2   3   4   &   5   6   7   8   &

2/2
(Right) Left Right Left Right Left Right Left Right Left
1   2   3   4   &   5   6   7   8   &

Juan de Dios Ramón Morejón, Raíces Profundas – photo by Peter Maiden – maidenfoto.com

Before leaving the topic of dancing, we should mention a subjective element that can be a source of confusion when watching dancers. There are many arrangements that combine a section that feels like it starts on the 2-side with one that feels like it starts on the 3-side. If you're used to starting on your left foot, you suddenly feel like you're starting on your right when the emphasis of the music changes. With inexperienced dancers, this often causes a "train wreck". To experience this for yourself, acquire a recording of *Todos vuelven,* from the album *Buscando América,* by Rubén Blades. It's a beautiful and brilliant arrangement, but as you dance through the whole track, you'll find that the beginning of the phrase seems to flip from your left to your right foot several times (at 1:50, 2:26, 3:03 and 4:10, to be exact). Many dance instructors offer special classes and techniques for learning how to deal with this type of situation gracefully. It's also explained in greater detail, with audio exercises, in our companion volume, *Understanding Clave and Clave Changes.*

Finally, with some songs, your dance partner will feel the music starting on the 2-side when you feel it starting on the 3-side. There's never a right answer – you just have come to an agreement.

Far more important than any of this left-brained madness is simply feeling the subdivisions as you dance. You don't have to know which beat you're "dancing on" as long as you're feeling a strong, physical connection to the subdivisions. The same attention to the subdivisions that will make you a better musician will make you a better dancer. *Feel the grid* – your dance partners will thank you.

Dancers starting young in Matanzas – 2012 – photo by Richard Robinson

131

Clave Patterns

The subject of *clave* is so important, so fascinating, and so mired in confusion and controversy that I've devoted a full book to it – *Understanding Clave and Clave Changes* (timba.com/clave). For our current survey, we'll settle for learning to play clave in its four most common forms and presenting a brief introduction to its most basic principles. The section below will make a lot more sense if you read it a second time after finishing the rest of the book. Clave is one of those mysteries of life that makes a little more sense each time you return to it over the course of a lifetime.

Exercise 3-7 is called *2-3 son clave.*

Exercise 3-7: 2-3 son clave • Audio Tracks 3-7a-d

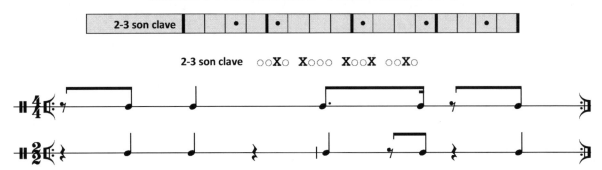

Each two-beat half of any clave cell is called a *side.* The side with two strokes is called the *2-side* and the side with three strokes, (wait for it …), is called the *3-side.* The chart on the next page illustrates and reviews the connections between tresillo and clave that we were getting so hot and bothered about in Exercises 2-2 (tresillo) and 2-3 (displaced tresillo).

								•		•		•	
tresillo								•		•		•	
2-3 son clave		•		•				•		•		•	
displaced tresillo		•		•			•						

Exercise 3-8 is called *3-2 son clave.*

Exercise 3-8: 3-2 son clave • Audio Track 3-8a-d

3-2 son clave	•				•				•				•				•			

3-2 son clave   X○○X ○○X○ ○○X○ X○○○

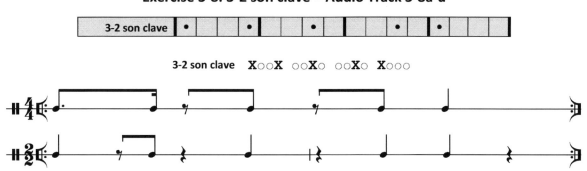

The difference between 3-2 and 2-3 clave is obvious on paper – you just swap the first two beats with the last two beats. You're simply starting at a different point in the same rhythmic cycle.

3-2 son clave	•				•				•				•				•			
2-3 son clave			•		•				•				•				•			

Or to look at it in another way:

3-2 son clave	•			•			•				•		•									
2-3 son clave											•		•				•			•		•

When listening, however, the difference between 2-3 and 3-2 clave is subjective because what you're hearing is the same loop cycling over and over. Where is the starting point? It all depends on where *you*, the individual listener, perceive the beginning of the musical phrase of the voices and instruments, and this can change as the song progresses. If you hear the beginning on the 2-side, you would say that the passage is "in 2-3 clave" and vice versa. What's *not* subjective is how the melody aligns "vertically" with the clave, regardless of its perceived starting point. Every singer and musician in a group must agree on this type of clave orientation. If one part is out of alignment with the others (i.e., playing the 2-side when everyone else is playing the 3-side), it's called *cruza'o* ("crossed") and will be obvious (and offensive) to experienced listeners, musicians and dancers.

If all this sounds horribly confusing, you're not alone. It *is* horribly confusing, so don't torture yourself trying to master clave in one sitting. It takes time and patience to fully internalize the reasons that clave is so important and so musically satisfying. The first step is to get the sound and feel of the rhythm into your blood. Later, when you can do these dancing and clave exercises in your sleep, try reading this section again.

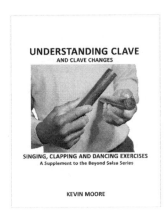
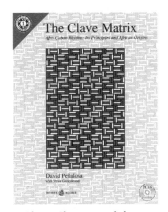

Everything You Always Wanted to Know About Clave ... *and then some*
Understanding Clave and Clave Changes, **by Kevin Moore** – timba.com/clave
The Clave Matrix, **by David Peñalosa** – bembe.com

Exercises 3-9 and **3-10** are called *rumba clave,* which also comes in two flavors: 2-3 and 3-2. Another name for rumba clave is *clave de guaguancó.*

Exercise 3-9: 2-3 rumba clave • Audio Tracks 3-9a-d

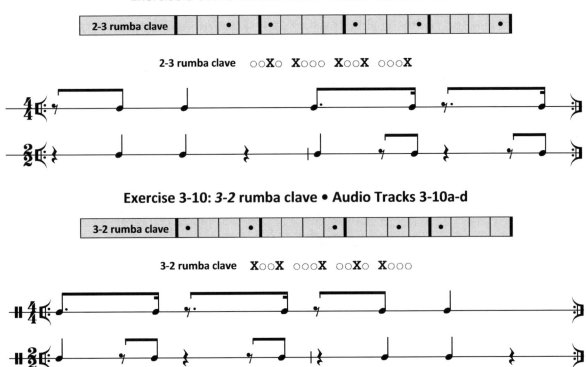

Exercise 3-10: *3-2* rumba clave • Audio Tracks 3-10a-d

The only difference between rumba clave and son clave is that the third stroke of the 3-side comes one subdivision later in rumba clave.

2-3 son clave		•		•				•			•				•		
2-3 rumba clave		•		•				•			•					•	

Our audio tracks start 2-3 rumba clave at the same point as 2-3 son clave, but starting on the third stroke of the 3-side is just as intuitive. If you examine the diagram carefully, you'll see that there are only two places in each cycle (shaded) where there are three consecutive silent subdivisions, and they're *not* between the two "sides" of clave. The last stroke of each 3-side is closer to the 2-side than it is to its 3-side siblings. Here are two ways of showing this graphically:

"correct" count	1		2			3		1		2		
common intuitive count	1		2			1			2		3	

As you can see, the final subdivision of the 3-side, the "rumba clave stroke", is closer to the 2-side than it is to the rest of the 3-side. When Cuban singers exhort the crowd to clap rumba clave, they often sing "pa – pa, pa-oom pa-pa,", where "oom" is the first main beat of the 2-side.

3-2 rumba clave	•		•			•		•		•			
vocalization	pa		pa			pa	oom	pa		pa			

The clave instrument of choice for most modern Cuban bands is the LP Jam Block.

Exercises **3-11** and **3-12** deal with a pattern I call the *clave markers* sequence. The concept is based on a paper entitled *Text to Tune Alignment in the Music of Charanga Habanera,* in which author Ryan Mead analyzes a large sample of Charanga Habanera's *coros* (vocal refrains) to see how their stressed syllables align with the clave. The conclusion of Mead's research is clear: of the eight subdivisions that comprise one side of the clave, four subdivisions are stressed much more often on the 2-side and the other four on the 3-side. As it turns out, this tendency is not limited to timba – it's at least as strong, and often stronger, in most Cuban music dating back to the mid-1940s.

While the clave marker sequence is very helpful for understanding clave in salsa and post-1950 Cuban music, the *son* and *danzón* music of the pre-1940s era danced to the beat of a different drummer, so to speak, marking the clave in different ways, as explained by Orlando Fiol ("The Great Clave Shift"), and David Peñalosa (the "clave motif versus offbeat onbeat" theory).

Don't overthink this for now – just learn the clave marker sequence and notice how helpful it is in quickly finding the clave. Also notice that if you dance "on 1", the first three clave markers go right with your feet. If you start dancing and, without counting or thinking, simply ask yourself which side of your dance step the music is reinforcing, you'll be amazed how often your first impression turns out to be the 2-side. Your brain may struggle to find the clave, but your body knows intuitively.

Exercise 3-11: 2-3 clave markers • Audio Tracks 3-11a-d

Exercise 3-12: 3-2 clave markers • Audio Tracks 3-12a-d

136

Bell Patterns

The great Johnny "Dandy" Rodríguez with the Mambo Legends Orchestra – Yoshi's Oakland – 2008 – photo: Tom Ehrlich

In **Exercises 3-13** and **3-14** we'll learn the most important pattern of the hand bell or bongó bell – a key instrument in *son, salsa* and *timba* rhythm sections. The hand bell is traditionally played by the bongosero but it's now often mounted and played by the timbalero or drummer. This bell's instantly recognizable main pattern states the tempo of the song and can be thought of as the "heartbeat" of the rhythm section, with a round open tone on each main beat, while the sharply-clanging closed end marks the clave. The pattern, sometimes called *campaneo,* is a clave-aligned, four-beat version of Exercise 2-1, and can also be played on the hihat or the timbalero's small *cha* bell.

A very important aspect of this pattern is that it requires two distinct timbres. When the bell is played near the open end, it produces a round, pitched tone, usually within a major third of A440 (A above middle C). These open tones are labeled with the letter "M" (for Mouth) in the standard notation. The other timbre is played on the neck ("N") or "heel" of the bell, producing a high, unpitched clang. The grey letters, (N) and bullets (•) are significantly less accented.

2-3 campaneo	M		N		M		N	N	M		N	N	M		N	N

Exercise 3-13: 2-3 campaneo • Audio Tracks 3-13a-d

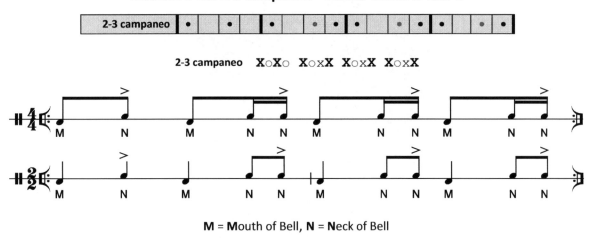

M = Mouth of Bell, N = Neck of Bell

Exercise 3-14: 3-2 campaneo • Audio Tracks 3-14a-d

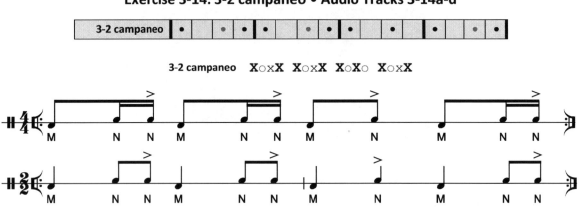

Remember that accentuation is particularly important with this pattern. In standard notation, we denote the unaccented strokes with accent marks, while in box notation, we show the bullets and text in grey. In **X**&○ notation we use a lower case x for the unaccented strokes.

It's also very important to accent the single "neck" stroke on the 2-side, one of the most important and audible clave markers as illustrated by the shading below:

3-2 campaneo	M		N	N	M		N	N	M		**N**		M		N	N
3-2 son clave	•			•			•				**•**		•			

Remember that you don't need a bell to learn these patterns. It's very useful to sing them.

This large pitched bell has many names, e.g., *hand bell, bongó bell, campana,* and so on. Although *campana* literally means "bell" – any bell, not just the hand bell – the term is also very frequently used to refer specifically to the hand bell we're discussing in this section. By the same token, the term *campaneo* literally means "a pattern played on a bell" – again, *any* pattern on *any* bell – but it's often used for the specific pattern above and we've chosen to follow that convention. Not everyone calls this pattern *campaneo*. In fact, not everyone has a name for it at all, but everyone knows how to play it. Which brings us to ... (drum roll, please) ... this volume's "Soapbox Sidebar".

Soapbox Sidebar: Terminology – Get Over It!

Nothing makes Latin music aficionados crazier, or hotter under the collar, than terminology. I have no doubt whatsoever that there are people reading this book who are pulling their hair out screaming *"No! No! No! Oh my God, NO! You can't call it campaneo! This is heresy!"* And if I called it something else, another group would be pulling out even larger handfuls of hair. But if I have to call it *"the pattern most frequently played by the larger bell, sometimes hand-held, sometimes mounted"* every single time I refer to it, *I'll* be the one pulling out my hair.

The truth of the matter is that you can play, and even teach music without ever saying a word. A salsa timbalero who speaks only Japanese can play in a band with a German-speaking bongosero. If the bongosero plays what this book calls *2-3 campaneo,* the timbalero will come in with what this book calls *2-3 contracampaneo* and everyone will be happy.

The bottom line is that rhythms are universal, but their names aren't, and never will be. Each pattern sounds the same no matter what you call it, so use the term that allows you to best *communicate* in each situation you find yourself. It's never worth arguing about, and always much easier to adapt to someone else's set of terms than it is to try to convince that person (who may feel very strongly about it) to use yours. And with that, another soapbox sidebar floats under the bridge.

Suggested Listening: In his fascinating Teaching Company audio course, *The Story of Human Language,* Professor John McWhorter explains that all languages are in a constant state of entropy – continuously breaking down and changing. The terms you'll need to communicate with other musicians today are different from those of 20 years ago and will need to be modified continually as you move forward.

Exercises 3-15 and **3-16**, called *contracampaneo* in these books, are played on a long, flat bell mounted on the timbalero's stand or somewhere on the drumset. Klímax drummer Giraldo Piloto mounts his on top of the kick drum.

Among the many names for this bell are *contracampana, mambo bell, timbal bell,* and *timbale bell.* (In Spanish, *timbal* is singular and *timbales* is plural, but, like *tamal* and *tamales,* English-speakers have incorrectly used "timbale" as singular for so long that now you'll often hear even native Spanish-speakers say "timbale bell" – an example of Prof. McWhorter's linguistic entropy in action).

If you hear someone use *campana* or *cencerro* to refer to this bell, don't panic. Remember that these words literally mean "bell" – *any* bell. It's only by convention that *campana, contracampana,* and *cha bell,* or *campana de cha,* have come into use to identify the three standard bells of the Latin rhythm section.

The contracampana is usually played in the middle of the bell, producing an unpitched sound that blends well with the hand bell. A rare example of using two timbres on this type of bell is Pello el Afrokán's *mozambique,* demonstrated by Calixto Oviedo in *Beyond Salsa Percussion, Volume 2.*

Calixto Oviedo during the filming of *Beyond Salsa Percussion, Volumes 2 and 3* – 2010 – photo by Tom Ehrlich
left to right: cha bell, contracampana, jam block – Calixto has his large campana mounted on his kick drum. Others mount a large campana just below the contracampana with the mouth facing towards them.

Exercise 3-15: 2-3 contracampaneo • Audio Tracks 3-15a-d

2-3 contracampaneo	•		•		•	•	•	•		•	•	•	•		•	•

2-3 contracampaneo   X○X○ XXXX ○XXX X○XX

Exercise 3-16: 3-2 contracampaneo • Audio Tracks 3-16a-d

3-2 contracampaneo		•	•	•	•		•	•	•		•		•	•	•	•

3-2 contracampaneo   ○XXX X○XX X○X○ XXXX

Calixto Oviedo, like Reinier Guerra, plays the contracampana with the left hand and the bongó bell mounted on the kick with the right. Piloto, of Klímax, mounts the contracampana on the kick and has a timbalero who plays the bongó bell.

2010 – Oakland, CA, during filming of Beyond Salsa Percussion Volumes 2 & 3 – photo by Tom Ehrlich

A Brief History of the Use of Bells in Cuban Music

modern bongosero's hand bell (campana, bongó bell)

The use of the bell in Cuban music was popularized by the son *sextetos* of the 1920s. During the louder and more exciting concluding sections of an arrangement, the bongosero would pick up and play a small hand bell (about the size of the modern *cha bell*). As time went by, *sextetos* added a trumpet to become *septetos*, which in turn became *conjuntos* by adding more trumpets, piano and congas. This, along with the advent of amplification, increased the volume level of live music, and hand bells gradually grew to the size of the large hand bell used today by bongoseros (or mounted on today's drumsets or timbal stands). As the size grew, the pitch got lower.

In contrast to their conjunto counterparts, which used bongó, trumpets, guitar, tres, claves and maracas, *charanga* groups used timbales, violins, flute and güiro. In reaction to the son explosion of the 1920s, charanga timbaleros added a small mounted bell, still retained today, and usually called the *cha bell* or *campana de cha.* The cha bell produces a pitch in the general vicinity of F, an octave above middle C (699Hz) and the large hand bell used today for the campaneo rhythm usually ranges from G to C above middle C (392-523Hz). If you practice matching the pitch of your voice to these bells, and the various pitched drums, you can develop a sense of how the many percussion sounds are arrayed from low to high, helping you pick out the nuances of the dense and intricate timbral textures of Latin music.

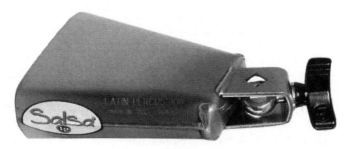

cha bell

Conjuntos and charangas had fairly rigid instrumentation formats. Prior to the Cuban Revolution, you could expect to hear only one bell in each. Conjuntos always had a bongosero with a hand bell and never had timbales while charangas always had timbales and never had bongó. Groups of both formats began adding conga and piano around 1940.

contracampana, timbal bell, timbale bell, mambo bell

The third main category of groups, the big bands, or *jazzbands,* were much more varied in both instrumentation and repertoire. These groups were originally formed in the early 20th Century to play North American jazz and pop for tourists, but, for a variety of reasons, began to adopt more and more Cuban rhythms. Jazzbands used multiple horn sections and usually a drumset, further increasing the volume level and resulting in the tiny mounted cha bell being replaced by the long, flat, mounted bell with much more volume and a much less distinct pitch *(contracampana, timbal bell* or *mambo bell).* Larger bands, more economically feasible in New York, began using both timbales and bongó, establishing the idea of two interlocking bell patterns, *campaneo* and *contracampaneo.* This became the status quo for *salsa,* and later, *timba.*

Examples of the Three Main Types of mid-20th Century Instrumentation

Conjuntos	Charangas	"Jazzbands"
Arsenio Rodríguez y su Conjunto	Antonio Romeu	Casino de la Playa
René Álvarez y Los Astros	Arcaño y sus Maravillas	Orquesta Julio Cueva
Conjunto Kubavana	Melodías del 40	Machito y sus Afro-Cubanos
Conjunto Gloria Matancera	Orquesta Aragón	Pérez Prado
Conjunto Modelo	José Fajardo y sus Estrellas	Beny Moré y su Banda Gigante
Chappottín y sus Estrellas	Orquesta América	Habana-Riverside
Conjunto Roberto Faz	Orquesta Broadway	Orquesta Chépin-Chóven
Conjunto Cheo Marquetti	Orquesta Sensación	Tito Puente
Sonora Matancera	Orquesta Sublime	Tito Rodríguez
Conjunto Clásico	Orquesta Estrellas Cubanas	Bebo Valdés y su Orquesta
Johnny Pacheco y su Tumbao Añejo	Orquesta Broadway	Mambo Legends Orchestra

As the traditional instrumentation categories of conjunto, charanga and jazzband began to break down, and as North American drummers demonstrated the tremendous expressive potential of the hihat and snare, the drumset found its way into more and more Cuban groups. All sorts of different combinations were tried. Players began experimenting with the idea of playing both bell patterns at once: Chuck Silverman reports doing this in Miami as early as 1974; Daniel Díaz of Ritmo Oriental used an array of half a dozen bells and played another with a foot pedal; Calixto Oviedo used multiple bells with drumset with Acheré in the early 70s; and Changuito, with Los Van Van, switched from seated drumset to standing timbales in the early 80s, using double bell patterns on many arrangements.

Changuito is usually credited with the specific pattern we'll call *contracampaneo 2,* shown in **Exercises 3-17** and **3-18.** As you can see, the key difference is that the main beats are silent, so as to avoid doubling the open strokes of the *campaneo* pattern played with the other hand.

Changuito's successor in Los Van Van, Samuel Formell (among many other modern Cuban drummers) uses this combination of campaneo and contracampaneo 2 regularly.

Exercise 3-17: 2-3 contracampaneo 2 • Audio Tracks 3-17a-d

Exercise 3-18: 3-2 contracampaneo 2 • Audio Tracks 3-18a-d

Patterns for Timbales

Calixto Oviedo's unique combination of cáscara with left-hand hihat – 2010 – Oakland CA – photo by Tom Ehrlich

Exercises 3-19 and **3-20** are often called *cáscara,* from the Spanish word for "shell", in this case the shell of the timbal drum, the sides of which are played with one or both sticks. The cáscara approach is used during softer, lower energy solos and sections of the arrangement such as the *cuerpo* (opening song form of an arrangement). *Cáscara,* like *campaneo* and *clave,* is yet another example where a general term is borrowed to refer to a specific rhythm. The term *cascareo* is sometimes used for the rhythm and is more consistent (with *-eo* denoting a pattern, as with campan<u>eo</u>). We'll call the rhythm cáscara, however, because it's more common.

Exercise 3-19: 2-3 cáscara • Audio Tracks 3-19a-d

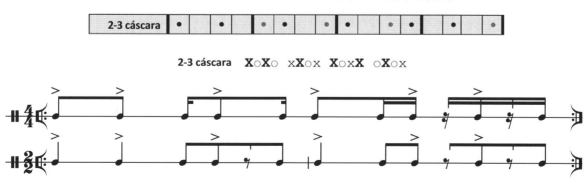

Exercise 3-20: 3-2 cáscara • Audio Tracks 3-20a-d

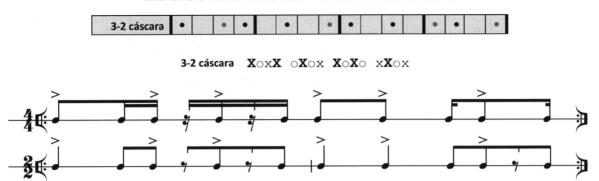

3-2 cáscara   X○X○ ○X○x X○X○ xX○x

This version of cáscara is played with one hand, with the other usually playing clave on the jam block, a *soba'o* pattern on the timbal, or a combination of the two. There are also two-handed approaches. For example, Exercise 3-19 can be played with one hand, while the other hand, playing the side of the other timbal, fills in every empty subdivision. Calixto Oviedo demonstrates all of this in detail in *Beyond Salsa Percussion, Vol. 3* in the *marcha abajo* chapter. The sides of the timbales are also often used for a clave-neutral maraca pattern. As you can see below, one of the limitations of graphic notation is the difficulty of showing three subdivisions in the space of two.

Maraca-style Cáscara Pattern (no audio)

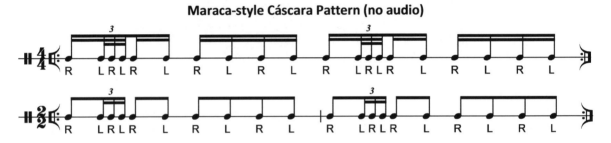

Of all the rhythms studied here, cáscara has the most extreme contrast between the accented (•) and unaccented (•) strokes. Sometimes, as in the case of **Exercises 3-21** and **3-22**, the accented strokes are played alone to produce a new pattern. The earliest example I've found of this approach is by Walfredo de los Reyes, in the 1950s, on *Descarga cubana #2* (see Listening Tour 1).

Exercise 3-21: 2-3 cáscara accents • Audio Tracks 3-21a-d

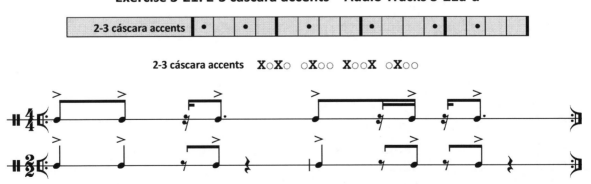

2-3 cáscara accents   X○X○ ○X○○ X○○X ○X○○

Exercise 3-22: 3-2 cáscara accents • Audio Tracks 3-22a-d

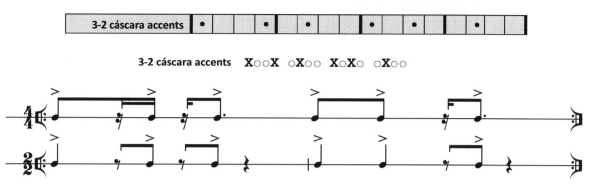

The cáscara rhythmic cell is also played on other instruments. It's often used on the ride cymbal or the hand bell during horn mambos in dance bands. In *guaguancó (rumba)* ensembles, cáscara is one of the two most common patterns played on the *guagua,* a piece of hardwood or bamboo played with sticks. When the guaguancó groove is borrowed for dance band arrangements, the timbalero usually plays the figure on a wood block or jam block.

Exercises 3-23 and **3-24** show another rumba guagua pattern, somewhat more commonly used in the slower *yambú* genre of rumba. For lack of a better term, we'll call it *cáscara de rumba.*

Exercise 3-23: 2-3 cáscara de rumba • Audio Tracks 3-23a-d

Exercise 3-24: 3-2 cáscara de rumba • Audio Tracks 3-24a-d

Exercises 3-25 and **3-26** show the main pattern of the güiro in danzón, often called *baqueteo* (still another example of deriving a specific term from a general one). *Baqueta* means drumstick, so *baqueteo* literally means "a pattern played with a drumstick".

Another dictionary definition for *baqueteo* is "an annoyance", which, ironically, is what certain terminology purists experience when they hear the term used for this specific danzón rhythm. So, as always, feel free to call it "a common pattern played by the güiro and timbales in danzón". *Baqueteo* works just fine for me, thank you very much.

Danzón began in the late 1800s, predating the *son* sexteto craze of the 1920s, and making it probably the first commercially recorded popular music genre to use a clave-like rhythm. Baqueteo, as you can see, uses cinquillo (Exercise 2-4) on its 3-side, while its 2-side contains both strokes of the 2-side of clave.

Exercise 3-25: 2-3 baqueteo • Audio Tracks 3-25a-d

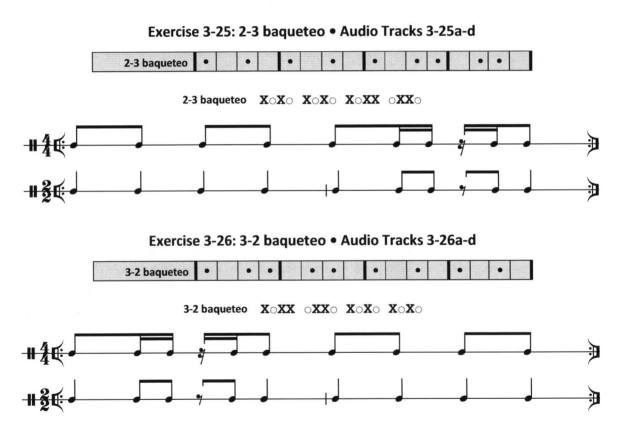

Exercise 3-26: 3-2 baqueteo • Audio Tracks 3-26a-d

The term baqueteo is also sometimes used for the overall part of the timbalero in many sections of a danzón arrangement. Used this way, *baqueteo* is differentiated from *paseo,* a different part that the timbalero plays at a very specific point near the end of each A-section of a danzón arrangement.

For much more on playing timbales in danzón, please see *Beyond Salsa Percussion, Volume 2 – Calixto Oviedo: Basic Rhythms.*

Drumset Patterns

Walfredo de los Reyes, Sr. – one of the pioneers of the drumset in Cuban music – drummerworld.com

To review, the drumset first found its way onto the Havana music scene in the 1920s and 30s when it was used in jazz and pop big bands playing North American music for tourists. Gradually these *jazzbands*, as Cubans called them, began to add Cuban material to their repertoires, creating a third type of ensemble format to compete with *conjuntos* (trumpets, bongó, clave, maracas, tres) and *charangas* (violins, flute, timbales, güiro). By this point, all three instrumentation styles used congas, bass and piano.

By the 1970s and 80s, the drumset had begun to play a critical role in the rhythms themselves at the hands of drummers such as José Luis "Changuito" Quintana (Los Van Van), Enrique Pla (Irakere), Daniel Díaz (Ritmo Oriental), and Calixto Oviedo (Acheré, Pacho Alonso, and Adalberto y su Son).

In the *timba* era that began in the early 1990s, the drumset, or at least the kick drum, became an integral and indispensable part of most rhythms. In groups without a drumset, the timbalero would add a kick drum and play it from a standing position. The presence of the kick drum had become mandatory in modern Cuban music. Oviedo and Changuito were joined by a new generation of phenomenal drummers and timbaleros with kick drums, among them: Giraldo Piloto (NG La Banda, Issac Delgado, Klímax), Eduardo Lazaga (Charanga Habanera), Yoel Páez (Paulito FG, Issac Delgado, Manolín), Alexis and Angel Arce ("Los Pututi") (with Manolín), Reinier Guerra (Manolín), Georvis

Pico (Issac Delgado), Ludwig Núñez (Bamboleo), Roicel Riverón (Manolito y su Trabuco), Samuel Formell (Issac Delgado, Los Van Van), Yulién Oviedo (Charanga Habanera), Andy Fornet (Revé), Pavel Díaz (Azúcar Negra, Charanga Habanera) and Bombón Reyes (Issac Delgado, Los Que Son Son).

Kick Drum Patterns

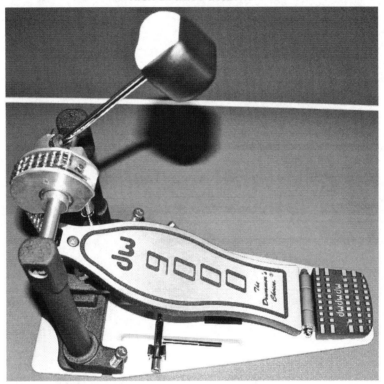

The use of the kick drum in modern Cuban music is a fascinating subject covered in great depth our *Beyond Salsa Percussion* series. For now, we'll learn the two most common patterns.

Exercises 3-27 and **3-28** cover the most common timba kick pattern used in the call and response vocal portions of the *montuno* section, or, described in gear terminology, in *marcha arriba* gear.

Exercise 3-27 • 2-3 common timba marcha kick • Audio Tracks 3-27a-d

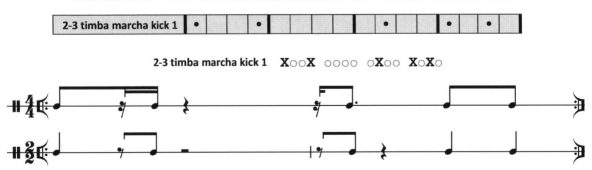

Exercise 3-28 • 3-2 common timba marcha kick • Audio Tracks 3-28a-d

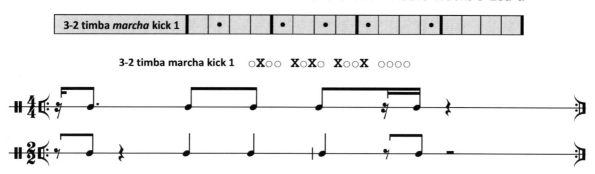

3-2 timba marcha kick 1 ○**X**○○ **X**○**X**○ **X**○○**X** ○○○○

Exercises **3-29** and **3-30** cover one of the most common kick patterns used during the timba breakdown portions of the *montuno* section, or, described in gear terminology, in *presión* gear.

Exercise 3-29 • 2-3 common timba presión kick • Audio Tracks 3-29a-d

2-3 timba presión kick ○○○○ **X**○**X**○ ○**X**○○ **X**○**X**○

Exercise 3-30 • 3-2 common timba presión kick • Audio Tracks 3-30a-d

3-2 timba presión kick ○**X**○○ **X**○**X**○ ○○○○ **X**○**X**○

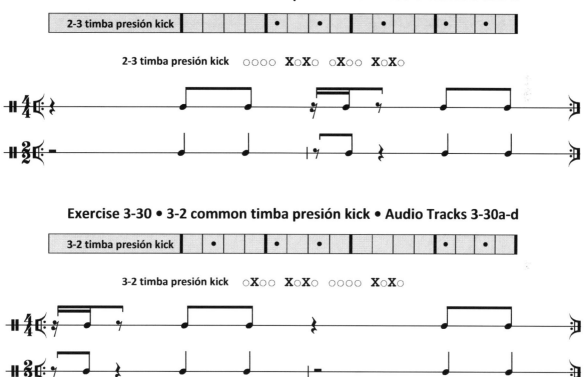

The single stroke on the second subdivision of the 3-side falls on the most common accent of the *quinto* drum in *rumba* (and therefore sometimes called the *quinto pulse*). Since the rest of the pattern is identical on each side of the clave, we say that the drummer uses the kick on the quinto pulse to "mark the clave".

The quinto pulse is also often omitted to create a clave-neutral pattern (Exercise 2-10).

Snare Drum Patterns

Reinier Guerra – jamming with Walfredo de los Reyes, Sr. – 2009 – photo by Tom Ehrlich

The snare drum is used to produce two distinct timbres in Cuban music: open and ghost. Let's start with the extremely familiar open stroke we're so used to hearing in rock, funk, blues, and even country music – a loud, bright, aggressive burst of sound, often fattened by an open hihat. In North American music this is played on the second and fourth main beats, usually called the *backbeats* (as in Chuck Berry's classic lyric "*it's got a backbeat you can't lose it, any old time you use it*"). In Cuban music, however, the backbeat is only used this way in sections meant to invoke a North American groove. Otherwise, the open snare is only played on the backbeat of the 2-side of the clave.

both backbeats				•								•			
2-3 son clave			•	•				•			•			•	
clave-aligned backbeat				•											

Exercise 3-31 • 2-3 timba kick & snare • Audio Tracks 3-31a-d

2-3 timba kick & snare	K			K	S				K			K		K	

2-3 timba kick & snare   KᵒᵒK Sᵒᵒᵒ ᵒKᵒᵒ KᵒKᵒ

Exercise 3-32 • 3-2 timba kick & snare• Audio Tracks 3-32a-d

3-2 timba kick & snare		K			K		K		K				K	S		

3-2 timba kick & snare   ○**K**○○ **K**○**K**○ **K**○○**K** **S**○○○

The snare can also mark the clave on the quinto pulse, just as the kick marked it in the exercises above (note that in the chart below, you'd use the snare *or* the kick on the quinto pulse, but not both at once).

2-3 rumba clave		•		•				•		•				•	
backbeat and quinto pulse				•					•						
standard kick drum	•			•					•			•		•	

Another interesting approach to the snare evolved when Pupy Pedroso left Los Van Van in 2001 to form Los Que Son Son, enlisting the help of his old friend and colleague Changuito to create a new rhythm section approach, featuring Changuito's young protégé, "Bombón" Reyes. Among other innovations, Changuito moved the snare to the *frontbeat*, or first main beat, of the 2-side.

Bombón Reyes with Pupy y Los Que Son Son — Yoshi's SF — 2010 — photo by Tom Ehrlich

To look at it in a different way, Changuito and Bombón took the standard timba kick part and changed the timbre of the first stroke from kick drum to snare:

Los Que Son Son kick & snare	S		K				K		K		K	
standard timba kick	K		K				K		K		K	

Exercise 3-33 • 2-3 Los Que Son Son kick & snare • Audio Tracks 3-33a-d

Los Que Son Son kick & snare	S		K				K		K		K	

2-3 Los Que Son Son kick & snare   S○○**K** ○○○○ ○**K**○○ **K**○**K**○

Exercise 3-34 • 3-2 Los Que Son Son kick & snare • Audio Tracks 3-34a-d

Los Que Son Son kick & snare		K		K	K	S		K			

3-2 Los Que Son Son kick & snare   ○**K**○○ **K**○**K**○ **S**○○**K** ○○○○

At the hands of such masters as Clyde Stubblefield (of James Brown's late-1960s group), the funky, conversational interjections of the ghost snare stroke became a major component of North American funk, R&B and other genres. Calixto Oviedo (NG La Banda) and Yoel Páez (Issac Delgado) used ghost notes extensively in the 1990s.

As of this writing, the leading proponent of the ghost snare style is Roelvis "Bombón" Reyes of Los Que Son Son. In this group, the timbalero is responsible for holding down both bell parts while Bombón (who plays only drumset) plays a provocative running commentary on snare and toms.

Exercises 3-35 and **3-36** show one typical pattern used by Bombón, but keep in mind that the ghost snare is, by its nature, improvisational and conversational rather than prone to being played as a repeating figure or *ride*. In this particular format, the rhythm differs by only one stroke (underlined below) from Cachao's *chanchullo* rhythm, better known to modern ears as the main riff of *Oye como va*, made famous by Tito Puente and even more famous by Santana (**X**○<u>**X**</u>○ ○**X**○**X** ○○○**X** ○**X**○○).

Exercise 3-35 • 2-3 Los Que Son Son ghost snare • Audio Tracks 3-35a-d

main snare	•															
ghost snare						•		•				•		•		

2-3 Los Que Son Son ghost snare   S○○○ ○S○S ○○○S ○S○○

Exercise 3-36 • 3-2 Los Que Son Son ghost snare • Audio Tracks 3-36a-d

main snare									•							
ghost snare				•		•								•		•

3-2 Los Que Son Son ghost snare   ○○○S ○S○○ S○○○ ○S○S

Hihat, Toms and Cymbals

Cuban hihat wizard Calixto Oviedo during the filming of *Beyond Salsa Percussion, Vol. 3* – photo by Tom Ehrlich

The most common hihat part is the güiro pattern (Exercise 2-1), but the hihat has endless potential, having been developed into an extremely flexible and expressive instrument by North American drummers. The leading Cuban drummer in the category of hihat artistry remains Calixto Oviedo, who played with NG La Banda and Adalberto Álvarez, and is the subject of *Beyond Salsa Percussion, Volumes 2 and 3,* which includes many examples of Calixto's hihat-playing. Bombón Reyes, whose brilliance seems to come up every few pages, makes an entirely different use of the instrument. To compare them, Calixto uses the hihat as his main ride in some gears and a powerful spice in others, while Bombón, who has no bells in his drumset, plays left-hand hihat as a ride in almost every gear and adds his own jambalaya on snare and toms. With still a different approach, Keisel Jiménez of Havana d'Primera creates an irresistible groove with a hard-driving, rolling two-handed hihat ride. In summary, the hihat is a fantastically versatile instrument that's currently undergoing a period of continuous and very exciting development in timba.

The toms are used in many creative, and often song-specific ways. Other common uses of the toms are the *bomba sicá* pattern (Exercise 2-5) and the drumset adaptations of *guaguancó* studied in *Beyond Salsa Percussion, Volume 1.*

As mentioned, the ride cymbal is often used during *mambos* (high energy horn sections) to play the *cáscara* pattern (Exercises 3-19 and 3-20). It's also used for reinforcing efectos and horn figures.

Conga Patterns

Denis "Papacho" Savón has played congas with Issac Delgado since 1998.
Juan "Wickly" Nogueras, playing bongó bell here, was the innovative founding conguero of NG La Banda.
photo by Tom Ehrlich – San Francisco – 2007

We'll cover the vast range of this all-important instrument in *Beyond Salsa Congas,* but even for those who don't play congas, it's critical to be aware of the most basic conga marchas.

Many dance instructors teach their students to dance to the congas alone, pointing out that each of the variations on the basic steps can be anchored to the conguero's slap, open tones or both. Only the louder "speaking tones" are notated, with "**S**" for **S**lap and "**C**" for the high drum (**C**onga) played open. A conguero would of course fill in the unmarked subdivisions with softer *manoteo* strokes.

basic conga slaps (S) and opens (O)		S			C	C			S			C	C	
dancers' count	1	2		3	4		5		6		7		8	

Exercises 3-37 and **3-38** show the speaking tones of the simplest clave-aligned, one-drum marcha, with a single tone on the 3-side of the clave and a double tone on the 2-side.

Exercise 3-37 • 2-3 clave-aligned standard conga marcha • Audio Tracks 3-37a-d

2-3 clave-aligned standard conga marcha			S			C	C			S				C	

S = **S**lap, C = **C**onga (higher drum open)

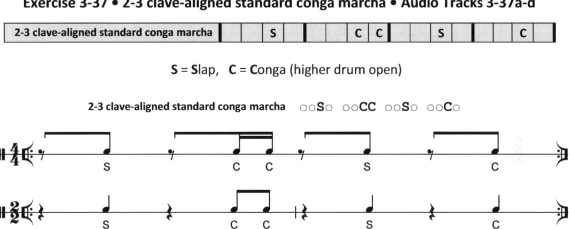

2-3 clave-aligned standard conga marcha   ○○**S**○ ○○**CC** ○○**S**○ ○○**C**○

Exercise 3-38 • 3-2 clave-aligned standard conga marcha • Audio Tracks 3-38a-d

3-2 clave-aligned standard conga marcha			S			C			S				C	C

3-2 clave-aligned standard conga marcha   ○○**S**○ ○○**C**○ ○○**S**○ ○○**CC**

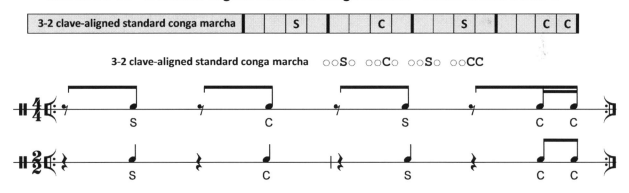

Note that this clave-aligned version is actually much less common in modern salsa and timba than the clave-neutral marcha shown in the dancing discussion above (and immediately below). If you *do* alternate between single and double tones, it's important to play the single tone on the 3-side.

clave-neutral standard conga marcha			S			C	C			S			C	C	

By 1960 or so, nearly every conguero had added a second drum, the lower-pitched *tumba*, and today, some congueros use three drums, with the *tres dos* pitched between the other two.

Tomás Cruz was among the first to introduce the revolutionary idea of doubling or even quadrupling the length of conga marchas. Combined with his creative use of muffs and melodic placement of tones and slaps, this geometrically increased the possibilities for recognizable *song-specific* marchas. The congas have begun to join the piano and bass in the ongoing trend away from formulaic, genre-specific patterns and toward composed, song-specific ones. Given the precedent of batá music, song-specificity in the congas is a hugely important evolutionary step. Multi-clave patterns also emerged in 1990s *guarapachangueo* groups such as Clave y Guaguancó (see Listening Tour 4).

In traditional two-drum playing, some congueros use the tumba (lowest drum) as a clave marker, as shown in **Exercises 3-39** and **3-40**. Most salsa congueros follow this convention. We use "**T**" for **T**umba and "**C**" for **C**onga, the higher drum. Note that the "big drum on the 3-side" rule of thumb is discarded completely in the styles of some timba congueros (Cruz himself among them).

Exercise 3-39 • 2-3 2-drum conga marcha • Audio Tracks 3-39a-d

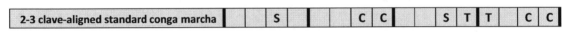

S = **S**lap, C = **C**onga, T = **T**umba (low conga)

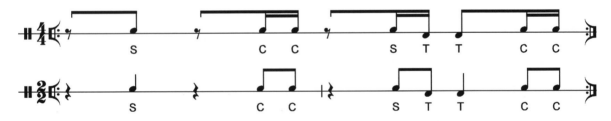

S = **S**lap, C = **C**onga, T = **T**umba (low conga)

Exercise 3-40 • 3-2 2-drum conga marcha • Audio Tracks 3-40a-d

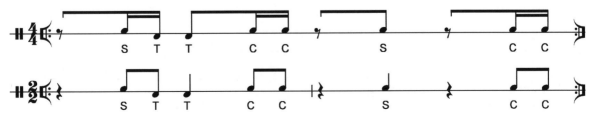

158

Rhythm Exercises 4: Rhythmic Perspective

Historically speaking, Afro-Cuban music, changüí and rumba came before the popular music we've studied in Listening Tours 1, 2 and 3, but each has rhythmic perspective issues that cause many non-Cuban listeners to hear them incorrectly, so before asking you to immerse yourself in Listening Tour 4, we'll need to do a few preparatory exercises.

What is Rhythmic Perspective?

The easiest way to understand what we mean by rhythmic perspective is to look at the graphic above and then turn the book upside down. To paraphrase the old Jimi Hendrix song, "6 turns out to be 9". But we don't mind. We English readers have been taught from birth that the spine of the book goes on the left. I can be confident that all readers of this book will recognize the symbol above as a "6", but this might not be apparent to a person who knows Arabic numbers, but has only been exposed to Arabic and Semitic language books, which are read from right to left, with the spine on the right. Such a person would hold the book with the spine on the right and see a "9".

So it is with rhythm. Each musical culture has hundreds of subliminal cues that give us the audio equivalent of knowing how to hold the book right-side-up. But with music, we're not concerned with up, down, right or left. Music exists in time, not space, and to hear it as the artist intends it to be heard, we have to agree on three rhythmic factors:

1. the speed of the main beats

2. how the beats are grouped – in threes, fours, fives, sevens, etc.

3. where each cycle of beats begins, or, colloquially speaking: "where '1' is"

If you aurally "rotate the book" by choosing a different combination of these three parameters, your ear will still hear a coherent rhythm, just as "6" looks like "9" when the book is upside down. It will sound like music – it might sound like very good music – but it won't sound like the music the artists who played it had in mind, and this can cause all sorts of fear and loathing on the dance floor.

The Problem

The human sense of hearing did not evolve for the purposes of enjoying music. It evolved to keep us from getting eaten by sabre-tooth tigers. Our ancestors were those humans who were able to identify the sounds of approaching predators and avoid them well enough to allow time for procreation. As the progeny of these sharp-eared, quick-thinking, horny ancients, our brains instinctively pounce on each little morsel of sound that floats our way and start parsing it for vital information. In the case of music we look for a tempo, for logical groupings, and for "1". We can't stop ourselves from making initial guesses and drawing all sorts of musical conclusions from them. This works wonderfully as long as we're dealing with familiar musical cues. For example, within the first seconds of a rock track we've situated the snare on the backbeat and started to listen for the harmonies changing on the frontbeats. But for the Afro-Cuban music and changüí we're about to study, we'll need some serious boot camp training before venturing out among the tigers.

Mixed Signals

Try this experiment:

1. Go to YouTube and search for "cream sunshine of your love". If you've never heard it, all the better. This 35-year old bit of hippie nostalgia is contemporaneous with *changüí-68* in Cuba and the debut of the Fania All Stars in New York. *Sunshine of Your Love* owes its structure to the blues, its groove to chachachá, and the concept of its essential hook, the guitar/bass riff, to our old friend Arsenio Rodríguez.

2. Now, listen to the snare drum. What do you hear? Is there any question as to where "1" is? Probably not, but there's something strange nevertheless. The snare is on the frontbeats, not the backbeats. If you had only the drum track to listen to, you might well hear the snare as the backbeat because that's where it is in every

160

other rock song you've ever heard. But the blues chord progression and the phrasing of the guitar/bass riff powerfully outweigh the snare drum – at least for me.

3. Now go back to YouTube and search for "la rumba esta buena changui". If you've never heard *this* one, again, all the better. There's no snare, no clave, no bass other than the marímbula, and no chord instrument other than the tres, which is often doubling the vocals. Later in this section, when you start to get the feel for changüí and its cultural auditory cues, you'll learn to ground yourself to the *guayo* (the changüí güiro) and the maracas, and correctly hear the vocals and tres as strings of offbeats. But many North American listeners hear the vocals and tres *on the beat,* as reportedly anecdotally by Benjamin Lapidus, author of *Changüí: Origins of Cuban Music and Dance,* and someone who has taught changüí to dozens of non-Cubans. As with *Sunshine of Your Love,* once you decide where "1" is in the melody and harmony, the percussion parts get flipped around and the guayo sounds like the offbeats. Like the upside down "6", *it still sounds like recognizable music.* If you'd been born in Guantánamo you'd be unable to hear the guayo incorrectly, but if you were born in Peoria, Illinois, you may never have heard a guayo, maracas or a melody comprised of all offbeats, so you hear the melody on the beat and the accents of the guayo and maracas on the offbeats. If you're not a changüí insider, the guayo sounds just fine on the offbeats – perhaps like an offbeat hihat part.

Warning: if you found yourself hearing the vocals and tres on the beats, *stop listening to changüí immediately until you've completed the exercises in this section!*

How Rhythmic Perspective Affects Our Listening Tour Strategy

Up to this point, the strategy we've been using has been to listen over and over to a playlist until we feel a strong emotional connection to the individual songs and artists, making it fun and easy to then study the history and rhythms of that music. With son, danzón, son montuno, songo, salsa and timba, this should be working like a charm, especially since you've gotten this far into the book. But if we use this approach with changüí, rumba and Afro-Cuban folkloric music, there's a strong danger that you'll learn to hear the music incorrectly, so before moving on to Listening Tour 4, we'll study a series of interesting exercises designed to train you to instinctively hear some of the trickier elements of these genres from the correct rhythmic perspective.

Rhythmic Perspective Problem 1: Changüí offbeats

If you've never heard *changüí,* you're in for treat, but before plunging in, make sure you've fully mastered **Exercises RP-1** and **RP-2**. Changüí is fast, intensely syncopated, and *very* prone to being felt incorrectly by non-Cubans. The reason is that most of the vocal and accompaniment notes come on the offbeats, tempting the uninitiated to hear the music as if it were a very square melody consisting entirely of onbeats. It winds up sounding like a simple, boring tune with funny sounding percussion. Hearing the relentless syncopations of changüí correctly is like learning to ride a bicycle – or perhaps a unicycle. When you're able to keep your balance in the stream of rapid-fire offbeats, it's exhilarating, but at first it's very easy to fall off. The tres *guajeo* that begins the highlighted track for changüí in Listening Tour 4 uses these offbeats exclusively and the vocals sing right along with the tres. The starting point (>) of Exercise RP-1 (before the first main beat) is particularly important because that's where the harmony changes, establishing the perceived "beginning" more conclusively than an unpitched percussion pattern.

Exercise RP-1: main beats + changüí tres • Audio Tracks RP-1a-d

main beats	•			•			•			•		
changüí tres		•		•		•		•		•		•
starting point												>

```
        main beats   Xooo  Xooo  Xooo  Xooo
changüí tres (and vocals)   oXoX  oXoX  oXoX  oXoX
    starting point   oooo  oooo  oooo  ooo>
```

Exercise RP-2 is the part of the changüí marímbula. It's the same as the standard conga marcha so we can use the audio tracks from Exercise 2-11. In actual practice the tones of the marímbula are played with a "swing" or "fix" feel, pulled slightly in toward the triplet.

Exercise RP-2: changüí marímbula • (use Audio Tracks 2-11a-d)

changüí marímbula			S			O	O		S			O	O

```
changüí marímbula   ooSo  ooOO  ooSo  ooOO
```

S = Slap (slapping the body of the marímbula)   O = Open tone produced by the metal tongue

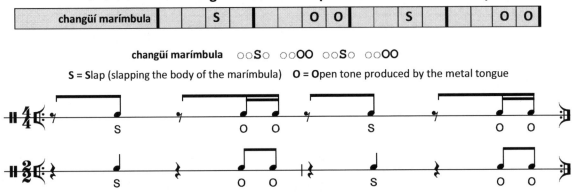

Little attention is paid to the pitches of the marímbula – it's as much a percussion as a bass instrument. When a contrabass is used, however, it leads to our next rhythmic perception problem.

Rhythmic Perspective Problem 2: The Anticipated Bass

The horrific era of slavery in the Western Hemisphere provides perhaps the most far-reaching example of the unintended effects of politics and economics on music history. It's always the same type of story: those in power are driven by greed and megalomania and usually oblivious to music, but their machinations never fail to alter its development – often dramatically, and often for the worse, but sometimes, as in this case, for the better. The musical cultures of Europe and Africa, having separately developed to incredible levels of sophistication over the centuries, were suddenly thrown together – and like nitrogen and glycerin, they produced a sustained musical explosion without which almost none of the music we listen to today could have emerged. At ground zero of this musical explosion we find our next rhythmic perspective conundrum: the anticipated bass.

Our exploration of this phenomenon will be a three-step process. First we'll learn a typical, basic, Afro-Cuban rhythm. Then we'll learn a song with European harmonies. Finally, when we try to put them together, we'll discover a problem, and the magical compromise that makes it all work.

Step 1: The African Rhythmic Component

Exercise RP-3: tumba part for guaguancó • Audio Tracks RP-3a-d

tumba	H	F		M	H	F	O		H	F		M	H	F	O
subdivision 7 (ponche)							•								•

H=**H**and or **H**eel; **F**=**F**ingertips; **M**=**M**uff (or **M**ute); **O**=**O**pen Tone

tumba	HFoM	HFOo	HFoM	HFOo
subdivision 7 (ponche)	oooo	ooOo	oooo	ooOo

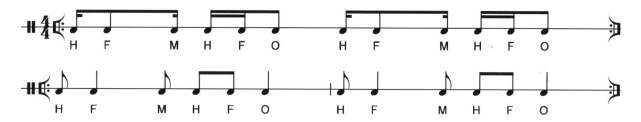

As a right-handed conguero, you'd play the **H** and **F** with your left hand and the **M** and **O** with your right. Drop the whole left hand down (**H**); then tap with the fingers (**F**); then, while the left hand stays down, strike the drum with your right hand to produce a muff or muted tone (**M**); then repeat the **H** and **F**. Finally, as you lift your left hand, play the drum open with your right (**O**). It's the open tone that provided the inspiration for the development of the modern bass tumbao.

If you don't have a conga, learning to sing the exercise will be just as valuable for our purposes – perhaps even more so since the physical technique of playing the drum won't distract you from the main goal of hearing and feeling a low pitched tone on Subdivision 7 instead of on Subdivision 1, where your European sensibilities would otherwise lead you hear it.

After you master the exercise, listen to some guaguancó tracks and try to identify the tumba part.

Step 2: The European Harmonic Component

Now let's learn to sing one of the coros of the old Cuban standard, *Pare cochero*. The chords change four times, from C to F to G to F. Except for the pickup, each harmony changes right on the beat. *Pare cochero,* probably written in the 1940s or early 1950s, is far more modern and Latin-sounding than 19th Century European music, but its harmonies change on the beat, so it'll serve our purposes well. I originally designed this little demonstration with a Mozart melody but decided that the point could be made more clearly with *Pare cochero*.

Pare cochero – harmonized • Audio Track RP-3e

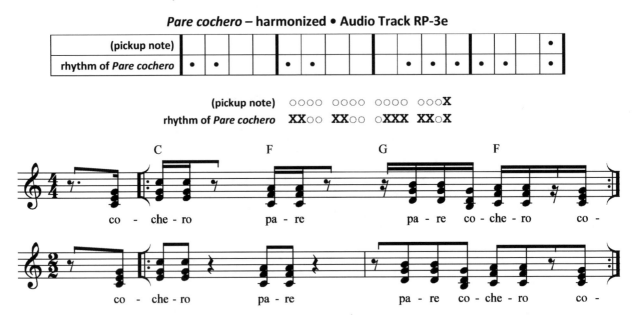

Step 3: The Problem and its Solution

So, imagine for a moment that you've never heard salsa, rock or jazz – only African drum rhythms – and that someone has given you an acoustic bass and asked you to come up with a bass line for *Pare cochero* – sung, as it is here, in full three-part harmony. Common sense would dictate that you play a rhythm that would keep your pitches in sync with the pitches of the voices. **Audio track RP-3f** demonstrates three ways of doing this, one after they other. How do they sound? Well, the first two sound hopelessly square and the third sounds like 1950s rock & roll, but to your sophisticated African rhythmic sensibilities, none of them is satisfying. You want to hear something that feels more like **Audio Track RP-3g**, which combines the guaguancó tumba part with the voices but has no bass part. How can you come up with a bass part that captures the African feel of the conga part but that doesn't clash with the lovely three-part vocal harmony?

The solution ... drum roll please ... is the anticipated bass, **Audio Track RP-4a**. If you listen to the slow version, **Audio Track RP-4b**, you can hear that the voices temporarily clash with the bass. The shaded subdivisions represent areas when the bass and voices are out of sync. But at a normal speed, it sounds fantastic – and this is exactly what's happening on most salsa tracks and many son and timba tracks. What started as a workaround and a compromise turns out to have an artistic value that transcends the original musical idea.

Exercise RP-4: *Pare cochero* + anticipated bass • Audio Tracks RP-4a and RP-4b

(pickup note)																•
rhythm of *Pare cochero*	•	•			•	•			•	•	•	•	•			•
rhythm and notes of bass			F			G					F			C		
harmonies of voices	C	C	C	C	F	F	F	F	G	G	G	G	F	F	F	C

(pickup)	○○○○ ○○○○ ○○○○ ○○○**X**
rhythm of *Pare cochero*	**XX**○○ **XX**○○ ○**XXX** **XX**○**X**
rhythm and notes of bass	○○○**F** ○○**G**○ ○○○**F** ○○**C**○
harmonies of voices	**C**○○○ **F**○○○ **G**○○○ **F**○○○

Rhythmic Perspective Problem 3: 4 Groups of 3 or 3 Groups of 4?

Hearing the beat correctly in 12/8 Afro-Cuban rhythms is the most common category of Latin music rhythmic perspective issues. To see it in action, all you need to do is attend a concert, class or clinic on Afro-Cuban songs and rhythms. Scan the crowd, focusing on the tapping feet and nodding heads of the audience members. You'll find that some are tapping at one tempo while others are happily grooving away to a completely different tempo.

To understand why this is so common, think about the number 12. It's divisible by both 3 and 4. The following table uses shading to show the two common ways that 12 subdivisions can be grouped, followed by the two most common folkloric rhythms, shown without shading.

3 groups of 4 (3/4)	1				2				3			
12 subdivisions	1	2	3	4	5	6	7	8	9	10	11	12
4 groups of 3 (12/8)	1			2			3			4		
standard 12/8 bell pattern	•		•		•	•		•		•		•
12/8 clave (3-2 "rumba")	•		•			•		•		•		

Of course, not all music uses 12 subdivisions. Various genres use three groups of three, or (as in all the rhythms we've learned up to this point), four groups of four. But no major Cuban genre is grouped in three groups of *anything*. (The exception that proves the rule is *frenté,* from the *tumba francesa* family, which uses three groups of four). You can *hear* the rest of the Afro-Cuban folkloric rhythms in 3 groups of 4 (or 6 groups of 2), and you can enjoy what you're hearing, but that's not how the performers and dancers are feeling the groove.

So let's look at the table again, this time adding the proper shading to the bell and clave patterns:

the wrong way to feel it!	1				2				3			
the 12 subdivisions	1	2	3	4	5	6	7	8	9	10	11	12
4 groups of 3 (shuffle)	1			2			3			4		
standard 12/8 bell pattern	•		•		•	•		•		•		•
12/8 clave (3-2 "rumba")	•		•			•		•		•		

As with changüí, it's the absence of a chord instrument that makes it so easy for people who didn't grow up with Afro-Cuban folkloric music to feel it incorrectly. Let's use North American pop to get our heads around this concept:

1. Go to YouTube and search for *My Favorite Things,* a Broadway show tune in 3/4.

2. When you hear *"rain-drops on ro-ses and"*, count 1-2-3, 1-2-3.

3. Now, listen to the musical accompaniment. You can hear the chord changing very clearly with each group of 1-2-3.

4. Now search for "huey lewis if this is it", an example of a 12/8 rock shuffle.

5. When it gets to the chorus, start counting 1-2-3-4. If you're counting correctly, you should be saying "1" on the bold capitalized syllables below and you should hear the chords changing with each line.

> *If this is*
> **IT** *... please*
> **LET** *me know ... if*
> **THIS** *ain't love you'd better*
> **LET** *me go*

Without the chord changes and other subliminal cues that North American pop provides, it's much less clear to a new listener whether Afro-Cuban singing and drumming is in 4 groups of 3, or 3 groups of 4 – but rest assured that it is absolutely meant to be felt in 4 groups of 3, something that you should train yourself to do with **Exercise RP-5** before immersing yourself in Listening Tour 4.

Exercise RP-5 is by far the most common and most important 12/8 bell pattern.

Exercise RP-5: main beats + standard 12/8 bell • Audio Tracks RP-5a-d

| main beats | • | | | • | | | • | | | • | | |
| 12/8 bell | • | | • | | • | • | | • | | • | | • |

main beats	**X**oo	**X**oo	**X**oo	**X**oo
12/8 bell	**X**o**X**	o**XX**	o**X**o	**X**o**X**

166

It's very important to learn this pattern *with the main beats* from the very beginning. The most common student mistake is to hear this pattern as three or six groups of two subdivisions instead of four groups of three subdivisions – or, as Michael Spiro would say, as a waltz instead of a shuffle.

To drive this point home, let's review the wrong way to feel this pattern.

wrong main beats!	•		•		•		•		•		•	
12/8 bell	•		•		•	•		•		•		•
correct main beats	•			•			•			•		

What about "6/8"?

Using a 6/8 time signature instead of 12/8 is just another way of notating the same rhythms. Just as the rhythms we've learned up to this point (with four groups of four) can be written as 4/4 or 2/2, rhythms that use four groups of three subdivisions can be written as either 12/8 or 6/8.

12/8 in Latin Popular Music

Suggested Listening: Elio Revé y su Charangón – *Oyan coro* **(1980) – (EGREM Siboney vinyl only)**

I hate to recommend a track that's not available on CD, but there are so few examples of 12/8 in Latin pop and this arrangement is *so good!* Fortunately, you can find several live video performances on YouTube. Search for "orquestas cubanas recorrido 1981". This was the breakthrough Revé band that introduced the "charangón" instrumentation, combining elements of charanga, conjunto, changüí, rumba and batá (See Listening Tour 2).

To be exact, the breakthrough in *popularity* came with the next band, with musical director Juan Carlos Alfonso, the future leader of Dan Den. That band was so popular in the 1980s that it earned the nickname *La explosión del momento*. It very much deserved its success, but the previous band, featuring Félix Baloy and Ignacio Herrera, which made only the one vinyl LP pictured above, was as good in its own way and, of course, pioneered many of the innovations. The 12/8 section of *Oyan coro* begins at 0:40 of the YouTube video.

After hearing the above suggested listening track, you might wonder (as I do) why 12/8 isn't used more often in Cuban pop. In North American pop, we find many examples of 12/8. The most logical answer is that no one has started a 12/8 Cuban popular dance craze – in spite of the fact that every 12/8 Afro-Cuban religious rhythm has its own special dance moves. If you're a dancer or choreographer, there's your homework assignment for this chapter!

Metric Modulation

Most examples of 12/8 in Latin pop are interludes in arrangements that are otherwise in 4/4, bringing up the interesting question of how to execute the transition. In the case of *Oyan coro* above, the tempo stays the same while the time feel goes from four subdivision per main beat to three. Another approach occurs in *Changó* by the Nuyorican group Saoco (co-led by Henry Fiol, father of *Beyond Salsa* guru, Orlando Fiol). The track is available on YouTube as of 2012. In this case, the transition, at 0:58, uses a device called "metric modulation". While *Oyan coro* holds the tempo constant and changes the speed and grouping of the subdivisions, *Changó* does just the opposite – holding the speed of the subdivisions constant, but grouping them in threes instead of fours, resulting in a faster tempo.

The Beatles' *Happiness is a Warm Gun* is similar to *Changó*. At 1:47 *("when I hold you, in my arms")*, it keeps the subdivisions constant but instead of going from four to three subdivisions, it goes from two to three, creating the effect of slowing the tempo instead of speeding it up.

Suggested Reading: In *Rhythmic Illusions* and *Rhythmic Perspectives,* drummer Gavin Harrison catalogs dozens of these combinations, as well as inventing quite a few of his own. Each book includes lots of fascinating and well-played audio files.

12/8 in North American Pop

Steely Dan	*Black Friday*
Doobie Brothers	*Minute by Minute*
Toto	*Hold the Line*
Toto	*Make Believe*
Huey Lewis	*If This is It*
Yellowjackets	Monmouth College Fight Song

Swing and "Fix"

Note that there's also a family of North American grooves (jazz and R&B "swing", some blues "shuffles", and various hip-hop grooves) that blur, or stretch, the distinction between three and four subdivisions per beat. These grooves start with a four-subdivision pattern and "swing" the subdivisions toward the triplet, creating a feel that isn't pure duple or pure triple, but something in-between.

This bending, or swinging of rhythms is not studied in this book, but it does have a critical connection to Cuban music, discussed in Volume 3 of *Beyond Salsa Piano*. The leading author on this subject is Michael Spiro, who covers it in great depth in *The Conga Drummer's Guidebook* and demonstrates it in his instructional videos on congamasterclass.com.

Rhythmic Perspective Problem 4: "Where's '1' in 12/8?"

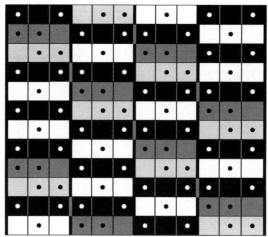

The 12 possible displacements of the standard 12/8 bell pattern

(If you really want to induce a headache, note that the first line is the same pattern as the intervals of a major scale.)

After you've learned to comfortably feel Exercise RP-5 as four groups of three, you'll be ready for your next challenge. Even after you're feeling the beat in four groups of three, the absence of chordal instruments in Afro-Cuban folkloric music also makes it hard to hear which one of those four beats is the strongest, or the beginning. In musicians' parlance, "where's '1'?"

Let's take a look at one of the nastier of the 12 possible displacements of Exercise RP-5 with **X**&○ notation (it's the sixth row from the top in the chart above):

12/8 bell	**X**○**X**	○**XX**	○**X**○	**X**○**X**
12/8 bell starting on its 5th stroke	**X**○**X**	○**XX**	○**X**○	**XX**○

Ouch! They differ by only one stroke and it's the very last one. So, let's say you walk into the room in mid-performance. Your brain instinctively tries to find "1". You've studied Exercise RP-5 so you don't have to worry about hearing it as a waltz. So far so good. Now you start listening for the familiar bell pattern. If you hear it as shown directly above, you won't realize you're wrong for four beats! By this time, your brain has already started hearing the offbeats of the vocals as onbeats and you're well on your way to learning the song incorrectly.

One solution is to look at everyone's feet – the musicians, the dancers, and those people in the audience who seem to know what's going on. Once you get the main beats properly situated, you've narrowed it down to these four permutations, three of which give themselves away as being wrong after one beat of less:

correct
beat 2 reveals the problem
absence of beat 1 reveals the problem
absence of beat 1 reveals the problem

In summary, if you don't immediately hear Exercise RP-5, watch the feet of the musicians and dancers and then make your first guess. If you don't hear a bell on beat 1 or if you *do* hear a bell on beat 2, it's wrong. This should get you into the saddle as quickly and painlessly as possible.

Exercise RP-6 isn't a *displacement* of Exercise RP-5 – it's a *variation*, delaying the first stroke by one subdivision while keeping the rest of the pattern intact. This one is a legitimate, fairly common, and very funky variation that you'll love once you get used to it.

standard 12/8 bell	•		•		•	•		•		•		•
alternate 12/8 bell		•	•		•	•		•		•		•

Getting used to it, however, can be tricky. That stroke on the first main beat of Exercise RP-5 is by far your most powerful anchor, and when it suddenly disappears – especially with a new song at a fast tempo – it can make you second-guess yourself if you're not prepared for the possible substitution of Exercise RP-6 for Exercise RP-5 at any point.

Exercise RP-6: alternate 12/8 bell + main beats • Audio Tracks RP-6a-d

main beats	•			•			•			•		
alternate 12/8 bell		•	•		•	•		•		•		•

main beats	Xoo	Xoo	Xoo	Xoo
alternate 12/8 bell	oXX	oXX	oXo	XoX

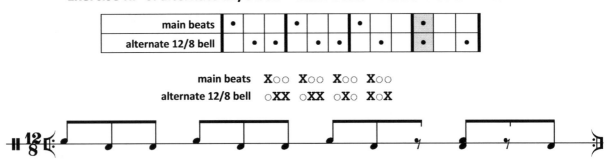

Sometimes, especially in the Yoruban *güiro* genre, this alternate bell is used exclusively for a whole song, but sometimes, especially in the Congolese *palo* subgenre, the bell player switches between the standard and alternate patterns like a jazz drummer mixing ride cymbal patterns.

12/8 Clave

To review, here are the four types of 4/4 duple pulse clave that we learned in Exercises 3-7 to 3-10:

3-2 rumba clave	•			•				•			•		•			
3-2 son clave	•			•			•				•		•			
2-3 rumba clave			•		•				•			•				•
2-3 son clave			•		•				•			•			•	

To arrive at the 12/8 equivalents, simply delete the second column from each beat group:

3-2 rumba clave in 12/8	•		•			•		•		•		
3-2 son clave in 12/8	•		•		•			•		•		
2-3 rumba clave in 12/8		•		•			•		•			•
2-3 son clave in 12/8		•		•			•		•		•	

It's questionable, of course, to use the terms "rumba" and "son" for clave. Rumba and son are genres that developed centuries after the 5-stroke patterns shown above. Nevertheless, son clave and rumba clave are the most widely used terms for this important distinction, and so far no one has come up with a better system of terminology. In this context, the adjectives "son" and "rumba" simply refer to the placement of the third stroke of the 3-side. It's like saying "french-fried burrito", with "french" referring to a cooking method, not a nationality.

The terms "2-3" and "3-2" are also often frowned upon. With very few exceptions, the clave part enters on the 3-side in folkloric music, even when the songs themselves are phrased in 2-3. The concept of "2-3" infers that the listener is subjectively hearing the melody starting on the 2-side, as explained in excruciating detail in *Understanding Clave and Clave Changes.* For this book, we'll learn the most common pattern, 3-2 rumba clave in 12/8, but if you find yourself getting more deeply into Afro-Cuban vocal music, you should learn the other three patterns.

An example of 3-2 rumba clave in 12/8 occurs at the beginning of the highlighted track *Palo monte* in Listening Tour 4.

Exercise RP-7: main beats + 12/8 rumba clave • Audio Tracks RP-7a-d

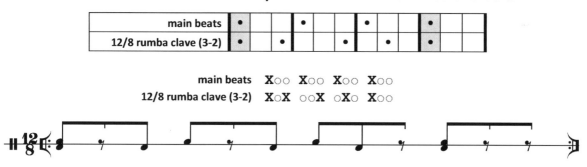

Exercise RP-8 is an 8-beat cycle used in various *arará* rhythms, alternating four main beats with a pattern that *begins* just like the standard 12/8 bell pattern. A good example of this can be found on *Tierra arará* by Los Hermanos Arango, one of the highlighted tracks in Listening Tour 4.

Exercise RP-8: main beats + 12/8 arará sabalú bell • Audio Tracks RP-8a-d

Exercise RP-9 is an alternate version of the sabalú bell as transcribed in Fernández's *The Afro-Cuban Folkloric Musical Tradition.*

Exercise RP-9: main beats + 12/8 alt. sabalú bell • Audio Tracks RP-9a-d

main	•			•			•			•			•			•			•			•		
alt bell	•	•		•	•		•		•	•		•	•		•			•	•		•	•		•

```
main beats      Xoo  Xoo  Xoo  Xoo  |  Xoo  Xoo  Xoo  Xoo
alt sabalú bell  XXo  XXo  XoX  XoX  |  XoX  oXX  oXX  oXo
```

Like Exercise RP-8, Exercise RP-9 also contains all four main beats in its first measure, but adds an additional offbeat stroke to each beat group. Peñalosa points out a fascinating connection: if we ignore the beat groups, Exercise RP-5 uses the same pattern three times in a row:

XoXXoXXo

XoXXoXXo

XoXXoXXo

This is the same pattern as "alt sabalú bell" above, starting on the fifth **X**. It also uses the same spacing of strokes as our old friend *cinquillo*, Exercise 2-4! So Exercise RP-8 is a common duple-pulse rhythm superimposed over a triple-pulse grid, and Exercise RP-9 is simply a subset of that, putting special emphasis on the main beats.

Having covered most of the issues having to do with bell patterns, our next group of exercises will demystify several common 12/8 *drum* parts that have a tendency to throw new listeners off the track as they try to latch onto the 12/8 bell.

Exercise RP-10 can be heard in context on the track *Bríkamo* from Grupo AfroCuba de Matanzas: *Raíces africanas.*

Exercise RP-10: abakúa drum cell 1 • Audio Tracks RP-10a-d

main beats	•			•			•			•		
abakuá drum cell 1			H	H	L				H	H	L	

```
main beats           Xoo  Xoo  Xoo  Xoo
abakuá drum cell 1   ooH  HLo  ooH  HLo
```

H = High drum; **L** = Low drum

172

Exercise RP-11 can be heard in context on the track *Abacuá* from Grupo AfroCuba de Matanzas: *Raíces africanas.* (When referring to a specific CD track, I substitute that track's spelling.)

Exercise RP-11: abakúa drum cell 2 • Audio Tracks RP-11a-d

main beats	•			•			•			•		
abakuá drum cell 2	H				L		H		M	M	L	

main beats	X○○	X○○	X○○	X○○
abakuá drum cell 2	H○○	○L○	H○M	ML○

H = High drum; **M** = Middle drum; **L** = Low drum

Exercise RP-12 can be heard in context on the track *Ritmo abacuá* from Los Muñequitos de Matanzas: *Guaguancó matancero,* one of the highlighted tracks from Listening Tour 4.

Exercise RP-12: abakúa drum cell 3 • Audio Tracks RP-12a-d

main beats	•			•			•			•		
abakuá drum cell 3	H	H			L		H	H	M	M	L	

main beats	X○○	X○○	X○○	X○○
abakuá drum cell 3	HH○	○L○	HHM	ML○

H = High drum; **M** = Middle drum; **L** = Low drum

Comparison of Open Tone Patterns in 12/8 Rhythms

H = High drum; **M** = Middle drum; **L** = Low drum

Below is a summary of the three abakuá drum cells and several other common 12/8 patterns:

12/8 bell	•		•		•	•		•		•		•
abakuá drum cell 1		H	H	L				H	H	L		
abakuá drum cell 2	H			L		H		M	M	L		
abakuá drum cell 3	H	H		L		H	H	M	M	L		
rumba columbia Havana		H	H	L	L			H	H	L	L	
rumba columbia Matanzas		H		L	L			H		L	L	
palo	L		M	M	H			M	M	LH		

173

Exercise RP-13 can also be heard in context on the track *Bríkamo* from Grupo AfroCuba de Matanzas: *Raíces africanas.* The bell player can use it as a variation, creating something along the lines of a timba "gear change". This pattern is a displacement of the very first 4/4 pattern we learned back in the Exercise 2-1, the pattern commonly played by the güiro in salsa and timba:

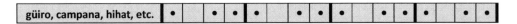

Used in 12/8, however, the pattern becomes a cross-rhythm, with its four subdivisions creating tension against the three-subdivision groove, just as the sabalú pattern did in Exercise RP-9.

Exercise RP-13: abakúa displaced shaker pattern • Audio Tracks RP-13a-d

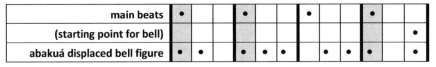

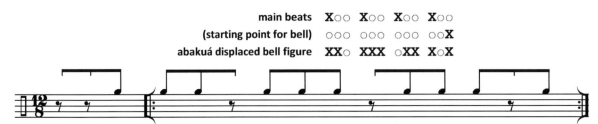

Another family of folkloric rhythms we'll hear in Listening Tour 4 is *tumba francesa,* brought to Eastern Cuba by Dahomeyan refugees of the Haitian slave rebellion. A tumba francesa performance usually has three movements – *masón, yubá* and *frenté* – each with a rhythmic twist that will be much easier to grasp with a bit of preparatory study.

The first, masón, is the easiest. In fact, on paper, it looks like it should be extremely easy. It's in 4/4, and the bell pattern is cinquillo (Exercise 2-4). The cause for confusion is the fast tempo combined with the open low tone on the ponche. At this speed, the ear latches onto the regular low tone first, hearing it as "1" and then, incorrectly, hearing the bell pattern as X○X○ XX○X.

Exercise RP-14: Tumba francesa masón + main beats • Audio Tracks RP-14a-e

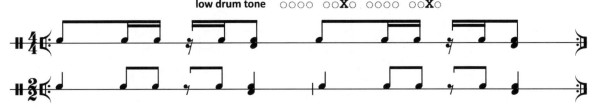

After mastering the exercise, sing or clap along with the special additional track **RP-14e**, which gradually accelerates to 160 beats per minute.

The second and third movements of the tumba francesa suite – *yubá* and *frenté* – are related in a fascinating way. The technical musical term is *metric modulation.* The bell part is the same but the grouping of subdivisions switches from 4-groups-of-3 to 3-groups-of-4. As mentioned earlier, *frenté* is the only example I've found of a Cuban rhythm played in 3 groups of anything, perhaps because tumba francesa had its origins in slaves parodying the courtly dances of their French masters, many of which were in 3/4 *(menuet, courante,* etc.). To master the transition, we'll learn each *catá* part separately and then practice switching between yubá and frenté while holding the catá steady.

Exercise RP-15: Tumba francesa yubá + main beats • Audio Tracks RP-15a-d

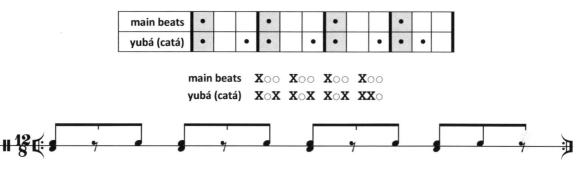

main beats	•			•			•			•		
yubá (catá)	•		•	•		•	•		•	•		•

main beats   Xoo Xoo Xoo Xoo
yubá (catá)   XoX XoX XoX XXo

Exercise RP-16: Tumba francesa frenté + main beats • Audio Tracks RP-16a-d

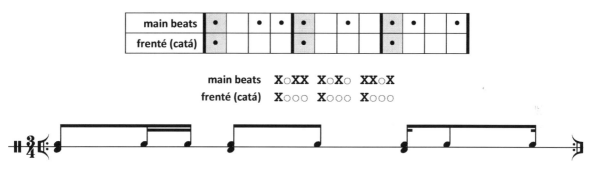

main beats	•		•	•	•		•	•	•		•	
frenté (catá)	•			•			•					

main beats   XoXX XoXo XXoX
frenté (catá)   Xooo Xooo Xooo

Exercise RP-17: Tumba francesa yubá to frenté loop • Audio Track RP-17

catá (starting at halfway point)   XoXXXoXoXXoX
main beats for yubá   XooXooXooXoo
main beats for frenté   XoooXoooXooo

X&o notation is the only good way to show this relationship. **Audio Track RP-17** contains the catá rhythm continuously in the left speaker. **Note:** the *mid-point* of the yubá pattern is the *starting-point* of the frenté pattern. The right speaker plays the main beats for yubá for two cycles, then the main beats for frenté for two cycles, then back to yubá and so on. The base tempo begins at 60 BPM (beats per minute) and gradually increases to the maximum performance speed of 200 BPM.

The best way to learn Exercise RP-17 is to dance in place on the main beats while clapping or singing the catá part.

Rhythmic Perspective Problem 5: Clave Direction – Dancing in 2-3 versus 3-2

Clave direction is an incredibly puzzling subject that drives both students and teachers to the brink of madness – usually beyond that brink, but take heart! *Dancing is the key to understanding clave direction.* Your body has to understand it first in order to give your brain a fighting chance.

Exercise RP-18 teaches you to clap clave in each "direction" while dancing. The kick drum represents your feet. *When the 3-side of clave lines up with the beginning of your dance step, the "clave direction" is 3-2.* It's that simple. (For a full tutorial, see *Understanding Clave and Clave Changes*.)

Exercise RP-18: basic dance step + 3-2 son clave • Audio Tracks RP-18a-d

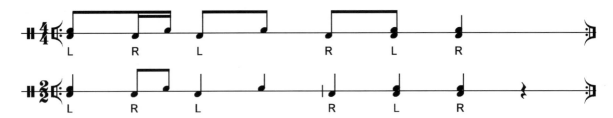

```
basic dance step ("on 1")   XoXo  Xooo  XoXo  Xooo
        3-2 son clave        XooX  ooXo  ooXo  Xooo
```

Exercise RP-19: basic dance step + 2-3 son clave • Audio Tracks RP-19a-d

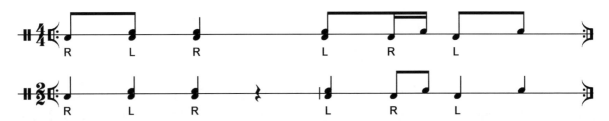

```
basic dance step ("on 1")   XoXo  Xooo  XoXo  Xooo
        2-3 son clave        ooXo  Xooo  XooX  ooXo
```

Dancing is also the quickest way to *find* the clave in the first place. Start dancing first, and then see which side of your dance step seems to lock in with and reinforce the bass and vocals. That side is (almost always) the 2-side and the side on which you feel more rhythmic tension is the 3-side.

Listening Tour 4: Folkloric Music

Category	Song	Source
Yoruba: batá	*Oru seco*	Abbilona – any of Volumes 1-8 – EGREM
Yoruba: güiro	*Ensamble*	*Antología de la música afrocubana, Volume 8* – EGREM
Yoruba: iyesá	*Cantos a Ochún y Oyá*	Afroamérica: *Chants et rythmes afrocubains* – VDE-Gallo
Yoruba: bembé	*Eleguá*	Grupo AfroCuba de Matanzas: *Raíces africanas* – Shanachie
Carabalí: abakuá	*Ritmo abakuá*	Muñequitos de Matanzas: *Guaguancó matancero* – TCC
Bantú: palo	*Palo-monte*	*Les danses de dieux* – Ocora (Harmonia Mundi)
Bantú: makuta	*Makuta*	Iyabakuá: *Afrekete* – Pan
Bantú: yuka	*Palo, yuka and makuta*	Conjunto Folklórico Nacional – YouTube video – Latidos
Dahomey: arará	*Tierra arará*	Los Hermanos Arango: *Las estrellas del folklor* – BIS
Dahomey: tumba francesa	*Tumba francesa*	Ballet Folklórico CUTUMBA de Santiago: *Ritmos Afrocubanos, Vol. 1* – Academy of Cuban Folklore and Dance
Dahomey: vodú	*Vodú*	Ballet Folklórico CUTUMBA de Santiago: *Ritmos Afrocubanos, Vol. 1* – Academy of Cuban Folklore and Dance
12-8 in popular music	*Oyan coro*	*Elio Revé y su ritmo changüí* – (vinyl-Siboney)
Changüí	*Loma del chivo es*	Grupo Changüí de Guantánamo: *Bongó del monte* – EGREM
Conga de comparsa	*Conga oriental*	Ban Rarrá: *Con sabor del guaso* – Mayulí
Rumba: guaguancó	*La gitana*	Muñequitos de Matanzas: *Rumba abierta* – West Side Latino
Rumba: yambú	*Conga yambumba*	Muñequitos de Matanzas: *Live in New York* – QBADisc
Rumba: columbia	*Campana de oro*	AfroCuba de Matanzas: *Cuba in Washington* – Smithsonian
Rumba: guarapachangueo	*Callejón de los rumberos*	Yoruba Andabo: *Callejón de los rumberos* – Universal Latino

In our first three Listening Tours, we strongly suggested that you begin by immersing yourself in the highlighted and further listening tracks, waiting to study the history and rhythms until you'd developed an emotional attachment to each genre. First become a fan, *then* become a student. And with these carefully selected lists of masterpieces, becoming a fan should be easy and thrilling.

With Listening Tour 4, however, it's extremely important to use the opposite approach. Please study the previous section on rhythmic perspective carefully *before* listening to these tracks. If you haven't gotten a feel for the hands-on exercises taught in the previous section, there's a strong danger that you'll hear some of these rhythms incorrectly. The absence of bass and chordal instruments makes it very easy to be lured into the wrong rhythmic perspective and once you get a song into your ear from a given rhythmic perspective, it can be *brutally* hard to unlearn it.

If not for these critical rhythmic perspective issues, Listening Tour 4 would of course have been presented as Listening Tour 1, as all of these folkloric genres were present in Cuban culture well before the development of son, danzón and recording technology. In fact, those familiar with the first three tours will have already heard many references to the folkloric songs we're about to study.

Afro-Cuban Folkloric Music

Grupo AfroCuba de Matanzas – 2004 – photo by Mary Brassell

Our final Listening Tour begins where Cuban music itself began: with the vast, complex and awe-inspiring world of Afro-Cuban folkloric music.

By "folkloric" we mean music that was originally played non-commercially in religious or social settings. By "Afro-Cuban", we mean genres that developed in Africa, were brought to Cuba by slaves, and over time took on unique Cuban qualities. Later in this Listening Tour, we'll cover other folkloric genres, such as *rumba* and *changüí,* that were actually created in Cuba.

Researching, collecting and understanding Afro-Cuban folkloric music is no small challenge. There's an incredible amount of it, it's incredibly complex, and until recently, it was seldom recorded or transcribed, surviving over the centuries by being passed down aurally – by rote – from generation to generation in the religious communities and *cabildos* (municipal cultural preservation societies) of various, sometimes remote, regions of Cuba.

In the last 30 years, folkloric music has become the subject of intense interest, resulting in many new recordings, instructional books, videos and academic papers. Unfortunately, the research has been unevenly distributed. Some genres, such as *batá,* have been the subject of so many excellent publications of all types that it's hard to decide where to start, while it's frustratingly hard to find anything at all on many others, such as *vodú* and *yuka*.

A lot of serious academic research has also been devoted to the original African roots of Afro-Cuban folkloric music – how the same genres are played in Africa today, and how they might have been played in Africa at the time the ancestors of today's Afro-Cubans crossed the Atlantic Ocean. Musicologists can only guess how and when the genres we're about to study first developed in Africa and how different today's African music is from the way it was played in the 17th Century, but we *can* identify major differences between the way the various genres are now played in regions like Havana and Matanzas, and massive differences between either of these and present-day Africa.

From a theological point of view, it's especially important to modern practitioners of this music to play, sing and understand it as it was originally intended. The prevailing musical aesthetic also strongly emphasizes tradition. An analogy could be drawn to the recent "original instrument" movement in European classical music, which seeks to make each piece sound as it did during the composer's lifetime. With what I like to think of as "African classical music", it's significantly more difficult to do this because it wasn't preserved nearly as well, having been passed down by ear from generation to generation, without a notation system and without the written anecdotal observations of contemporaries that European period instrument scholars use to help formulate their performance practices. Despite these difficulties, the desire for authenticity is very strong. The amount of curiosity, mystery and debate over "the real way" and "the right way" to play each genre of Afro-Cuban folkloric music renders *The Da Vinci Code* uncontroversial in comparison.

But even to a music fan with little interest in theology or musicology, it's saddening to ponder how much of the African classical music of the last millennium has been lost – or altered beyond recognition. It's like imagining what Mozart might have created had he not died at the age of 35 when Beethoven was just publishing his first compositions, or to imagine how the two might have influenced each other. On the other hand, as you'll see shortly, the treasure of African classical music that we *do* have is large enough to consume several lifetimes of study. And while it may differ from its original African sources by many levels of metamorphosis, today's Afro-Cuban folkloric music – taken entirely on its purely musical merits – is breathtakingly beautiful and complex.

So, we've established the importance of learning about Afro-Cuban folkloric music, hinted at its extraordinary beauties, and given fair warning of the many confusing difficulties involved in understanding and collecting it. The next step is to get a foot in the door by creating an overarching outline of all the genres and rhythms. Finally we'll start filling in each category with recordings, videos, books, historical information, and of course, rhythms.

There are many organizational approaches to categorizing this massive and unruly body of music:

- sacred versus secular
- African point of origin
- Cuban point of arrival
- vocal versus instrumental
- types of drums used
- triple- versus duple-pulse structure
- Havana versus Matanzas versus Santiago
- … and so on!

The most successful strategy I've found is what I call the "big four" approach – dividing everything into four large groups corresponding to the four West African ethnic groups brought to Cuba in the largest numbers: Bantú, Carabalí, Yoruba, and Dahomey.

Our goal in this brief survey is to make you aware of Afro-Cuban folkloric music, to show the critical a role it played in the development of Cuban popular music, to get enough of it into your ears to inspire you to seek out some of the more detailed reference materials listed in the **For Further Study** sections, and to help you build a collection through the Listening Tour approach.

In each section I'll recommend specialty books and videos that focus exclusively on the genre under study, but first let's look at five indispensable study aids that paint the big picture, each one covering the complete range of Cuban folkloric music in a more general way.

Further Study Materials for an Overall Understanding of Folkloric Music

We'll start with books and then move on to videos and in-person courses. *The Afro-Cuban Folkloric Musical Tradition* is a concentrated, well-explained, and meticulously accurate survey of all the major Afro-Cuban folkloric genres, plus *comparsa* and *rumba,* with professionally recorded and sung examples on an audio CD. Robert Fernández, an excellent percussionist, teaches at California State University at Los Angeles and spends at least two months each year in Cuba researching and gathering material for future books. He's also made significant contributions to the *Beyond Salsa* series. The audio CD also features Luca Brandoli, whose work we'll explore in the section on batá.

Ned Sublette has done an extraordinary job of researching the African roots of Western Hemisphere music, but it's his genius for storytelling that makes *Cuba and its Music* and *The World That Made New Orleans* so compelling and inspiring.

Curtis Lanoue's *Afro-Cuban Percussion Workbook* is based on the teachings of José Eladio, a top professor at Havana's famous ENA conservatory. The book and its DVD companion product cover a wide range of Afro-Cuban and popular music rhythms in text and transcription.

The subscription website, **congamasterclass.com**, is endlessly valuable, with detailed instructional videos on nearly every Cuban genre. Michael Spiro has the unique ability to cut through the mystery and hyperbole and break down these complicated rhythms to simple, down-to-earth English. It's like one musician explaining something to another at a gig between sets. The site also includes extensive videos from Jesús Díaz (leader of QBA), and guest appearances by Calixto Oviedo, Bombón Reyes, Karl Perazzo and many others.

Explorations in Afro-Cuban Dance and Drum is a week-long, live-in, immersion course given each July at Humboldt State University in Northern California. It offers an inexpensive package that includes access to non-stop daily classes and workshops, on-campus accomodations in the university's dormitories and three meals a day in a cafeteria setting with large tables allowing extensive informal access to the faculty – a large pool of Cuban masters and top U.S. educators. Whether you go as a beginner, a dancer, or simply as an observer, there's no faster way to jumpstart your knowledge of the folkloric music and dance scene and meet inspiring people.

Yoruba

Of the four ethnic groupings, Yoruba (often called *Lucumí* within Cuba) has gotten the most attention from scholars, fans and initiates of its *Santería* religion. And of the four major Yoruban subgenres – *batá, güiro, iyesá* and *bembé* – most of the research has centered on *batá*. In fact, batá music has probably been studied more than all the other genres of Afro-Cuban music combined.

Batá

highlighted track: *Oru seco* – **Grupo Abbilona:** *This track is on __each__ of Volumes 1-8* – **BIS**

The Abbilona series is as great from a musical point of view as it is confusing from a marketing point of view. There are 49 volumes in total, but only 16 have been released as of 2012. Each volume has beautiful vocal music devoted to one specific oricha (deity) – played and recorded brilliantly. The main musicians are members of the legendary López (Los Chinitos) clan, including, on itótole, the incomparable Manley "Piri" López, one of the most exciting musicians in the world today. So far, so good. The confusion centers around the "seco" (instrumental) batá tracks. Each volume has one such track. The first eight volumes contain a track called "Oru seco" that consists the first half of the Oru seco. This is our highlighted track and it's absolutely fantastic. I don't know why it's only the first half or why it's repeated on eight different CDs. The next eight volumes, each denoted with the Roman numeral II, have a different instrumental track, called Eggún, (the piece that closes a Santería ceremony), and this track is also repeated on each of the "II" volumes. The second half of the Oru seco is promised for the upcoming volumes. In spite of the repetition of the seco tracks, it would be worth buying all 16 of the existing volumes for their vocal tracks alone, so by all means, go forth and buy them, hopefully adding to the urgency for the other 33 volumes to be released. And if you find all this mystery and confusion unsettling, don't worry – welcome to the world of batá! In fact, welcome to the world of Afro-Cuban folkloric music – think of it as half treasure hunt and half mystery novel. The old adage "good things don't come easy" might well have been coined by a batá student.

time	tempo	meter	comments
0:00	62		call to Eleguá section 1 (tricky part: the 3rd sound – slap, tone, **tone** – is "1")
0:05		12/8	Eleguá section 1 (12/8 means 4 groups of 3)
0:37	70		call to conversation – 3 iyá (low) tones answered by 3 itótole (high) tones
0:40			call to Eleguá section 2 (the *absence* of the iyá tone is the call, but two beats go by before the itótole player has to change)
0:41			Eleguá section 2 (iyá starts with both hands together and leaves off last tone; last itótole tone added versus section 1)
0:50	71		call back to Eleguá section 1
0:51			Eleguá section 1 (brief reprise)
0:54			call to Eleguá section 3
0:57			Eleguá section 3
1:09	74		call to Eleguá section 4 (by omitting an iyá muff)
1:10			Eleguá section 4
1:18			call to Eleguá section 5 ("abukenke")
1:19	78		Eleguá section 5
1:42	116	4/4	call to Ogún section 1 (4/4 means 4 groups of 4)
1:45			Ogún section 1
1:54	123		(iyá variation – itótole unchanged)
2:10	131		Ogún section 2 – iyá changes w/out call, because there's time for itótole to change
2:16			Ogún section 1 returns (again, there's time for the itótole to change w/out call)
2:19	93	4/4	call to Ochosi section 1
2:30	110		Ochosi section 2 (no call needed)
2:42	107		Ochosi section 1 (return) (no call needed)
2:49	114		call to Ochosi section 3
2:51	118		Ochosi section 3 – the high-pitched itótole slaps in the right channel are offbeats (see exercise RP-1)
2:57			call to Ochosi section 4
3:00			Ochosi section 4
3:05			Ochosi section 5 (no call needed)
3:11	124		call to Ochosi section 6
3:12			Ochosi section 6 (always played 3 times)
3:17	130		conversation within Ochosi section 6 (4 low tones answered by 4 mid tones)
3:20			conversation repeated
3:26			Ochosi section 7
3:30		triple	continues through Obaloke, Inle, Babalú Ayé, Osún, Obatalá and Dadá

The batá ensemble consists of three double-headed, hourglass-shaped drums. The leader plays the largest, the *iyá,* and is responsible for playing the low, open and muted tones in each melody and initiating each of the many changes in rhythm by playing specific rhythmic cues, or calls *(llamadas).* The player of the smallest drum, the *okónkolo,* is primarily a time-keeper, switching accompaniments in response to the calls. Playing the middle drum, the *itótole,* is incredibly challenging. The smaller head, the *chachá,* locks in with both heads of the smallest drum to form the accompaniment for most rhythms, while the larger head, the *enú,* plays open and muted tones to complete the melodic phrases initiated by the leader.

The three batás provide the rhythm section for the singing and dancing that comprise the bulk of each Santería ceremony, but the opening and closing of each ceremony are played *seco* ("dry") by the batás alone. The opening piece, the *Oru seco,* is one of humanity's most unique and sublime creations. A performance can be as short as 15 minutes, or as long as the iyá player desires, and no two Oru secos are the same. The Oru seco combines the improvisational freedom of jazz with the formal and structural complexity of classical music. *Most astonishing is that the form itself is subject to improvisation* – not just the content of the individual drum parts. And all of this is accomplished without written music, verbal cues or visual cues. The iyá player establishes and conducts the large scale form of each performance through rhythmic signals alone.

As ceremonial religious music, the primary artistic aesthetic of batá music is to preserve tradition. Ideally, the songs and thematic drum material would be unchanged from their African origins, but it's an aural tradition, passed from generation to generation by rote, under the duress of forced emigration across oceans and the unthinkable hardships of slavery and post-slavery oppression. The result is that the Oru seco is played very differently in different regions such as Matanzas and Havana and with significant differences even between different communities of players within the same region. The batá style played by the Abbilona group on our highlighted track is representative of one of the more common approaches used in modern Havana.

Sidebar: Spelling of Afro-Cuban Folkloric Terms

The beautiful phonetic spelling logic of the Spanish language is unfortunately not applicable when it comes to these African terms. *Elegua, Eleggua, Ellegua, Elleggua, Elegba, Legba, Elewa, Elegbara,* and many more are used for just this one *oricha* (a.k.a., *orisha, orisa, orixa*) in various important books and recordings. Since there's no agreement, I use the Spanish rules for pronunciation, accent marks and double consonants. Like the majority of the world's 6,000 languages, these African languages are not written. For titles of CD tracks, however, I use the spellings used on the CDs themselves.

The Oru seco, as usually played in Havana, has 23 major sections, each a tribute to a different deity, or *oricha* (sometimes spelled *orisha* – see spelling sidebar above). The movements are usually played in a set order, always beginning with *Eleguá.* If the overall ceremony is devoted to a specific oricha, that oricha's movement is usually moved to the end of the sequence. Each movement contains from one to seven (or more, depending on how you count them) subsections, sometimes called "roads". Which subsections are included and how long each is played are left to the discretion of the iyá player. Within each subsection, the iyá player can improvise and play special calls to instigate conversations. The other two players train themselves to instinctively respond to each call and to know whether it's calling for a conversation within a road or calling for a switch to a new subsection.

If all of this sounds incredibly difficult, that's because it *is* incredibly difficult. Most Cuban percussionists can play some batá rhythms, but only an elite few are able to play the entire Oru seco, especially on the two larger drums.

In popular music and jazz, the three batás are often strapped together and played by one drummer.
Photo by Peter Maiden – Yoshi's Oakland - 2012

My favorite batá anecdote comes from Michael Spiro, who found himself playing itótole at a ceremony in Matanzas. In the middle of a section devoted to one oricha, he heard the call for another from a completely different part of the normal sequence. He switched his part accordingly but had to wait until after the performance to hear the explanation. An important member of the community had walked into the ceremony and the iyá player was offering a salute by switching to a rhythm played for that person's special oricha, or *santo*. Spiro, of course, had no way of knowing who the person was, or who his oricha was, but his training in the system of rhythmic cues served its purpose and the performance proceeded.

Further Listening Recommendations for Batá

Track	Source
complete Oru seco - separate tracks	Grupo Ilú Añá – *Sacred Rhythms* – Bembe
complete Oru seco	Wemilere: *Santería* – Harmonia Mundi
complete Oru seco with parts separated for practice	Grupo Olubatá – latinpulsemusic.com
Lázaro Ros series (one CD per oricha – vocal music, but each CD also has a long seco version of just that Oricha's toque).	multi-volume series - Unicornio
hundreds of oricha songs with batá accompaniment	Luca Brandoli - *Cantos Afrocubanos, Vols. 1-10* – cdbaby.com
beautifully harmonized oricha songs, with batá	Emilio Barreto: *Santísimo* – Luz Productions
oricha songs	Merceditas Valdés & Yoruba Andabo: *Aché IV* – EGREM

Further Study Materials for Batá

Passionate followers of all the other Cuban genres, from changüí to arará to timba, turn green with envy when they see how much incredible educational material is available on batá.

There's a mystery and mystique about these rhythms – and the culture, religion and iconography surrounding them – that's inspired some of our greatest musical minds to devote large parts of their lives to the subject.

Batá Drumming: The Oru Seco, by Don Skoog and Alejandro Carvajal, is a stunning achievement. The first half is a very thoughtful and eloquent history of Afro-Cuban music with a special emphasis on how there came to be so many approaches to batá-drumming, and how to deal with them as a creative musician. The second half is a meticulous roadmap to a Havana style Oru seco as played by Alejandro Carvajal. This approach is closer to the Abbilona recording while the Spiro roadmap book below is closer to the Ilú aña recording. (contemporarymusicproject.com)

Michael Spiro's and Justin Hill's ***Roadmap for the Oru del Igbodu,*** (lulu.com) is another complete notational guide to the Oru seco, based on Spiro's studies with the late great Regino Jiménez, whose playing he documented on the highly-recommended CD, *Ilu aña: Sacred Rhythms,* which includes the entire 23-movement Oru seco, with track divisions to easily locate each rhythm.

Batá Rhythms from Matanzas, Cuba, by Bill Summers and Neraldo Durán (kabiosile.org), is a complete Oru Seco roadmap in the Matanzas style, drastically different from either of the Havana books above.

Luca Brandoli's ***Cantos Afrocubanos*** project (cdbaby.com/Artist/LucaBrandoli) is a godsend for students of this music. Each of the 11 volumes covers about 50 of the best and most common folkloric songs, professionally recorded by incredible Cuban musicians in two ways. One version has a full and gorgeous batá accompaniment. More important for our purposes, the second version is just vocals with the 12/8 bell – always starting clearly on "1" – so you can learn each song (and the bell pattern itself) with absolute clarity from the very beginning. Remember – unless you've spent years with this music, the absence of bass and piano makes finding "1" like finding a needle in a haystack, and your overactive brain will immediately start learning the song the wrong way as soon as it makes its first random guess, so this series is *the* way to learn the vast repertoire of Afro-Cuban songs. Each volume has three CDs and a book with the lyrics and other information. Volume 1 is entitled *Cantos a Eleguá,* but the difficulty level is not progressive so you can start with any volume.

Carlos Aldama's Life in Batá, by Umi Vaughan and Carlos Aldama, is a fascinating biography of one of the elder statesmen of the batá world, a protégé of the legendary Jesús Pérez. The book provides many insights into the music, religion, and culture, and the ways they're passed down from generation to generation. Some parts are written in Aldama's voice and others from the point of view of the author, also a batá drummer.

Finally, ***Grupo Olubatá*** (latinpulsemusic.com) has a great Oru seco product using a "music-minus-one" approach. Each movement is also provided with either the iyá or itótole track muted. The performance, following the Regino Jiménez model, is extremely musical and well-recorded.

Pedrito Martínez plays iyá (left) and okónkolo (right) – photo by Tom Ehrlich

Pedrito Martínez plays three batás in a timba context.
Photo by Peter Maiden – Yoshi's Oakland - 2012

Güiro

highlighted track: *Ensamble para acompañar – Antología de la música afrocubana, Vol. 8* – EGREM

"Antología de la música afrocubana" is a very useful 10-CD project produced by (and with extensive liner notes by) the highly-regarded Cuban musicologist, María Teresa Linares. Each CD covers a different folkloric genre. One of the best features of this box set is that for most of the rhythms an attempt is made to supply educational tracks that solo the individual parts. The ultimate product of this type is by the late great Regino Jiménez, and includes almost all the rhythms covered in this listening tour. Unfortunately it's currently not available but may be by the time you read this so remember to google "Regino Jimenez Instruction" regularly.

time	tempo	comments
0:00	99	hoe blade *(guataca)* plays 12/8 bell pattern (Exercise RP-5)
0:10		chékere 1 enters (plays main beats: **X**○○ **X**○○ **X**○○ **X**○○)
0:12		alternate bell pattern (Ex. RP-6) is used (and again at 0:17)
0:19	101	chékere 2 enters (plays various rhythms)
0:34	102	chékere 3 enters (plays all subdivisions: **XXX XXX XXX XXX**)
0:50	106	supporting conga enters (plays doubled ponche in triple pulse structure: ○○○ ○**XX** ○○○ ○**XX**)
0:59		lead conga enters (improvisational)

Our second Yoruban genre is called *güiro,* but don't be confused. It doesn't use the popular music güiro instrument we studied in Exercise 2-1. Instead, it uses three chékeres.

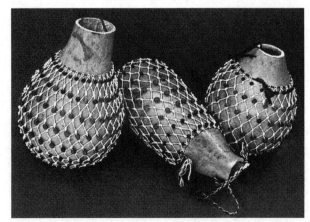

chékeres as used in güiro – photo from the recommended Soul Jazz recording

188

Like the güiro instrument, chékeres are made from dried, hollow gourds but instead of being scraped they're played by shaking and tapping. The higher frequency percussive sounds are created by a net of beads attached to the gourd.

The bell sound is produced by a metal hoe blade called a *guataca.* In the 20th century, congas were added to the mix. Güiro performances salute the same deities as batá performances but are less formal and can be played by anyone in the community, while only those who have had a specific initiation are allowed to play the *fundamento* batás designed for religious ceremonies. (It's now quite common for non-fundamento, or *aberíkula,* batás to be played in all settings, including popular music.)

Many güiro performances use the alternate 12/8 bell (Exercise RP-6) almost exclusively, except for the first entrance, which is always right on beat 1. For an example of this approach, listen to any of the tracks from the Echún Okiry CD recommended below. Make sure you master Exercise RP-6 or you'll find yourself lost in a world of rhythmic disorientation. Our highlighted track uses the standard 12/8 bell (Exercise RP-5) and mixes in the alternate bell occasionally. The Regino Jiménez instructional CD is another that uses the alternate bell.

Further Listening Recommendations for Güiro

Track	Source
Oshún	Grupo AfroCuba de Matanzas: *Raíces africanas* – Shanachie
all tracks	Echún Okiry: *Güiro for Elegguá* – Earth CDs
Güiro	Jiménez and Wardinsky: *Study Guide for Afro-Cuban Percussion*
multiple tracks	*Antología de la música afrocubana, Vol. 8* – EGREM
Canto y toque a Ochún	Afroamérica: *Chants et rythmes afrocubains* – VDE-Gallo
Güiro	Grupo Oba-Ilú: *Drums of Cuba* – Soul Jazz Records

Yosvany Terry at La Peña Cultural Center with Yé-de-gbé – Oakland, CA – 2007 – photos by Tom Ehrlich

Iyesá

CUBA
Afroamérica
Chants et rythmes afrocubains
Cantos y toques afrocubanos
Afrocuban songs and rhythms

highlighted track: *Cantos a Ochún y Oyá* – Afroamérica: *Chants et rythmes afrocubains* – VDE-Gallo

time	tempo	comments
0:00	107	first drum enters
0:03	109	first bell enters
0:05	110	second bell enters
0:08	112	second drum enters
0:11	114	lead vocalist introduces coro 1
0:28	120	coro 1
1:44	126	lead vocalist introduces coro 2a
1:52		coro 2a
2:07		coro 2b
2:17		lead vocalist introduces coro 3
2:23		coro 3
3:02	130	instrumental – drum variations

The term *iyesá* has two important meanings. It's the name of a duple-pulse (4/4) batá rhythm that, like *chachalokefún, ñongo* and *la lumbanché,* is one of the most common non-Oru seco rhythms used for accompanying vocal songs. But *iyesá* is also the name of a self-standing religious genre with its own special rhythms and even its own drums, although it's often played on congas in Cuba today.

In the iyesá genre, there are two main rhythms, one in 4/4 *(ochún)* and one in 12/8 *(ogún)*. Both use two interlocking bell parts. The 4/4 (duple pulse) rhythm uses four drums, and the 12/8 (triple pulse) rhythm uses two drums.

Some of the drums are played with sticks and some with stick and hand combinations (a practice we'll also encounter a little later in bembé and arará). Michael Spiro's indispensable 8-part video series on congamasterclass.com clearly explains and demonstrates all of the bell and drum parts for each rhythm.

All the iyesá rhythms, including the batá version, are represented in the Further Listening list. Our highlighted track above uses the 4/4 *ochún* rhythm.

Further Listening Recommendations for Iyesá

Track	Source
Ogún – (iyesá genre: 12/8 rhythm)	Grupo AfroCuba de Matanzas: *Raíces africanas* – Shanachie
Ogún – (iyesá genre: 12/8 rhythm)	Afroamérica: *Chants et rythmes afrocubains* – VDE-Gallo
Song for Ochún – (iyesá genre: 4/4 rhythm)	*Afro-Cuba: A Musical Anthology* – Rounder
(entire CD on iyesá genre)	*Antología de la música afrocubana, Vol. 3* – EGREM
Baba oba oba – (batá rhythm)	Luca Brandoli: *Cantos afrocubanos, Vol. 3, CD 3, track 42*
Iyesá (iyesá genre: 4/4 rhythm)	Jiménez and Wardinsky: *Study Guide for Afro-Cuban Percussion*

Bembé

highlighted track: *Eleguá (Bembé)* – Grupo AfroCuba de Matanzas: *Raíces africanas* – Shanachie

time	tempo	comments
0:00	rubato	vocalist enters alone
0:04	82	standard 12/8 bell (Ex. RP-5) enters, but on the third stroke of its pattern (!)
0:06	89	drums enter
0:24	96	coro 1
0:45	101	lead singer introduces coro 2
0:53	104	coro 2
1:00		coro 3
1:18	107	lead singer introduces coro 4
1:24		coro 4a
1:48	110	coro 4b
2:06	111	lead singer introduces coro 5
2:12		coro 5 (note that coro 5 is phrased to begin on the 2-side of the bell pattern)
2:28	113	lead singer introduces coro 6
2:34	114	coro 6 (now beginning on the 3-side again)
3:14		lead singer introduces coro 7
3:16		coro 7
3:48		lead singer introduces coro 8
3:54	115	coro 8

The term bembé can refer to a 12/8 rhythm, a family of drums, or a religious party where bembé rhythms are played. The standard 12/8 bell is used, with three drums, featuring a heavy accent on the frontbeat of the 3-side. There are many different styles of bembé in different regions, played with various combinations of hands and sticks.

Further Listening Recommendations for Bembé

Track	Source
field recording of bembé celebration	*Antología de la música afrocubana, Vol. 6* – EGREM
Bembé a Oggún	Afroamérica: *Chants et rythmes afrocubains* – VDE-Gallo
Bembé a Oyá	Afroamérica: *Chants et rythmes afrocubains* – VDE-Gallo
Bembé	Mongo Santamaría with Francisco Aguabella: *Afro Roots* – Concord
instructional videos	congamasterclass.com
tracks 3 through 10	Robert Fernández: *Afro-Cuban Folkloric Musical Tradition*
Bembé Matanzas and Havana	Jiménez and Wardinsky: *Study Guide for Afro-Cuban Percussion*

Carabalí drums and shakers – played by Pedrito Martínez – photos by Tom Ehrlich - 2012

Carabalí

The *Carabalí* category has its own distinct religion, drums, rhythms, and a mysterious, all-male, mutual aid society called *Abakuá.* The definitive English language resource on the rituals and history of Abakuá is Ivor Miller's epic *Voice of the Leopard: African Secret Societies and Cuba* (University Press of Mississippi). There's also an excellent online interview of Miller (by Ned Sublette) on afrocubaweb.com.

highlighted track: *Ritmo abakuá* – **Los Muñequitos de Matanzas:** *Guaguancó Matancero* – TCC
Be sure to master Exercise RP-12 to learn the correct orientation of the drum melody before studying this track.

time	tempo	comments
0:00	118	3-2 12/8 rumba clave, with drum melody starting on the ponche of beat 4 (Ex. RP-12)
0:07	120	vocal intro (analogous to the *diana* of guaguancó) – clave switches to Ex. RP-13
0:21	123	cuerpo
1:24	125	characteristic responsorial *rezo* (prayer) chant
1:44		second diana-esque passage (unusual)
2:00	129	coro

Carabalí rhythms, all in 12/8, are usually divided into the faster *Efik* (or *Efí)* style and the slower *Efó* style. The pitched drums tend to produce very interesting melodies that can easily be learned incorrectly by inexperienced listeners, so please make sure that you're comfortable with Exercises RP-10, RP-11, RP-12 and RP-13 before immersing yourself in this part of the Listening Tour.

Further Listening Recommendations for Abakuá

Track	Source
Bríkamo	Grupo AfroCuba de Matanzas: *Raíces africanas* – Shanachie
Abacuá	Grupo AfroCuba de Matanzas: *Raíces africanas* – Shanachie
Abakuá - Efik	Jiménez and Wardinsky: *Study Guide for Afro-Cuban Percussion*
multiple tracks	*Antología de la música afrocubana, Vol. 10* – EGREM
Wemba of the Abakwa	*Les danses des dieux* – Harmonia Mundi
Brícamo	Mongo Santamaría: *Afro Roots* – Fantasy Records
Appapas del Calabar	Los Van Van: *Llegó Van Van* – Pimienta (about abakuá, not the rhythm itself)

Bantú

The first and largest wave of Africans to come to Cuba were of the *Bantú* ethnic group, originating in the vast Congo River area, in and around present-day Congo (Zaire) and Angola. The three most important Bantú musical genres are *palo, makuta* and *yuka*.

Palo

This album contains live performances from religious ceremonies as opposed to the usual recording studio approach, giving the listener the sense of being a "fly on the wall" at a performance meant for the participants, not an audience. Players switch instruments in mid-song and the music has a rough, authentic feel and a hypnotically torrid groove. This palo recording is about 13 minutes long – with many singers, coros, bell patterns and probably different bell players. To help you get comfortable, here's a breakdown of what the bell does for the first minute:

time	tempo	comments
0:00	167	12/8 clave (Exercise RP-7)
0:37		bell stops (another player probably takes over)
0:39		bell enters on 2nd stroke of clave and cycles twice, then switches to the alternate 12/8
0:41		After playing the alt. 12/8 bell (Exercise RP-6) 3 times, the bell-player switches to the standard bell 6 times, then back, then continues to switch at the bell player's discretion – just feel the main beats and three subdivisions and hang on!

Like Santería, the Palo religion is still practiced extensively in Cuba, although palo tends to be a much less public religion. Some people practice both religions. Herbalism plays a major role in Palo so you'll often hear the term *yerbero* or *hierbero* in lyrics such as Los Van Van's *Hierbero ven*.

The palo rhythm, in 12/8, is very fast and very intense. The bell, or *guataca* (hoe blade), generally plays the standard 12/8 bell (Exercise RP-5) but in some recordings jumps freely and unpredictably to the alternate 12/8 bell (Exercise RP-6). Our suggested listening track for palo is a very challenging one because of the alternate bell and the blisteringly fast tempo (167 BPM). It's best not to attempt to listen to it until you're extremely confident of your mastery of Exercises RP-5 through RP-7. To help you get your foot in the door, you might want to try using a software program like Transcribe™ or Amazing SlowDowner™ to listen at a slower tempo until you're comfortable.

Further Listening Recommendations for Palo

Track	Source
Canto y toque de palo	Afroamérica: *Chants et rythmes afrocubains* – VDE-Gallo
Palo	Jiménez and Wardinsky: *Study Guide for Afro-Cuban Percussion*
Palo	Los Calderones: search YouTube for "palo, Los Calderon"
Palo	Grupo AfroCuba de Matanzas: *Raíces africanas* – Shanachie
instructional videos	Michael Spiro: congamasterclass.com

Makuta

highlighted track: *Makuta* – Iyabakuá: *Afrekete* – Pan

time	tempo	comments
0:00	104	bell enters alone (cinquillo)
0:02		drums enter one by one
0:07		lead vocalist introduces coro 1
0:11	106	coro 1 (final tempo: 111 BPM)

Makuta is another rhythm and dance of the Bantú group, this time in duple pulse structure (4/4). The dance is a fertility rite and is considered a forerunner of *guaguancó,* a type of rumba with a famous dance featuring pelvic thrusts that we'll study later in this Listening Tour.

In most versions of makuta, the bell part consists of cinquillo (Exercise 2-4) on both sides of the clave. It's usually easy to hear, but at faster tempos it can cause the type of rhythmic disorientation that we dealt with in Exercise RP-14.

Further Listening Recommendations for Makuta

Track	Source
Makuta	Afroamérica: *Chants et rythmes afrocubains* – VDE-Gallo
Mama Chola	Luca Brandoli y Grupo Barracón: *Cantos de palo* – Barracón
Makuta	Regino Jiménez and Scott Wardinsky: *Guemilere: Study Guide for Afro-Cuban Percussion*
Makuta	Ballet Folklórico CUTUMBA de Santiago: *Ritmos Afrocubanos, Vol. 1* – Academy of Cuban Folklore and Dance – Seattle, WA

Yuka

highlighted video: Conjunto Folklórico Nacional: *Palo, Yuka and Makuta* – Latidos

time	tempo	comments
0:00	approx. 110	a cappella coro 1 and lead
0:46		a cappella coro 2
1:01	168	(video edit) yuka – in *"con qué"*, *"qué"* is "1"
1:57	112	makuta
2:24	147	(video edit) short clip of palo

Yuka is often sung in Spanish or a mixture of Spanish and Bantú. It's a very interesting style of secular (non-religious) music and dance in which the *catá* (a type of woodblock) plays in double-time, triple-pulse structure while the supporting drums and vocalists sometimes play much closer to duple pulse. The improvising drum (the lowest in tuning) can switch between the two time feels.

Yuka dancing near Pinar del Río – c. 1990 – photo courtesy of Robert Fernández

Unfortunately, yuka has become quite rare, even in Cuba. It's among the hardest of the folkloric genres to find on CD and many tracks labeled "yuka" don't actually use the double time triplet *catá* figure. I've used a YouTube performance as our highlighted track because I couldn't find a good example of the pure rhythm on a non-instructional CD. The Regino Jiménez, Robert Fernández and congamasterclass.com products all include great-sounding examples of the rhythm.

It's very interesting to watch the dancers in the highlighted Conjunto Folklórico Nacional video. You can see the characteristic catá part mirrored in the shoulders of the dancers as they imitate the movement of chickens *(gallinas)*.

While pure yuka is rarely played, even in cabildos, some of its songs live on as quotes in timba. The most common is *"con qué, gallina va a chapear cantero, con qué"*.

Further Listening Recommendations for Yuka

Track	Source
Yuka	Afroamérica: *Chants et rythmes afrocubains* – VDE-Gallo
Yuka	Ballet Folklórico CUTUMBA de Santiago: *Ritmos Afrocubanos, Vol. 1*
El bla bla bla (quote at 1:40 from *"con qué, gallina"* on a timba song)	Charanga Habanera: *Charanguero mayor* – Ciocan Records (1999) (After the initial quote, the next coro also quotes the yuka song.)
Yuka (this version is all 12/8)	Jiménez and Wardinsky: *Study Guide for Afro-Cuban Percussion* An excellent part by part breakdown of this style can be found on congamasterclass.com.
Garábato (yuka with only sticks)	Jiménez and Wardinsky: *Study Guide for Afro-Cuban Percussion*
Cantos de Yuka	*Afro-Cuba: A Musical Anthology* – Rounder Records

Yuka drummers near Pinar del Río – c. 1990 – photo courtesy of Robert Fernández

Dahomey

Pedrito Martínez and Román Díaz playing arará drums with Yosvany Terry and Yé-de-gbé
La Peña – Oakland, California – 2007 – photo by Tom Ehrlich

The last African ethnic group to be brought to Cuba in large numbers were from Dahomey (present-day Benin). Some were brought directly to Matanzas and Havana, and their music, and Cuban descendants, are called *arará,* a term probably derived from the name of the African city Allada.

Dahomey people also came to the other side of the island by a more circuitous route. In the turmoil following the famous Haitian slave rebellion of 1791, tens of thousands of French and African refugees fled from Haiti to the eastern or *Oriente* region of Cuba – to cities like Santiago, Holguín and Guantánamo, and to dozens of smaller towns whose names have been celebrated in the lyrics of so many classic Cuban songs – Baracoa, Alto Songo, Alto Cedro, Cueto, La Maya, Mayarí, Marcané, Los Hoyos, Yateras, Yumurí, Guayacán, Cayo Hueso and so on.

The sacred genre of *vodú* and a variety of secular genres had already evolved in Haiti before arriving in Cuba. The most important secular genre was *tumba francesa,* which combines Africanized parodies of 18th Century French couple-dancing with African drumming. Tumba francesa consists of three dances, usually performed as a suite: *masón, yubá* and *frenté.*

In gripping fashion, Ned Sublette's *The World That Made New* Orleans recounts the horrific ordeals – and transcendent musical contributions – of the Dahomey people in Haiti, New Orleans and Cuba. In the previously recommended *Changüí: Origins of Cuban Music and Dance,* Benjamin Lapidus connects the musical dots, establishing a musical chain of custody from *arará*, to *vodú* and *tumba francesa*, to the Eastern Cuban folk genres of *kiribá* and *nengón*, to *changüí*, and finally to *son*, bringing us full circle back to Listening Tour 1. And remember, of course, that this current tour would have *been* Listening Tour 1 if not for the need to master the challenges of rhythmic perspective before tackling these older but more difficult genres. Make sure to study Exercises RP-8 and RP-9 before embarking on this part of the Listening Tour.

Arará

highlighted track: (DVD) – *Tierra arará* – Los Hermanos Arango: *Las estrellas del folklor* – BIS

This track is jazz-fusion arará, as opposed to the pure folkloric tracks in the Further Listening section. Because of the chordal instruments, there's never a doubt as to "where 1 is", so you can learn Exercise RP-8 easily in this context.

time	tempo	comments
0:00	rubato	a cappella vocal intro
0:23		bass enters (Feliciano Arango, founding bassist of NG La Banda)
0:43	87	coro 1
1:15	89	band enters (jazz/funk)
1:37	130	sabalú bell begins (Exercise RP-8)
2:02		sax solo - funk groove with sabalú bell
2:46	132	bass and keyboard theme
3:26		coro 2
4:13	135	coro 3 (with bomba bass against sabalú groove)
4:37		coro 4
5:14		coro 5
5:25		back to coro 2
5:57	132	coda

Arará music is extremely complex, endlessly fascinating, and – like rumba and batá – has begun to find its way into popular music and jazz.

Our highlighted track is by Los Hermanos Arango, an excitingly innovative group that combines the virtuosic bass-playing of NG La Banda founder Feliciano Arango with Afro-Cuban folkloric percussionists and vocalists. *Tierra arará* is from their Cubadisco-winning *Los Hermanos Arango y las Estrellas del Folklor*, released as a CD and also in DVD form with an excellent documentary (including English subtitles).

Another pioneer in the use of arará rhythms in jazz is the Cuban saxophonist and percussionist Yosvany Terry, whose group, Yé-de-gbé, features Román Díaz and Pedrito Martínez. More traditional performances are listed in the Further Listening section below.

The two most common arará rhythms are devoted to the deities *Afrekete* and *Ebioso* (there are *many* spellings, including *Gervioso, Jebioso,* etc.), corresponding to the Yoruban deities *Yemayá* and *Changó*, but there's a full pantheon of arará deities, just as in Yoruban music, though far less well preserved in Cuba. Robert Fernández and Luca Brandoli have done extensive research on this and are planning to release a recording of an arará Oru seco. In the meantime, you'll find more recordings of arará than of yuka, but not nearly so many as of batá.

The currently available tracks are primarily spread across the now-familiar anthologies and compilations already recommended above, and offer a musically excellent, but frustratingly incomplete snapshot of this quirky and exceptionally creative genre, with the many inconsistencies in naming and rhythmic details that have resulted from centuries of aurally passing down the varying approaches of different cabildos and different ethnic subgroups (e.g., *sabalú, majino*).

It's painful to imagine how much of the rich musical legacy of the Dahomeyan culture has been lost over the course of Cuba's and Africa's long and tumultuous histories.

Further Listening Recommendations for Arará

Track	Source
Afrequete, Gerbioso, Mase	Afroamérica: *Chants et rythmes afrocubains* – VDE-Gallo
Culte arará	*Les danses des dieux* – Harmonia Mundi
Afrekete, Jevioso, Asuano	Jiménez and Wardinsky: Study Guide for Afro-Cuban Percussion
tracks 36 through 44	Robert Fernández: *Afro-Cuban Folkloric Musical Tradition*
all tracks	*Antología de la música afrocubana, Vol. 4* – EGREM
all tracks	*Yosvany Terry & Ye-dé-gbé: Afro-Caribbean Legacy*

Tumba Francesa

highlighted track: *Tumba francesa* – Ballet Folklórico CUTUMBA de Santiago: *Ritmos Afrocubanos, Vol. 1*
Academy of Cuban Folklore and Dance – Seattle, WA

time	tempo	comments
0:00	rubato	a cappella vocal introduction
0:35	131 4/4	**MASÓN** – The first three percussive strokes are pickups; the cinquillo starts on fourth stroke; the first two drum strokes are bombo-ponche: ○○○**X** ○○**X**○.
0:42		masón coro 1
1:15	133	masón coro 2 – introduced by lead singer first
2:11		masón coro 3 – introduced by lead singer first
2:57	200 12/8	**YUBÁ** – Note the insanely fast tempo. The first eight percussive strokes are pickups; the first five (before the low drum enters) are: **X**○**X** ○**X**○ **X**○○ **X**○○. Then, with the first low tone, three more pickups: **X**○**X** ○**X**○. With the second low drum tone, the pattern (Exercise RP-15) begins – ‖: **X**○**X** **X**○**X** **X**○**X** **XX**○ :‖
3:16	200-207	yubá vocals – switches between lead and coro but has more of the character of a *rezo* or rumba *diana* than a normal coro call and response section
5:47	132 3/4	**FRENTÉ** – The transition demonstrates the metric modulation described in Exercise RP-16. The 3/4 section begins on beat 3 of the 12/8 ‖ **X**○**X** **X**○**X** ‖ ¾ ‖: **X**○**XX** **X**○**X**○ **XX**○**X** :‖ The speed of the pattern itself stays constant, but the tempo is now perceived as one beat for each four subdivisions instead of one beat for each three subdivisions.
5:50		The steady low thumps come on the beat in groups of three.
5:55		vocals enter – the drum improvisation in the right channel converses (or duels) with the single male dancer
8:51	150	**MASÓN** – The idea of returning to masón was not part of the traditional format but is often used by modern groups for performance. The transition consists of two repetitions of tresillo (Exercise 2-2).

Tumba francesa combines stately 18th Century French dance and costumery with as challenging, intricate and blazingly fast African-based drumming as you'll find anywhere in Afro-Cuban music. I'm not sure how much – if any – humor was intended by the original creators of this music and dance genre, but in my twisted little brain, I can't help but think of it as sort of an 18th Century version of

The Daily Show. Most humor, after all, is based on absurd juxtapositions, e.g., *"a duck and a unicorn walk into a bar ...".* Now, if Jon Stewart had been a Dahomeyan slave in Saint-Domingue, imagine the comedy routine he might have come up with to divert his friends from the reality that their lives were being made miserable – to put it lightly – by a bunch of pompous, stiff, sadistic French aristocrats, whose idea of a good time was to dress up in elaborately silly costumes and dance with all the airs of Louis XIV the Sun King and his court, and all the rhythmic nuance of a kitchen broomstick. To the sophisticated rhythmic sensibilities of the Dahomeyans, these rhythms and body movements must have seemed unfathomably primitive. You spend two hours getting all dolled up and then you dance like *that?* Watching Europeans trying to dance was already as humorously incongruous as the duck walking into the bar, but what stroke of comedy genius could bring the unicorn into the equation and turn humor into absurd hilarity? How about having them dance to the fastest, most syncopated rhythms imaginable, laced with every conceivable trick of rhythmic perception? The final irony was that the slave owners had no idea that the joke was on them, and were getting their own laughs from the spectacle of "silly savages", whom they assumed were unable to master the stately European rhythms.

Whether the humor was intended or – more likely – a complete and utter figment of my overactive and admittedly demented imagination, let this ridiculous little tangent serve as fair warning: don't even *think* about trying to follow tumba francesa until you've studied Exercises RP-14 through RP-17. Each of the three main rhythms has extremely challenging rhythmic perspective issues.

Further Listening Recommendations for Tumba francesa

Track	Source
all tracks	*Antología de la música afrocubana, Vol. 7* – EGREM
first three tracks	Air Mail Music: *Cuba* – Celluloid Records

Vodú

highlighted track: *Vodú* – Ballet Folklórico CUTUMBA de Santiago: *Ritmos Afrocubanos, Vol. 1*
Academy of Cuban Folklore and Dance – Seattle, WA

time	tempo	comments
0:00	151	lead singer introduces coro 1 alone
0:04		percussion enters – first stroke is "1" – *guataca* (hoe blade) plays standard 12/8 bell throughout (Exercise RP-1) ‖: X∘X ∘XX ∘X∘ X∘X :‖
1:24	159	coro 2 – note that each cycle (including the lead vocal) lasts 5 claves, or 5 repetitions of the bell pattern
4:40	170	coro 2 fades out after reaching a tempo of 170

The Afro-Haitian immigrants also brought their religious music to Cuba. As with Santería, the *vodú* religion has a large pantheon of deities, multiple sects, multiple drum ensembles, and is marked by *syncretization,* the process of using the terms and symbols of one religion to represent those of another, in this case Catholicism. The best-known example of this is Santería, in which, for example, "Santa Bárbara" is understood to mean Changó, "St. Peter" to mean Ogún, "La Virgen de Regla" to mean Yemayá, and so on.

Unfortunately, it's very hard to find recordings and performances of vodú, even in comparison to the arará music practiced in Matanzas and Havana.

Further Listening Recommendations for Vodú

Track	Source
Culte Vaudou (3 tracks, also including *rará* and *yanvalou*)	Les danses des dieux – Harmonia Mundi
Vodú	Ballet Folklórico CUTUMBA de Santiago: *Ritmos Afrocubanos, Vol. 1 – Academy of Cuban Folklore and Dance – Seattle, WA*
Vodú	Grupo Ban Rarrá: *Con sabor al guaso* – Mayulí

Dancing for Changó (Yoruba) - Sandy Pérez and José Francisco Barroso
(www.obakoso.org) – photo by Tom Ehrlich – 2010

In conclusion, all of today's popular music, whether Latin or North American, owes its existence to the music brought to the New World from West Africa. Hopefully this short listening tour has made it clear that this incredible rhythmic legacy has many more musical treasures waiting to be enjoyed and assimilated.

Folkloric Music of Cuban Origin

We've been using the term *Afro-Cuban folkloric music* to refer to genres based on music brought to Cuba by specific African ethnic groups. *Changüí, conga de comparsa* and *rumba* are examples of folkloric genres that *developed in Cuba* by Cubans of African ancestry.

Changüí

highlighted track: *Loma del chivo es* – Grupo Changüí de Guantánamo: *Bongó del monte* – EGREM

time	tempo	comments
0:00	116	tres enters (playing all offbeats – see Exercise RP-1)
0:04		bongó del monte, maracas, guayo and marímbula enter
0:14		tres plays *paso de calle* figure
0:18	118	cuerpo (lyrics explain that Loma del Chivo is a barrio of inspiration, where the new generation maintains the traditions of changüí, *tumba francesa*, etc.)
0:25		the paso de calle figure disrupts the duple-beat phrase structure – one of the reasons that changüí is among the few Cuban genres that don't use clave
0:58		montuno section – coros and pregones
1:34	120	bongó and tres soloistic passages
2:51	122	coros and pregones

Changüí originated in the mountains around Guantánamo. Like rumba, it was already a vibrant folk genre by the turn of the 20th Century and had profoundly impacted popular music for many decades before any record company saw fit to record it. Today's changüí discography, beginning in the 1980s, is woefully small, but extremely good, especially in the case of Grupo Changüí de Guantánamo.

When you learn to recognize the changüí influence, you'll be able to hear it everywhere in Cuban pop – in groups like Los Van Van and Revé, and in the styles of individual musicians such as Lilí Martínez, Emiliano Salvador, Tony Calá, Los Pututi, Denis "Papacho" Savón and the afore-mentioned Bombón Reyes, all of whom hail from Oriente (Eastern Cuba) and credit changüí as a major component of their styles.

In one crucial way, the changüí influence on popular music is even more extensive than that of rumba: while rumba used only voices and percussion, changüí combined harmonic instruments with African rhythms, introducing the forerunners of the modern Cuban piano and bass – the *tres* and *marímbula*, respectively.

Carmelo Ivanes Sulterán of Grupo Changüí de Guantánamo – photo by Gabriel García – Guantánamo – 2012

The changüí tres is a small guitar-like instrument with three widely-spaced pairs of strings. It was the first instrument in any genre to use the arpeggiated, offbeat-dominated ostinatos that evolved into son's tres *guajeos,* and later the piano *tumbaos* (a.k.a., *montunos)* that are omnipresent in almost all subsequent genres of Cuban popular music.

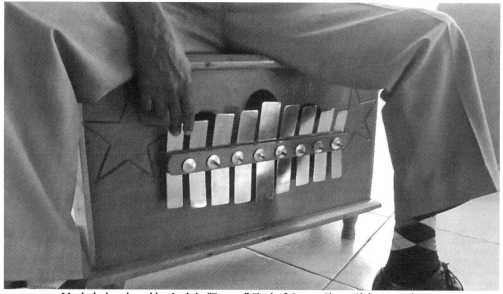

Marímbula, played by Andrés "Tavera" Fistó of Grupo Changüí de Guantánamo
photo by Gabriel García – Guantánamo – 2012

Changüí's bass instrument is the *marímbula,* a huge kalimba. The player sits on the wooden resonating box reaching down to play large, tuned metal tongues and tap the box percussively. The rhythmic pattern is a clear ancestor of both the modern bass tumbao and the basic conga marcha.

The changüí percussion section includes maracas, a güiro-like scraper *(guayo)*, and a large *bongó del monte* that's played in a syncopated and improvisational way, like the quinto in rumba, the caja in palo, and so on. The *son* genre borrowed the bongó and maracas, but used claves instead of guayo.

Elito Revé – 2010 – Yoshi's San Francisco – photo by Tom Ehrlich

No discussion of changüí is complete without mentioning Orquesta Revé, also covered in Listening Tours 2 and 3. For reasons explained earlier, many Cuban bands can boast of careers spanning over 50 years, but Revé is the only group to stay consistently at the creative vanguard of Cuban music for that stretch of time. In 1956, timbalero Elio Revé brought his group from Guantánamo to Havana. It was a charanga with the traditional instrumentation of violins, flute, timbales, bass and piano, but Revé marketed it as "changüí" – not because it played changüí, but because its charanga music was imbued with changüí's rustic flavor and attitude. That said, it's primarily in the lyrics that the changüí element can be heard. A decade later, having already enlisted pianist Pupy Pedroso, Revé brought in Juan Formell as musical director. Formell introduced North American pop and rock elements and the new style, *changüí-68,* had even less to do with changüí than Revé's original conception. Ironically, it was Formell, in 1974, now the leader of Los Van Van, who gave pop music its first jolt of pure changüí energy. The song, a massive hit called *Güararey,* used Van Van's songo-charanga instrumentation but was otherwise a relatively faithful cover of *El güararey de Pastora,* by Pedro Speck of Grupo Changüí de Guantánamo.

In about 1980, 25 years after his original changüí marketing idea, Revé had a true stroke of pop music genius, creating a new instrumentation called *charangón.* To the charanga instrumentation he added bongó and tres from changüí, as well as trombones and sometimes batá and quinto. Beneath the surface, he also developed a unique style of playing the timbales emulating the changüí bongó del monte in various ways. The group's arrangements, by Ignacio Herrera and later by Juan Carlos

Alfonso and Tony García, also included changüí elements. For example, the trombones fills in the cuerpo of *Negra con pelo* mimic the *pasos de calle* of the traditional changüí arranging format.

Casa del Changüí (poster for the Festival Nacional) – photo by Michelle White – 2007 – Loma del Chivo

When Elio Revé died in 1997, his son Elito took over leadership and has continued his father's success at finding brilliant arrangers, singers and musicians to keep the band on the leading edge of Cuban popular music. Elito Revé has also been a champion of introducing pure, authentic changüí to a larger public, adding authentic changüí tracks to his timba CDs and serving as honorary president of the *Festival Nacional del Changüí Elio Revé Matos* held in Guantánamo every other year.

The best way to get more familiar with changüí is to hear it and dance to it live. Grupo Changüí de Guantánamo tours Europe and México frequently and is well-represented on YouTube.

Further Listening Recommendations for Changüí

Year	Song	Source
1998	*El Güararey de pastora*	Estrellas Campesinas – *Changüí* – Traditional Crossroads
2001	*Los fundadores*	Grupo Changüí de Guantánamo – *La rumba está buena* – Disky
2001	*La rumba está buena*	Grupo Changüí de Guantánamo – *La rumba está buena* – Disky
2007	*Vamos a bailar el changüí*	Elito Revé y su Charangón: *Fresquecito* – BIS
2010	*Changüí tradicional*	Elito Revé y su Charangón: *De qué estamos hablando* – BIS

Further Reading on Changüí

Changüí: Origins of Cuban Music and Dance, by Benjamin Lapidus (Scarecrow Press) – The definitive English-language book on changüí.

Conga de Comparsa

highlighted track: *Conga oriental* – Grupo Ban Rarrá: *Con sabor al guaso* – Mayulí

time	tempo	comments
0:00	178	a cappella introduction
0:06		bloque based on 3-2 rumba clave (Exercise 3-10)
0:08		coro 1
0:25		lead singer introduces coro 2
0:36		coro 2
1:09		percussion interlude
1:14	176	coro 3
1:39	175	coro 4
2:23		clave efecto (some percussion continues playing time)
2:28	179	coro 5
2:49		solo – corneta china (an oboe-like double reed instrument)
3:19	177	corneta china introduces melodies to coro 6
3:25		coro 6 alternating with corneta china
3:49		lead vocalist introduces coro 7
4:11		ends on clave bloque

Like Brazil and New Orleans, Cuba has a tradition of yearly parade-like festivals of music, dance and general debauchery. The events themselves are called *comparsas* and the family of rhythms is called *conga,* or *conga de comparsa.* YouTube is well stocked with footage to acquaint you with the general ambience. There are two distinct styles – Occidental (Havana, Matanzas) and Oriental (Santiago, Guantánamo, etc.) – with many regional differences in provinces such as Cienfuegos and Camagüey.

While it's relatively easy to find the beat and meter, conga rhythms are extremely fast, dense and complex. Fernández's transcription of *Conga Oriental* includes six hand drum parts, four different bass drum parts, four brake drum parts (yes, the brake drum from a car), plus bells and shakers. The Havana style (with snare drum) is quite different, and most regions between Havana and Guantánamo have their own distinct variants as well.

Conga rhythms and dance are quite familiar outside Cuba (for example the ubiquitous "conga line" dance and the novelty hit *Pico and Sepulveda)*, and have continually informed Cuban popular music – from Arsenio Rodríguez's *Todos seguimos la conga* (and other tracks), to countless big band hits throughout the 1950s, to the stage acts of many timba bands such as Issac Delgado and Wil Campa. Conga rhythms were also a primary influence on Pello el Afrokán's famous *mozambique* genre of the 1960s.

Further Listening Recommendations for Conga de Comparsa

Year	Song	Source
various	various	YouTube (particularly appropriate for comparsa because of the dance element and the visual aid of being able to see the dense texture of percussionists)
1980	*Conga de Santiago*	*Carnaval in Cuba* – Smithsonian Folkways
various	*Congas y comparsas del Carnaval Habanero*	Panart Vinyl (fidelseyeglasses.blogspot.com)
instr.	tracks 71-79	Robert Fernández: *The Afro-Cuban Folkloric Musical Tradition* audio CD
instr.	*Comparsa habanera*	Jiménez- Wardinsky: *Study Guide for Afro-Cuban Percussion*
instr.	various instructional videos	congamasterclass.com

Master Rumberos: Piri López of Los Chinitos (left) – San Francisco 2012 – photo by Peter Maiden
Sandy Pérez, former director of Grupo AfroCuba de Matanzas (right) – San Francisco 2010 – photo by Tom Ehrlich

Rumba

Rumba is the quintessential Cuban genre – a perfect composite of the island's inimitable rhythms, melodies, dances, slang, humor, sensuality, creativity, and *cubanismo*. It informs every type of Cuban popular music in the same primordial ways that the blues genre informs jazz, rock, soul and hip-hop.

The term *rumba* can refer to a complex of secular folkloric rhythms, songs and dances, or a party where these are performed. Rumba developed gradually as a form of social dancing and entertainment on slave plantations, and later in shipyards, and in the barrios and *solares* in urban areas. The rhythms, forms, gestures, language and attitudes of rumba have profoundly influenced every subsequent Cuban genre. Even today, most Cuban popular musicians engage in rumbas as a regular part of their social lives. In the 1930s, the word *rhumba* was misused to describe a watered down form of commercial son and the word *guaguancó* was used in the 1940s by Arsenio Rodríguez to describe a specific variant of his son montuno style. Arsenio's "guaguancós" are a seminal genre in their own right, but it wasn't until the 1950s that true rumba was first commercially recorded, most prominently by Guaguancó Matancero, a group that changed its name to Los Muñequitos de Matanzas in response to the popularity of one of its early hits, *Los Muñequitos.*

There are three traditional genres of rumba. With its syncopations and sexy dance rituals, *guaguancó* is by far the most popular and most influential on popular music. Less common are the earlier, slower, more G-rated *yambú,* and *rumba columbia* – a fast, 12/8 rhythm with a single male dancer interacting with an improvisational lead drum. All three types are still played in their traditional forms, but unlike most genres, rumba has proven immune to fossilization, continuing to grow and develop rather than settling into the exclusive domain of "heritage acts". At the hands of artists like Clave y Guaguancó, Yoruba Andabo, and Los Chinitos, modern rumba, often called *guarapachangueo,* has become incredibly sophisticated and complex, incorporating batás and cajones in a variety of interesting ways.

Rumba performances usually include examples of yambú, guaguancó and columbia, but unlike tumba francesa, the three rhythms are not performed in any specific order. Guaguancó accounts for the lion's share of the repertoire of rumba groups, with an occasional yambú, columbia, or even an *abakuá* number added for variety.

Like all folkloric genres, the rumba complex can vary from region to region. The best known example of this is the difference between Havana and Matanzas guaguancó in terms of the melodies of the open drums:

```
XooX oooX ooXo Xooo   3-2 clave de guaguancó (rumba clave)
oooo ooLo HooH ooLo   Havana guaguancó open tones (L=Low; H=High)
oooo ooLo Hooo ooLo   Matanzas guaguancó open tones
```

This often-cited difference is but the tip of the iceberg. Percussionist and author Robert Fernández travels all over the island each year and never returns without having discovered many new ways that each folkloric genre is played in this or that province or cabildo. Just as a cop from South New Jersey speaks English differently from a Texas cattle rancher, you'll find many different "dialects" of guaguancó, bembé and conga de comparsa throughout Cuba's 43,000 square miles.

Guaguancó

highlighted track: *La gitana* – Muñequitos de Matanzas: *Rumba abierta* – West Side Latino

time	tempo	comments
0:00	110	clave enters alone (on 3-side of rumba clave)
0:04		drums enter – listen for their melodic "answer" to the clave pattern
0:06		lead vocal enters with *diana* (melody without words) to set key and mood
0:12	114	cuerpo A – exquisite 2-part harmony – ground yourself rhythmically with the main beats of the chékere and the call and response of the drums.
0:44	118	cuerpo B – note contrary motion (low voice goes up while high voice goes down)
1:55	131	montuno section – coros and pregones (dancers would enter here)
2:15		vocals stop, highlighting the *quinto* (the highest of the three drums)
2:27	135	coros and pregones

The fact that Los Muñequitos were the first group to produce widely distributed commercial rumba recordings is secondary to the pure musical value of the recordings themselves. Their groove, lead vocals, quinto playing and beautiful, otherworldly harmonizations place them among the greatest popular music recordings in any genre or language. To collect all of the original group's output from the 1950s, you'll need the *Rumba abierta* CD shown above, *Guaguancó Matancero* on Tumbao Cuban Classics, and a dozen vinyl transfers from the Rosy label that can only be found on YouTube. The current Muñequitos still tour regularly and their recordings from 1970 onward are excellent.

Any of the classic early recordings could have served as our highlighted track, but there's something particularly haunting about the vocal harmonies of *La gitana,* and it has a famous coro, *para la niña y pa' la señora,* that resurfaced later on *Quindiambo,* from Irakere's historic first album in 1974. You'll hear Muñequitos quotes – intentional and subliminal – in the work of almost every subsequent Cuban group.

Further Listening Recommendations for Guaguancó

Year	Song	Source
1977	*El currito*	Los Muñequitos de Matanzas: *Rumba caliente* – QBADisc
1992	*Oh humanidad*	Carlos Embale – EGREM
1970	*Enigue nigue*	AfroCuba de Matanzas: *Óyelos de nuevo* - QBADisc
1996	*Enigue nigue*	AfroCuba de Matanzas: *Raíces africanas* – Shanachie
instr.	*Guaguancó*	Jiménez and Wardinsky: *Study Guide for Afro-Cuban Percussion*

Guaguancó dancing – Grupo AfroCuba de Matanzas – photo by Mary Brassell

The following list of guaguancó in popular music could easily be much longer. Even when not explicitly invoking the specific drum parts of guaguancó, timba, songo and Cuban genres all the way back to son constantly reference rumba in lyrics, attitude and phrasing.

Guaguancó in Cuban Popular Music

Year	Song	Source
1980	*De la Habana a Matanzas*	Los Van Van: *El baile de buey cansao (Vol. 7)* – EGREM
1981	*Ese atrevimiento*	Irakere: *El coco, also on Para bailar son (Vol. 5)* – EGREM
1985	*Rumberos latinoamericanos*	Revé: *Elio Revé y su Charangón, Vol. 2* – BIS
1988	*Qué cuento es ése*	Revé: *Elio Revé y su Charangón, Vol. 2* – BIS
1988	*Recuerdos de aquel solar*	Revé: *Qué cuento es ése* – (Areíto – vinyl only)
2011	*A Matanzas*	Revé: *De qué estamos hablando* – BIS
2000	*Ven Siroco, Ven*	Manolito y su Trabuco: *Para que baile Cuba* – Eurotropical
1989	*Los Sitios entero*	NG La Banda: *En la calle* – QBADisc
1996	*De la Habana a Matanzas (2nd version)*	Los Van Van: *Ay Diós ampárame* – Caribe
1999	*Somos Cubanos*	Los Van Van: *Llegó Van Van* – Pimienta

Yambú

highlighted track: *Congo Yambumba* – Muñequitos de Matanzas: *Live in New York* – QBADisc (1999)

time	tempo	comments
0:00	80	X○○X X○○X X○X○ X○○○ yambú style clave enters
0:03		X○○X X○○X X○X○ XX○X guagua or catá enters (first time is irregular)
		○○○○ ○○X○ ○○○○ ○○X○ middle cajón enters
0:06		X○XX ○X○X X○X○ XX○X guagua for this track (Ex. 3-20)
		XX○X XX○X X○X○ XX○X (more common guagua – Ex. 3-22 – not used for this track)
		In general, yambú uses Ex. 3-22, but this track uses the standard cáscara pattern.
0:07		○○○X X○○○ ○○○○ ○○○○ low cajón enters
0:12	81	high cajón enters with vocal diana
0:40	82	cuerpo sung in harmony
2:18	84	lead – coro 1
4:12	93	coro 2
4:38	94	drums drop out (like a timba gear change – this is not traditional, but rather an example of the ongoing growth and innovation in rumba – note that the date of this performance is 1999, near the peak of the timba explosion)
5:03	101-107	drums return (again like a gear change, and with an exciting entrance)

Yambú was the first of the three rumba genres to develop. Its dance depicts a graceful and stately couple, sometimes feigning old age in their movements, in contrast to the gymnastic and overtly sexual guaguancó. Yambú is often played with son clave and on *cajones* – wooden boxes without skins – instead of congas. The first cajones were simply wooden shipping boxes from the docks, but today, cajón-building has become a fine art. Artisan cajones are used in guarapachangueo ensembles and there are now even batá cajones *(batajones)*. The rhythms of yambú – shown in the track map above – are relatively easy and not prone to rhythmic perspective problems.

Further Listening Recommendations for Yambú

Year	Song	Source
1983	*Congo yambumba* (studio version)	Los Muñequitos: *Guaguancó columbia yambú* – QBADisc
1995	*El tahonero*	Los Muñequitos: *Vacunao* – QBADisc
instr.	*Yambú*	Jiménez and Wardinsky: *Study Guide for Afro-Cuban Percussion*
1996	*Pa' los mayores*	AfroCuba de Matanzas: *Raíces africanas* – Shanachie
unknown	*Ave María Morena*	*Afro-Cuba: A Musical Anthology* – Rounder Records

Rumba columbia

highlighted track: *Campana de oro* – AfroCuba de Matanzas: *Cuba in Washington* – Folkways

time	tempo	comments
0:00	153	12/8 bell: X∘X ∘XX ∘X∘ X∘X open tones: ∘∘∘ XX∘ ∘∘∘ XX∘ catá: xx∘x xx∘x x∘x∘ xx∘x (swing or fix timing)
0:08	156	quinto enters
0:12	160	lead vocal
3:00	164	coro 1
5:09		coro 1 returns
5:42		coro 2
6:46		coro 3
7:42	166	coro 4
8:53		coro 5
9:34		coro 6
9:48		coro 7

While played much faster, the basic rhythmic patterns of rumba columbia are similar to abakuá in so far as they both use the standard 12/8 bell (Exercise RP-5) and both feature interesting conga parts in which the open tones of the congas create melodies centering around the bombo and ponche, with variations depending on the region, era and in some cases the individual performance (see the table on p. 173). Columbia is usually danced by a single male dancer (often incorporating knives into his routine) interacting with the lead drum (the quinto).

Our highlighted track is in one of the more interesting styles, from Matanzas. The bell is in 12/8 (Exercise RP-5), but the catá plays cáscara de rumba (Exercise 3-24), with a time feel that can range from pure duple to a slightly "swung", or "fix" feel, to a double time 12/8. This is a very interesting track to listen to at half-speed with AmazingSlowDowner™ or Transcribe™. The drums are essentially in 12/8 but can also "swing" toward duple at certain points and the vocals are all over the map. After obsessing with this amazing track for many hours, my best advice is to try to hear the open tones like a North American backbeat. Using this to lock yourself into the groove, you can sit back and enjoy the endless subtleties and nuances provided by the musicians of AfroCuba de Matanzas.

Further Listening Recommendations for Rumba Columbia

Year	Song	Source
1970	La calabaza	Folklore Matancero (became AfroCuba de Mat.): Óyelos de nuevo – QBADisc
1989	Campana de oro	Grupo Afro-Cuba de Matanzas: Cuba in Washington - Folkways
unknown	Rumba columbia Malanga murió	Afro-Cuba: A Musical Anthology – Rounder Records
instr.	Columbia	Jiménez and Wardinsky: Study Guide for Afro-Cuban Percussion
1996	Aguado Koloya	AfroCuba de Matanzas: Raíces africanas – Shanachie

Rumba columbia dancing – Grupo AfroCuba de Matanzas – photo by Mary Brassell

Guarapachangueo

highlighted track: *Callejón de los rumberos* – Yoruba Andabo: *Callejón de los rumberos* – Universal Latino

time	tempo	comments
		The group consists of 5 percussionists: player 1: clave player 2: catá (guagua) player 3: high conga (quinto) (Román Díaz) player 4: middle conga (tres dos or segundo) and middle cajón player 5: lowest cajón and 3 batás (Pancho Quinto) The middle drum plays the guaguancó melody (Ex. 6-15) every time. This, the clave, and the catá, are your life lines as a new listener. Everything else is highly improvisational. The best approach is to listen to the segundo and then focus on the conversational quality of the quinto drum with everything Pancho Quinto plays. The first entrances are shown below to get you started.
0:00	151	1st drum entrance: smallest batá (okónkolo) ○○X ○○○ ○X○ X○○ (from Eleguá) 2nd drum entrance: smallest conga (quinto) X○○○ X○○○ X○○○ X○○○ 3rd drum entrance: middle cajón ○○○○ ○○○○ X○○X ○○○○ 4th drum entrance: middle conga (tres dos) (Ex. 6-15) ○○○○ ○○○○ X○○X ○○○○ 5th drum entrance: middle batá (itótole) X○○○ ○○X○ ○○○○ X○○○ 6th drum entrance: low batá (iyá) ○○○X X○○○ ○○XX ○○○○ 7th drum entrance: low cajón ○○○○ ○○X○ X○○X ○○X○ (other than the tres-dos, these are simply the entrances, not repeating parts)
0:08		lead vocalist's *diana* (melodies in non-verbal syllables)
0:25	145	cuerpo sung in harmony, with lead vocalist singing diana-style between phrases
2:00	141	lead vocalist introduces montuno section with diana
2:08		lead vocalist switches from diana to Spanish
2:24		coro 1
2:41	140	coro 2

As explained in the introduction to this section, most folkloric music is about preserving tradition, often for reasons of religious worship. The songs and drum parts in the Oru seco differ drastically from the way they were played in Africa centuries ago, but this is not intentional. The intent is to salute the deity in the traditional way. Rumba, on the other hand, is non-religious and very much about self-expression of the individual. As such, Los Chinitos, Yoruba Andabo, Clave y Guaguancó, and Rumberos de Cuba are more aesthetically analogous to timba bands – with a premium on individuality and innovation. Each group uses different instruments in different ways, with different approaches to the rumba equivalents of gear changes, and song-specific patterns. Clave y Guaguancó's 1998 album, *Noche de la rumba,* is perhaps the best starting point for hearing these highly-creative and timba-like aspects of guarapachangueo.

Traditional guaguancó, while improvisational, has clearly defined roles for the players of the three drums – tumba, segundo and quinto – and three Cuban musicians who have never met will be able to sit down and play rumba by adhering to these roles – much like a group of jazz musicians playing a jazz standard. But guarapachangueo involves extensive rehearsal.

Further Listening Recommendations for Guarapachangueo and Modern Rumba

Year	Song	Source
1996	*Y ya se formó el rumbón*	Yoruba Andabo: *El Callejón de los rumberos* – AyVa Music
1997	*En el solar la cueva del humo*	Pancho Quinto: *En el solar la cueva del humo* – Round World
various	*various live performances*	Los Chinitos (YouTube)
1996	*No jueges conmigo*	Conjunto Clave y Guaguancó: *Déjala en la puntica* – EGREM
1998	*Baila mi guaguancó (batarumba)*	Grupo AfroCuba de Matanzas: *Raíces africanas* – Shanachie
2004	*Dónde andabas tú*	Rumberos de Cuba: *Rumberos de Cuba* – EGREM
2005	*Respuesta a María*	Conjunto Clave y Guaguancó: *La rumba no termina* – Cuba Chévere

Further Reading on Rumba

Rumba Quinto, **by David Peñalosa (Bembe Books)** – This extraordinary book analyzes the quinto style of Los Muñequitos in loving detail. If you're not a Muñequitos de Matanzas fanatic already, Peñalosa will make you one by the time you finish the first few chapters.

The Conga Drummer's Guidebook, **by Michael Spiro (Sher Publications)** – I usually bring this book up for its innovative work on time feel, but it also contains extensive sections on rumba. Spiro also has excellent instructional rumba material on congamasterclass.com.

Los Chinitos YouTube Videos – There's a large treasury of priceless YouTube videos show Piri López and the rest of the Chinitos clan playing, singing dancing and talking about guarapachangueo.

esquinarumbera.blogspot.com – This endlessly fascinating website is a paradise for rumba fans.

Most of the other books recommended in other sections here also have significant amounts of rumba information, e.g., Fernández's *The Afro-Cuban Folkloric Tradition*, Sublette's *Cuba and its Music,* and José Eladio's ***Afro-Cuban Percussion Workbook***.

Looking Ahead to The *Beyond Salsa* Series

Beyond Salsa: The Central Premise

The explosive Havana music scene of the 1990s produced a windfall of transformational musical breakthroughs, many of which have yet to be fully exploited: song-specific tumbaos, gears, gear changes, controlled improvisation, conga, piano and bass tumbaos of double or quadruple length, contrasting gestures, efectos, rhythmic counterpoint, new approaches to clave and clave changes, and so on. Working in relative isolation, Cuban musicians have reinvented popular music arranging in many ways that cry out to be understood, recombined, and carried forward to their full potential across the full range of popular music – from salsa and Latin jazz, to rock, funk and pop.

The goal of the *Beyond Salsa* project is to study this "Cuban timba revolution", and its history, from the point of view of each instrument in the rhythm section: *Beyond Salsa Piano, Beyond Salsa Bass, Beyond Salsa Bongó,* and so on. In *Beyond Salsa for Ensemble,* we study the rhythm section as a whole, with coordinated exercises for each instrument designed to be practiced together as a complete rhythm section, whether by students in an ensemble class setting or by professionals in a working band seeking to incorporate more modern Cuban rhythm section techniques into its arsenal. In *Understanding Clave and Clave Changes,* we clarify some of the confusion and mystery surrounding this enigmatic musical topic.

The early volumes on each instrument cover history and basic concepts. Subsequent volumes focus on the style of one specific artist. *Beyond Salsa for Beginners* is a special course designed for non-musicians: dancers, listeners, and beginners and *Beyond Salsa Percussion, Volume 1* is a preparatory course for non-musicians considering taking percussion lessons.

How the Series is Organized and Sold

With the exception of the *Understanding Clave and Clave Changes* book and audio package, each volume of the *Beyond Salsa* series consists of two or three separately sold products:

1) a book like this one with text and musical notation (hard-copy or eBook)

2) downloadable MP3 audio files demonstrating the musical examples, accompanied by a clave click track, at full-speed and in slow motion, panning certain elements hard left and right for more flexible study

3) when available, downloadable computer video files and physical DVDs showing a Cuban musician performing each musical example at full speed, in slow motion, and with variations

Book

The book you're reading now can be purchased at www.createspace.com/4035244 as a hard-copy, bound paperback book. Alternatively, it can be viewed online and/or printed on your computer's printer from the website www.latinpulsemusic.com/albums/show/433. All volumes show music notation for each exercise in both 8th notes (American-style) and 16th notes (Cuban-style), as well as explanatory text and historical information. If you don't read music and aren't interested in the explanations and history, you can choose to buy only the audio and/or video products and use them to learn the parts by ear.

Audio

The audio files do not come with the books. They're available as separate, downloadable products from www.timba.com/audio (or, in the cases of *Understanding Clave,* and parts of *Beyond Salsa for Beginners* and *Beyond Salsa Percussion, Vol. 1,* they're available as free downloads at clave.latinpulsemusic.com and timba.com/audio). For each notation example, there are two ultra-high quality MP3 files made directly from 24-bit wave files. Depending on the subject, some audio files are generated from MIDI files (often played by the musician) and some are actual live audio. In each case, we provide a slow motion version. The Alain Pérez books, for example, are about 90% live audio and 10% MIDI audio. The audio files can be burned to audio CDs or played on an MP3 player. If you have audio on your computer, I highly recommend taking advantage of the new generation of computer programs that will allow you to change the tempo and/or key of any of these audio files and to loop them to fit your style of practice. Particularly useful are: Amazing Slowdowner™, Transcribe!™ and Emulator X®, all of which can be downloaded from their respective websites. Audio samples for all books can be auditioned at timba.com/audio.

Video

Like the audio products, the videos are sold as separate downloads from timba.com/audio. So far, we have video for the Alain Pérez volumes *Beyond Salsa Bass* the Melón Lewis volumes of *Beyond Salsa Piano,* and the Calixto Oviedo volumes of *Beyond Salsa Percussion*. There are video files for each exercise, in which the musician will play slowly, then at full speed, and finally with variations such as might be used in a live performance. In the cases of Melón and Alain, there are three separate videos for each performance: camera angle 1, camera angle 2, and a split screen version showing both angles. Samples of each as well as some free performance videos of Melón can be found at www.timba.com/piano and www.timba.com/bass. Samples are also on YouTube.

The video products for Volume 2 and Volume 3 of *Beyond Salsa Percussion,* featuring drummer/timbalero Calixto Oviedo, are available at www.timba.com/percussion, as are several free previews. The two volumes Calixto volumes are combined on a hard-copy DVD available at www.createspace.com/324911. All hard-copy DVDs are sold for $25 and include the contents of two volumes, while the downloadable videos are sold separately at $10 per volume. Hard-copy DVDs for Alain and Melón may also be released.

At the end of this book is the **Beyond Salsa** Catalog and **price list** for all products released to date, with pictures, links and content descriptions.

Beyond Salsa Piano

Beyond Salsa Piano, with 11 volumes as of 2012, is a history and anthology of the role of the piano in the Latin rhythm section – from its first appearance to the present. In a broader sense, it's a study of the art of creating music from layers of repeating rhythmic and melodic phrases. Whether these syncopated figures are called *tumbaos, guajeos, montunos,* riffs or vamps, this Afro-Cuban concept lies at the heart of nearly every popular music genre from salsa to rock, funk, R&B, hip-hop and jazz. While presented as a set of method books, the series doubles as a history course and record-collecting guide for listeners, dancers, and musicians who play instruments other than piano.

Perhaps the most important goal of the piano series is to provide a comprehensive understanding of how tumbaos are constructed, their central role in the texture of Latin music of all eras, and the endless possibilities they provide for creative composing and arranging.

Volumes 1 to 5 – Ranging from beginning to advanced, these five volumes cover the full history of Cuban tumbao playing, from the tres and violin guajeos that were the predecessors of the piano tumbao to a thorough analysis of the modern timba style.

Volume 6 onward – Each book concentrates on the style of one Cuban pianist, with note-for-note transcriptions, often based on MIDI files performed by the volume's featured pianist. For example, the subject of Volumes 6 through 9 is Iván "Melón" Lewis, the phenomenally innovative pianist who played with The Issac Delgado group from 1995 to 1998. Volumes 10 and 11 begin our study of César "Pupy" Pedroso of Los Van Van and Los Que Son Son. Volume 12 will complete our survey of Pupy's work with Los Van Van, and Volume 13 will cover his first four albums with Los Que Son Son. Beginning with Volume 14, we hope to move on to Juan Carlos González and Tirso Duarte of Charanga Habanera, Rodolfo "Peruchín" Argudín of NG La Banda, Chaka Nápoles of Manolín ("El Médico de la Salsa"), Rolando Luna of Paulito FG and The Issac Delgado group, and many others. For beginners and intermediate players, we'll also be adding a special volume featuring Gustavo Ramírez, exploring the history of and the many possible bass and piano variations that can be used with the ubiquitous "guajira" progression, I – IV – V – IV, so fundamental to *salsa* and *son*.

Beyond Salsa Bass

Beyond Salsa Bass also begins with five introductory volumes of increasing difficulty (planned for 2013), covering the history of the bass tumbao chronologically. The subject of Volumes 6-9, Alain Pérez, played side by side in the Issac Delgado group with Melón Lewis, the subject of Volumes 6-9 of *Beyond Salsa Piano,* so the two series cover the same material in the same order. Each is arguably the leading figure of the timba era on his respective instrument, but even more important was their creative chemistry they shared with each other and with Delgado himself, producing a musical result that far exceeded the sum of its parts. The opportunity to study the same historical music from these two vantage points has been one of the most exciting parts of writing this series.

Beyond Salsa Percussion

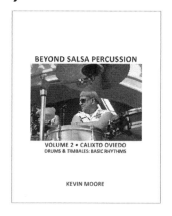

After an introductory volume for beginners and pre-beginners, the rest of the *Beyond Salsa Percussion* series focuses on individual timbaleros and drummers and analyzes the rhythm section practices of various bands from various eras of Cuban music. Volumes 2 and 3, on the inimitable Calixto Oviedo, of NG La Banda and Adalberto Álvarez fame, were released in 2011. There are extensive video products for these books, including special files for the Transcribe™ program with pre-stored video loop points that can be played back at any speed.

Understanding Clave and Clave Changes

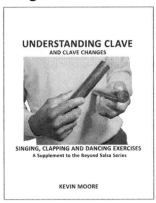

And ideal companion for the book you're reading now, **Understanding Clave and Clave Changes** is a special supplementary volume inspired by the arranging of Pupy Pedroso and Juan Formell during the period covered by *Beyond Salsa Piano,* Volume 11. It began as a short appendix, but the more I wrote, the more I thought about my years of discussions with other musicians, long nights spent with headphones, reading of endless clave threads on internet groups, and the many lectures and master classes I've attended. There seems to be an endless fascination with clave, clave direction and clave changes, as well as endless frustration, confusion and misinformation.

With *Understanding Clave* I was determined to end the confusion once and for all, and to keep it from being one more *"lose weight, quit smoking and make extra cash in your spare time"* self-help book. I designed a method that requires you to sing, clap and dance your way through memorized musical examples before even attempting to understand the terminology of concepts. In order to reach as large an audience as possible, the clave volume is sold at a reduced price, and with free downloadable audio files.

Beyond Salsa for Ensemble

At 368 pages, with 464 audio files, *Beyond Salsa for Ensemble, Volume 1* is by far the longest book of the series. It's designed for college and high school Latin ensembles and/or working salsa bands seeking to add Cuban rhythm section techniques to their repertoire.

Volume 1, Part 1 takes a standard chord progression and shows how it can be converted from salsa to timba on an instrument-by-instrument basis.

Volume 1, Part 2, using the same progression, presents 16 rhythmic breaks, or *efectos* and shows how they can be executed in 3-2 and 2-3 clave by each instrument, with lead sheets for experienced players and detailed transcriptions for students who need or want to learn an exact and authentic way to orchestrate each break on their specific instruments.

Volume 1, Part 3 is a meticulously complete arrangement of Pupy Pedroso's timba standard *El buenagente,* with full lyrics, vocal harmony parts, horns, piano and bass, the latter two provided both as lead sheets *and* note-for-note transcriptions. There's also a conductor's score.

Beyond Salsa for Ensemble, Volume 2, scheduled for 2013, will extend the same approach to timba gears.

Beyond Salsa Bongó and *Beyond Salsa Congas*

Beyond Salsa Bongó, featuring Carlos Caro of Opus 13 and Paulito FG, and starting with a volume for complete beginners, will be released in late 2012 or early 2013.

Beyond Salsa Congas is coming in 2013.

Appendix 1: Glossary

Abakuá	1. a 12/8 rhythm brought to Cuba from the Calabar River area of West Africa 2. a mysterious, all-male, mutual aid society
abanico	1. a special timbal figure used to introduce a new section; originated in danzón 2. Spanish for "fan", female danzón dancers would fan themselves during the A-sections of danzones and then collapse their fans on their partners backs just as the B-section began, perhaps the original reason for applying the term to timbales
aberíkula	un-consecrated batá drums for use in non-religious settings
ahí na'má'	slang for ahí nada más ("keep it there – no more"), shouted by singers after a passage or at the end of a song- the meaning is more like "that's perfect ... just like that"; sometimes *así ná má'* is substituted ("like that, nothing more is needed")
akpón	the lead singer and director in a traditional Afro-Cuban religious ceremony
apodo	nickname – many Cuban musicians have them and the nickname is often a good-natured jab about some physical attribute, e.g., *bombón* for someone who is short and dark-skinned, *gordo* or *flaco* for the fat and skinny, *melón* for someone with a big round head and so on. Only rarely is an apodo complimentary, e.g. *Changuito* (a smaller version of the revered deity, Changó). Other apodos refer to racial appearance or skin color, e.g., *El Indio, Chino, Niche (dark black), Chocolate,* or personality traits, e.g. *Tosco (rough and crude).*
Arará	1. an Afro-Cuban ethnic group from Dahomey whose music, drums and religion have been carried on in Western Cuba 2. a special batá rhythm adapted from the arará repertoire for use with specific types of songs
Bantú	an Afro-Cuban ethnic group of Congolese origin; more slaves were brought from this region than any other; principal musical genres are palo, makuta and yuka
BPM	Beats Per Minute – the unit of measurement for tempo (the speed of the main beats)
backbeat	subdivision 5; the second main beat of each side of the clave; the subdivision commonly played by the snare drum in North American music; as opposed to "frontbeat" the first main beat of each side of the clave
baqueteo	1. the principal timbal and güiro rhythm of danzón 2. (general) a rhythm played by a stick or *baqueta*
basic step	a six-step dance movement lasting one clave in duration
batá	1. one of three sizes of hourglass-shaped, double-side drums used in Yoruban music 2. the most extensively practiced and studied Afro-Cuban religious genre
batería	Spanish for drumset
bembé	1. a family of Yoruban drums in Cuba 2. one of the four main Yoruban music genres of Afro-Cuban folkloric music
bloque	a longer rhythmic break played by two or more rhythm section musicians (as opposed to *efecto,* a shorter rhythmic break)
bolero	1. a type of slow song with romantic lyrics, very popular throughout the 20th Century 2. a specific rhythmic pattern often, but not always, used to accompany bolero songs

bomba	1. a large family of Puerto Rican folkloric rhythms, including *bomba sicá*, studied in Exercise 2-5. 2. an ultra-high-energy timba gear in which the bass plays thumps and slides and dancers dance apart from each other, with shoulders and hips, and with reckless abandon
bombo	1. subdivision 4; the middle stroke of the 3-side of clave 2. Spanish term for bass drum
bongó	a pair of single-headed, open-ended drums, attached to each other, held between the knees and played with the hands; the bongó originated in Cuba
bongosero	a musician who plays bongó (and also the hand bell in most genres)
bongó bell	a synonym for hand bell or campana
bongó del monte	a very large, low bongó used in changüí
bota	1. a member of the songo family of rhythms that stresses subdivision 6 and 8 of each side of the clave; created by José Luis "Changuito" Quintana 2. Spanish term for boot (as in "kicking up the energy of the band")
botija or botijuela	a large jug used as a bass wind instrument; replaced by the marímbula in changüí and early son, and later replaced by the contrabass in son
cabildos	cultural preservation societies, some still in existence in Cuba, dating back hundreds of years when they were permitted by the government to allow African slaves to preserve their culture
caja	1. the lowest drum in many folkloric ensembles, often used for improvisation 2. Spanish for snare drum
cajón	1. one of a family of drums serving a similar role to a conga or tumbadora but with both the body of the drum and the playing surface made of wood 2. Spanish term for box
campana	1. Spanish term for bell (any bell) 2. a specific bell, the hand bell or bongó bell; the lowest of the three common bells of salsa and timba
campaneo	1. Spanish term for a pattern played on any bell 2. a specific and extremely common pattern played on the hand bell (Exercise 3-13)
cáscara	1. a common rhythmic cell played with sticks on the sides of the timbales – also called *cascareo* (Exercise 3-19) 2. Spanish for *shell*
cáscara pulse	a term invented for these books to provide a descriptive name for subdivision 6, which is heavily accented on both sides of the clave in the cáscara or cascareo rhythm
casino	also known as Cuban-style salsa in the dance sense; a term for the typical way that Cubans dance to salsa and timba. In the United States casino is often distinguished from LA- and NY-style Salsa as being more circular and less linear.
catá	any of a variety of folkloric instruments used for time-keeping and consisting of hardwood struck with sticks; also call *guagua*
cencerro	Spanish term for a cowbell; synonym for campana
chachá	the smaller head of a batá drum (the larger head is called the *enú*)

chachachá	a Cuban genre created in the 1950s, originally played by charanga groups, with a special characteristic dance step
cha bell	a small higher-pitched bell, usually mounted on the timbalero's stand *(campana de chachachá)*
Changó	one of the most celebrated Santería deities, the oricha of thunder and lightning; associated with the color red; danced by a single male dancer with an ax (see p. 204)
changüí	a seminal Cuban genre from the eastern region of Cuba
charanga francesa	a group that includes violins, flutes, güiro, and timbales, but not bongó or horns; now called simply *charanga*; its original primary genre was danzón, then danzón-mambo, then chachachá, but the term refers to the instrumentation; examples: Orquestas Aragón, Sublime, Sensación, América, Revé, Ritmo Oriental, Melodías del 40, Arcaño, Fajardo, etc.
chékere	a pitched gourd with beads netted around the outside, played with the hands (sometimes spelled *shékere);* a primary instrument in the Yoruban güiro genre
cinquillo	1. an important 5-stroke cell built around the 3-side of clave – *not* equally spaced 2. literally, a *quintuplet,* a group of five *equally spaced* strokes
clave	1. one of two sticks played together *(claves)* 2. one of several 5-stroke rhythms, regularly alternating between two "sides", one more syncopated than the other, and around which most Cuban genres are built
clave-aligned	a rhythmic cell of at least 4 beats, with a different rhythm for each of its internal 2-beat halves, such that one 2-beat cell is meant to be played against the 2-side of clave and the other against the 3-side. If the listener has experience in the genre and style the clave-aligned cell should establish the clave direction even if the actual clave is not present.
columbia	the fastest of the three original rumba genres; in 12/8; featuring a virtuosic single male dancer aggressively dancing with knifes and other implements and interacting with the quinto or lead drum
comparsa	a carnaval parade celebration, with floats, common all over Cuba, featuring a variety of fast, dense *conga* rhythms and sexy dancing in elaborate costumes
conga	1. a tall, rounded, single-headed Cuban drum, played with the hands, also called *tumbadora* 2. a specific sized drum of the conga family, larger than the quinto and smaller than the tres dos and tumba 3. a fast Cuban carnaval rhythm played by *comparsa* groups
conjunto	a group with trumpets, tres (optional), and bongó but not timbales; its original primary genre was son montuno but the term refers to the instrumentation; e.g. Arsenio Rodríguez, Chappottín, Roberto Faz, Conjunto Casino, Rumbavana, Son 14, etc.
contracampana	a long flat bell mounted on the timbalero's stand, also called timbal bell, or mambo bell
contracampaneo	a specific pattern played on the contracampana bell
contratiempo	literally "against the beat" – used to refer to dancing "on 2"
corneta china	a double-reed wind instrument used in comparsa, especially in Eastern Cuba
coro	1. a repeating call and response vocal riff sung during the montuno section 2. the whole section where a repeating coro and lead vocal *guías* or *pregones* are sung

cubanismo	the essential quality of "being Cuban"
cuerpo	1. the lower volume song, or verse, sung by the lead vocalist alone at the beginning of most Latin arrangements; the "body of the song" 2. Spanish term for *body*
Dahomey	1. an African kingdom in and around present-day Benin; some Dahomeyans were brought directly to Matanzas and Havana (called Arará); others came to Eastern Cuba via Haiti 2. a secular genre from the Vodú family, brought to Eastern Cuba from Haiti by people of Dahomeyan descent
danzón	seminal Cuban genre dating from the late 19th Century that combined clave-based rhythms with European orchestral instruments and the European *contradanza;* the first danzón was *Las alturas de Simpson* by Miguel Faílde in 1879
despelote	a non-couple style of sexy, undulating dance, performed to timba gears; literally, to strip off or throw down; from "despelotar"
danzonete	a 1930s modification of the danzón, adding vocals to compete with the popularity of son; the first danzonete was *Rompiendo la rutina* by Aniseto Díaz in 1929
descarga	a jam session – from the verb *descargar* – to discharge, to unload, or *descargarse* – to unburden oneself
diablo	Arsenio Rodríguez's term for the concluding sections of his son montuno arrangements, with repeating horn riffs juxtaposed against coros and sometimes solos; a direct predecessor of the mambo
diana	a free-form vocal sung by the lead singer, with non-verbal syllables instead of words, at the beginning of a guaguancó. The diana sets the mood and key before the cuerpo begins.
duple-pulse structure	music in which each main beat is felt as being subdivided into two or four parts; most Cuban popular music is in duple-pulse structure
efecto	a rhythmic break played by two or more members of the rhythm section
enú	the larger head of a batá drum (the smaller head is called the *chachá)*
estribillo	in general, a repeated vocal chorus; used specifically as a part of a danzón arrangement
frontbeat	subdivision 1, the first main beat on each side of the clave, as opposed to backbeat, the second main beat on each side of the clave
gear (gear changes)	a term coined by the author to describe any specific rhythm section orchestration that the members of the rhythm section have rehearsed and can switch in an out of on cue. All genres have gears, but timba has a unique group of gears involving the absence of the bass tumbao and often accompanied by changes in the dance moves.
guagua	1. a piece of hardwood or cane, played with sticks, creating a woodblock-like sound, used in rumba and other folkloric genres; also called *catá* 2. Cuban slang for *bus*
guaguancó	one of the three genres of the seminal Cuban folkloric *rumba* complex; characterized by a specific mating ritual dance; incredibly influential on all Cuban popular music genres
guajeo	a syncopated, looped figure used for accompaniment; guajeo is primarily used for violins and tres but also sometimes used for piano; synonyms are tumbao and montuno

guajiro/guajira	1. a person from the country (also campesino/campesina) 2. guajira – a type of vocal/guitar folk music with minimal percussion, from the same family that includes trova, canción, bolero and punto guajiro. 3. guajira – a special medium-slow type of arrangement popular in Nuyorican salsa
guaracha	originally a type of Cuban song used in operettas, featuring comical words and fast tempos, later adopted by son and charanga groups
guarapachangueo	a modern type of guaguancó adding cajones and sometimes batás to the rumba ensemble; the term was coined by a friend of Los Chinitos, who, upon first hearing, and not immediately comprehending, their rhythmic innovations, famously and pejoratively questioned: *"what's all this guarapachangueo?"*
guataca	a metal hoe blade used as a bell in many folkloric genres such as palo and güiro
guayo	a type of güiro (serrated gourd time-keeping instrument); used in changüí
güira	a metal güiro – like an open-ended metal thermos with a handle; used primarily in Dominican merengue and bachata, but sometimes in Cuban music; was played by musical director Joaquín Betancourt in Issac Delgado's mid-90s band
güiro	1. a serrated gourd played with a stick (like a washboard); one of the principal time keepers in Latin music; sometimes called *guayo* 2. an Afro-Cuban folkloric genre (Yoruban category) using multiple *chékeres*
habanera	1. a historically important rhythmic cell; sometimes called *tango* 2. a Spanish adjective meaning *Havanan,* or *of Havana* (habanero for masculine) 3. a female person from Havana (the Spanish term for Havana *is La Habana)*
hembra	the larger bongó, conga, or timbal in a group of two (the smaller being called *macho);* literally, hembra means female and macho means male
hihat	two small cymbals, facing each other, that can be opened and closed with a foot pedal, and/or played with sticks
hook	a short musical idea that draws a listener to a new piece of music, that sticks in the mind such that the listener wants to hear the song again. A hook can be rhythmic, melodic, harmonic, accompanimental, or lyrical – usually a combination.
itótole	the middle-sized drum of the three batás
iyá	the largest of the three batás, played by the leader, who cues the rhythmic changes
iyesá	1. one of four main genres of Yoruban music with its own type of drums 2. a specific rhythm adapted for use in batá music
jam block	originally the brand name for a rectangular instrument of red or blue plastic, producing a very loud clave-like sound, used primarily to play the clave rhythm and mounted on a drum or timbales set – now the term is used generically for any such instrument
jazzband	(pron: "yahz-bahng"); a group with the instrumentation of a North American big band, or a subset thereof, that later added Latin percussion, e.g. Orquestas Riverside; Casino de la Playa, Chepín-Chovén, Beny Moré's Banda Gigante, Tito Puente, Machito, etc.
jimagua	1. the 2-side of clave 2. Spanish for *twin*
kick or kick drum	a bass drum played with a foot pedal – in Cuban music sometimes played from a standing position by a timbalero

kiribá (or quiribá)	a simple folkloric genre from the mountains of Eastern Cuba; along with *nengón*, one of the precursors of *changüí*, and by extension, *son*
Lucumí	1. a term for Cubans of Yoruban ancestry 2. the language and religion inherited by Cubans of Yoruban descent
macho	the smaller bongó, conga, or timbal in a group of two (the larger being called *hembra*)
main beats	The four equally spaced beats of one cycle of clave. These are the beats on which you tap your foot to the music. Their speed is the *tempo* of the song. The first and third main beats are called *frontbeats* in this book and the second and fourth are called *backbeats*.
makuta	one of the three main Bantú genres, with its own type of drums (similar to congas), and a fertility rite dance considered a precursor of guaguancó
mambito	A short rhythmic figure shared by the flute and percussion in charanga music
mambo	1. a section of a Latin arrangement featuring repeating horn riffs, often with contrapuntal repeating vocal riffs, or *coros* 2. a Cuban genre, with a characteristic dance step, created in the 1950s
mambo bell	synonym for *contracampana,* the large flat mounted bell played by the timbalero
manoteo	the less-accented strokes of a conga marcha or bongó martillo, used to fill in the subdivisions for time-keeping purposes; also called *relleno*
maracas Maraca	1. a pair a small gourds with handles, filled with beads; one of the principal time-keeping instruments in Latin music 2. the nickname *(apodo)* of Orlando Valle, flutist and bandleader, who as a young man was very thin and had a huge afro, thus resembling the musical instrument
marcha	1. a repeating conga pattern used for accompaniment 2. a family of rhythm section gears that always includes a steady bass tumbao and conga marcha and has different percussion combinations depending on the part of the arrangement it's used for
marcha abajo	a term used in these books (and to some extent elsewhere) to mean the type of marcha gear used for cuerpos; uses cáscara and usually bongó, but with no bells.
marcha arriba	a term used in these books (and to some extent elsewhere) to mean the type of marcha gear used for coros, with two interlocking bell parts
marcha de mambo	a term used in these books (and to some extent elsewhere) to mean the type of marcha gear used for horn mambos, with bells, cymbals and lots of percussion fills
marímbula	a large wooden box with pitched strips of metal, like a large kalimba or lamellophone; used as the bass instrument in changüí and early *son*
martillo	1. the principal time-keeping pattern of the bongó 2. literally, Spanish for "hammer"
masacote	a term for a timba gear without bass tumbao, but with some sort of conga marcha
merengue	a fast Dominican genre that became popular in Cuban in the 1980s, spawning various hybrids such as Changuito's *merensongo*
meter	the regular grouping of main beats, e.g., 4/4, 2/2, 12/8 etc. The first number is the number of beats per group and the second is the duration used in standard notation for one beat. 12/8 is a "compound meter" meaning that each group of 3 is felt as one beat, such that 12/8 has four main beats, each felt with three subdivisions per beat.

moña	1. a type of horn riff similar to a mambo; sometimes invented on the spot in live performance 2. Cuban slang for recent North American R&B and Cuban pop influenced by it
montuno	1. as opposed to the *cuerpo,* the longer, more intense final section of a Latin arrangement, featuring coros, mambos, muelas, gear changes, and solos 2. a term used outside of Cuba for *piano tumbao*
mozambique	a genre of brief but extreme popularity created by Pello el Afrokán in the early 1960s and based on comparsa; a rare example of popular music with no bass or chord instruments, although electric guitar was later added; not related to the country of the same name; inspired a different genre of the same name in New York, of which the principal proponent was Eddie Palmieri
muela	1. a low intensity breakdown during a live performance where the band plays more softly and the singer engages with the audience 2. Spanish term for tooth (as in "chewing the fat with the crowd")
nengón	a simple folkloric genre from the mountains of Eastern Cuba; along with *kiribá*, one of the precursors of *changüí* and by extension, *son*
note	a pitched sound created by a musical instrument (as opposed to *stroke*, a sound, of optional pitch or no pitch, used in a percussion pattern)
nuevo ritmo	a name used by Arcaño and Cachao to describe the new type of montuno section added to the danzón format in the 1940s; sometimes also called mambo
okónkolo	the smallest of the three batá drums
on 1, on 2, on 3	terms referring to the dance count on which the longer step away from the body occurs
pachanga	a merengue/son flavored genre played primarily by charangas that became very popular in the late 1950s
pailas	synonym for timbales; literally, Spanish for "frying pans"
paseo	the 5th, 6th and 7th bars of a danzón A-section and the distinctive timbal/güiro figure used to accompany them; paseo repeats the rhythm of the 3-side of clave 3 times in a row and is always followed by a break (aka, bloque, cierre or efecto)
pega'o	popular, or in style; literally "stuck"; a hit song or a very popular artist is "pega'o"; contraction of "pegado", from the verb "pegar", to stick, or to hit
pilón	1. a long pole used to stir roasting coffee beans in a circular motion 2. a genre and dance based on this motion, created by Enrique Bonne and Pacho Alonso in the early 1960s; the genre is seldom played today but elements of the rhythm continue to strongly influence songo and timba
platillo	1. Spanish term for cymbal; literally "little plate" 2. occasionally used term for subdivision 8, the last subdivision of each side of clave
ponche	1. Spanish term for *punch* 2. subdivision 7, the next to last subdivision of each side of clave and the third stroke of the 3-side of son clave
pregón	an improvised phrase sung by the lead singer in-between coros; as opposed to *guía,* a similar, but non-improvised phrase; synonym: *soneo;* originally the exclamation that a street vendor *(pregonero)* uses to advertise his wares

presión	a dramatic timba breakdown gear where the bass drops out or plays pedal tones and the conga marcha and bells drop out; also called *pedal,* when the bass plays long tones
quinto	the lead drum in rumba (also the smallest and highest pitched of the conga family)
quinto pulse	a term for subdivision 2, the second subdivision of each side of clave
rezo	literally, a prayer – when used in Afro-Cuban folkloric music, the drums usually play in time while the sung prayer floats above, out of time
ride	a percussive figure played over and over to create a groove (also used in "ride cymbal", the cymbal used to play an important ride in jazz)
rueda (or rueda de casino)	"wheel" in Spanish; a circle of couples dancing casino in which all couples perform the same movements simultaneously as directed by a caller who cues the group verbally and with hand signals - originally developed in the late 1950s or early 1960s.
rumba	a critically important Cuban folkloric complex, the genres of which include *yambú, guaguancó* and *columbia*
rumba clave	a form of clave used in guaguancó, songo and very often in timba; also called *clave de guaguancó* (Exercise 3-9)
segundo	literally "second"; the middle drum in rumba, or in many folkloric ensembles
sello	literally "seal" or "stamp"; the trademark style of a band
slap	1. an accented "speaking tone" stroke on conga or bongó; unpitched, loud and sharp 2. an occasionally used term for subdivision 3, a subdivision on which the conguero often plays a slap; *tapado* in Spanish - *doble tapado* when a marcha uses two in succession
snare drum	(or snare) – a shallow drum with metal wires on the bottom head, used in North American drumset playing to play the backbeat; *caja* in Spanish
sobado or soba'o	literally "massaged"; refers to the left hand or stick playing a soft accompaniment on the timbales while the right stick plays a louder bell, cáscara or wood block part.
solar	an urban Cuban housing project, or large apartment complex, with a central courtyard where rumbas and other communal activities occur; plural: *solares*
son	a seminal Cuban genre developed in the 1920s
son clave	a form of clave used in son, salsa, some timba and many other Latin genres (Exercise 3-7)
son montuno	1. a genre represented by an augmentation of the instrumentation and arranging possibilities of son; pioneered by Arsenio Rodríguez; played by a conjunto (a son septeto with added congas, trumpets and piano) 2. an arrangement in the style of Arsenio Rodríguez and his followers; medium slow in tempo with a concluding *diablo* (aka, mambo) section and a higher degree (than son) of Afro-Cuban influence in the lyrics and rhythms.
songo	1. the self-described style of Los Van Van 2. a fast, syncopated rhythmic style typical of Los Van Van's 1970s style 3. a large and varied family of rhythms developed by José Luis "Changuito" Quintana, and including slower, R&B-related patterns as well as the better known fast songo above
song-specific	an accompaniment part (bass tumbao, piano tumbao, conga marcha, efecto etc.) composed to fit one particular song. For example, Tomasito Cruz's conga marcha on Paulito FG's *De la Habana.* The pattern is unique to that song and a discerning listener will be able to identify the song from the conga part alone. Often such a part is a *hook*.

stroke	a sound, of optional pitch or no pitch, used in a percussion pattern (as opposed to *note*, a sound of very specific pitch created by a musical instrument)
subdivision	the shortest, or quickest, unit of time in a rhythmic groove – sometimes called "pulse"
traps	drumset, *batería* in Spanish
trap drummer	a drumset player, *baterista* in Spanish (-ista is used for male *or* female)
tres	1. a guitar-like instrument with three pairs of strings, used in changüí and son 2. Spanish for the number 3
tres dos	the middle drum in rumba, also called *segundo*
tresillo	1. a three-stroke figure with unequal durations of 3-3-2 subdivisions; the 3-side of son clave (Exercise 2-2) 2. Spanish for *triplet,* three equally spaced strokes
triple-pulse structure	music in which each main beat is felt as being subdivided into three parts, e.g., 12/8
trova	troubador music with little or no percussion – an important influence on son; *nueva trova* was a movement in post-Revolutionary Cuba with politically conscious lyrics, typified by artists such as Pablo Milanés and Silvio Rodríguez.
tumba	the largest, lowest conga
tumbao	1. a syncopated, repeating ostinato figure played by the piano or bass 2. outside Cuba, a specific type of conga marcha that marks the 3-side of clave with the tumba 3. the personal quality of having a strong sense of rhythm or musicality, e.g., *"tiene tumbao"* ("he/she has a great groove") or Issac Delgado's lyric *"ya yo tenía mi tumbao pega'o"* ("I already had my musical style established early in my career")
tumbadora	another name for the conga drum; also applied to the Congolese ancestors of the conga
vacunao	the famous pelvic thrust dance move in *guaguancó*
yambú	the earliest, slowest, and most restrained of the rumba genres; originally played on cajones and using son clave, danced by couples, often feigning old age
Yoruba	one of the four main categories of Afro-Cuban folkloric music; includes four main genres: batá, güiro, iyesá and bembé
yuka	one of the three main genres of the Bantú complex of Afro-Cuban folkloric music

Appendix 2: Common Suffixes

-a'o	contraction for -ado, which is like -ed in English, e.g., cruza'o = cruzado = crossed; less formal, like changing "playing" to "playin'" in English
-eo	the rhythmic pattern played on a certain instrument, or the style of playing on a certain instrument, e.g., cascareo (pattern played on the shell of the drum), campaneo (pattern played on a bell , baqueteo (pattern played with sticks)
-ero, -era	a person who has a specific job, origin or cultural identity (conguero, Guantanamera, charanguera, bongosero, timbalero, etc.) -ero is masculine, -era is feminine
-ista	like -ero and –era, but used with different roots (violinista, dentista, Sandanista, pianista, bajista, trompetista, saxofonista, flautista); -ista is *not* gender specific
-ito, -ita	diminutive; a smaller version of something or someone, a person of small stature – señorita, timbalito, Manolito; can also be used like "Jr." – for example, Chuchito Valdés, the son of Chucho Valdés, is about 6'9"; Cubans love to add this suffix to almost any word.
-ón	a bigger, bolder version of something, e.g., danzón, charangón, vacilón, rumbón, Robertón (Los Van Van's bear-like lead vocalist)

Appendix 3: Spanish Explanations for English Speakers

If your native language is English, you'll find that Spanish – especially Cuban Spanish – takes a bit of getting used to. Some things will look wrong at first – such as only capitalizing the first letter in the title of an album or song. If you spend a little time studying Spanish, however, you'll be stunned to discover how exquisitely logical it is – and how obscenely ridiculous English is. After taking Spanish 101, you'll be amazed that anyone could ever learn English.

Pronunciation

When I say "exquisitely logical", I mean this: *there is only one way to pronounce any written Spanish word.* Conversely, in English, the same person will pronounce the same word in multiple ways. The old Cole Porter lyric, *"you say tomayto and I say tomahto"* is but the tip of the iceberg. And this is one iceberg that is *not* melting.

Try reading this sentence aloud: *"The only time I read the newspaper is when my internet connection is down."* Most North Americans will say *"**Thee** only time I read **thuh** newspaper …"*.

In Spanish, once you know a handful of rules, you can correctly pronounce any word in the dictionary even if you've never heard it spoken. Every vowel makes only one sound. There's never a double consonant unless it changes the pronunciation. Just as important, the stress of each syllable is also set in stone. If the word ends with a vowel, s, or n, the stress is always on the next-to-last syllable and if it ends with any other letter, the stress is on the last syllable. If you want to pronounce it any other way, you have to use an accent mark.

As an example, let's take the first name of the famous Cuban pianist Chucho Valdés. His first name ends in a vowel, which means that the next-to-last syllable is stressed. So, using English phonetics, it should be CHOO-choh. Right? You wouldn't call him choo-CHOH would you? Now, just for fun, let's say Chucho's mother had wanted to differentiate her young prodigy from the other Chuchos in the neighborhood and taught him to answer to choo-CHOH. This would be fine, but she'd have to change the spelling of his name to Chuchó. Got it? Now let's move on to Valdés. It's pronounced val-DEHS, but it ends with an "s" – and all words ending with "s" have the stress on the next-to-last syllable unless there's an accent mark. Without the accent, *Valdes* would have to be pronounced VAL-dehs. Now, go through all your Irakere records, and you'll find that some of them list Chucho as Chucho Valdez! And Chucho is among the most famous Cuban musicians. You can find three or even four different spellings of the names of many Cubans on their own albums! The reason is that *Valdez*, without the accent mark, is pronounced exactly the same as *Valdés,* because if a word ends with "z" (or any letter other than a vowel, s or n), it automatically gets a stress on the last syllable – so an accent mark would be redundant.

Finally, in Spanish there is no "z like zebra" sound. "Z" and "s" have exactly the same pronunciation (like an English "s"). Most English speakers tend to pronounce the name *Pérez* as per-EZZZZZ, but the correct pronunciation is PE-res.

Spanish Letter Combinations with the Same Pronunciation

option 1	option 2	option 3	English pronunciation
ll	y		**y**ellow (ñ is like the n in "no" followed by the "y" in "yellow"')
z	s	ce, ci	**s**ilver
j	ge or gi		**h**im
h			"h" is always silent in Spanish
k	ca, co, cu		**c**at
b	v		b and v are similar but not exactly like the b in **b**oy

So Chucho could write his last name Valdés, Valdez, Baldés or Baldez. What's really interesting is that some Cuban musicians will spell their own names differently from time to time. In English, people tend to be very snooty about spelling *("No! no! no! It Terri with an 'i' not Terry with a 'y'!!")*.

Accent Marks in Spanish

Showing the stress of syllables accounts for most accent marks but they have a few other uses:

Function	Example
separating two consecutive vowels into two syllables	*Mario* versus *María*
exclamations	*¡qué locura!* (what madness!)
questions	*¿cuándo?* (when?)
same word, different meanings	*más* = more; *mas* = plus

Finally, we have ñ, which makes *mañana* sound like man-YA-na, and ü, which makes an English "w" sound, like "water", as in güiro (GWEE-row).

Let's use everything we've learned to understand the word *changüí.* It's pronounced "chan-GWEE". If the "u" didn't have the two dots over it, it would be pronounced "chan-GEE" (like *guitar).* Since changüí ends with a vowel, it needs an accent on the í, or it would have to be pronounced "CHAN-gwee".

Accent marks also indication questions (cuándo = when?) and exclamation (qué locura = what madness!) and differentiates similar words (si = if; sí = yes; él = him; el = the).

Test Your Skills

The typical North American baseball announcer's pronunciation of *Oscar Hernández* is AH-skur hur-NAN-dezzzz. There are six errors. How many can you spot?

> 1 & 2. AH-skur (as in stir) should be oh-SKAR
>
> 3. the H should be silent
>
> 4. hur should be air
>
> 5. nan (like nanny goat) should be nahn (or non, like non-sequitur)
>
> 6. dezzz should be des

Capitalization in Spanish

In Spanish, only the first word is capitalized in song titles, book titles, and album titles, but all main words are capitalized in names of musical groups. For example, I recommend that you listen to the song *No te lo creas,* from the album *Con la conciencia tranquila,* by the group Paulito FG y su Élite. While we're on the subject, capitalization isn't used in Spanish for the names of days *(sábado),* months *(octubre),* adjectives for nationality *(la música cubana),* or languages *(inglés, español).*

Appendix 4: Other Style Conventions in this Book

Italicization

This book italicizes all song, book and album titles, and Spanish words the first time they come up in a section. For example:

"For his 1980 album, *Elio Revé y su ritmo changüí,* Revé created new a instrumentation called *charangón.* Charangón combines elements of *charanga, conjunto, changüí, rumba* and *batá.*"

I also use italicization to stress the meaning of English words, for new English terms that appear in the glossary (e.g., *basic step),* and to quote lyrics, whether in English or Spanish.

Appendix 5: For Further Study
Suggested Reading

Other *Beyond Salsa* Volumes:

Beyond Salsa Piano, Vol. 1 – The Roots of the Piano Tumbao, by Kevin Moore

Beyond Salsa Piano, Vol. 2 – Early Cuban Piano Tumbaos: 1940-1959, by Kevin Moore

Beyond Salsa Piano, Vol. 3-4 – Cuban Piano Tumbaos: 1960-1989, by Kevin Moore

Beyond Salsa Piano, Vol. 5 – Introduction to Timba, by Kevin Moore

Beyond Salsa Piano, Vol. 6-9 – Iván "Melón" Lewis, Pts. 1-2-3, by Kevin Moore

Beyond Salsa Piano, Vol. 10-13 – César "Pupy" Pedroso, by Kevin Moore

Beyond Salsa Bass, Vols. 6-7 – Alain Pérez, by Kevin Moore

*Beyond Salsa Percussion, Vol. 1-3 – Intro (1) and Calixto Oviedo (2-3) – by Kevin Moore

Understanding Clave and Clave Changes, by Kevin Moore

Beyond Salsa for Ensemble, Vol. 1, by Kevin Moore

Books on Instrumental Technique:

A Collection of Basslines, by Feliciano Arango and Cherina Mastrantones, www.createspace.com/3739479

A Contemporary Bass Technique, by Feliciano Arango and Cherina Mastrantones, createspace.com/3671152

Changuito: A Master's Approach to Timbales, by Chuck Silverman, Manhattan Music Publications

Yoel Páez Método (abmusica.es)

The New Method for Afro-Cuban Drumming, by Jimmy Branly, Hudson Music

Conversations in Clave, by Horacio "El Negro" Hernández, Alfred Publishing

Melodic Drumming, by Raúl Valdés

The Tomás Cruz Conga Method, by Tomás Cruz, Kevin Moore, Mike Gerald & Orlando Fiol, Mel Bay

El tres cubano, Cuban Master Series: Piano, both by Jon Griffin, www.createspace.com

Cuban Music Overview:

Cuba and its Music, by Ned Sublette, Chicago Review Press

The Clave Matrix, by David Peñalosa, Bembe Books

The *Salsa Guidebook* and *101 Montunos,* by Rebeca Mauleón-Santana, Sher Music

Text to Tune Alignment in the Music of Charanga Habanera, by Ryan Mead – Honors Thesis at Stanford University, 2007. Available at: ryanmead.com/Thesis.pdf

Roots of Timba – free online book covering bass tumbaos of Arsenio Rodríguez, Ritmo Oriental, etc.

Books and Videos on Afro-Cuban Folkloric Music and Rumba:

The Conga Drummer's Guidebook, by Michael Spiro, Sher Music (also at www.latinpulsemusic.com)

Rumba Quinto, by David Peñalosa, Bembe Books

The Afro-Cuban Folkloric Musical Tradition, by Robert Fernández, Leisure Planet Music

Afro-Cuban Percussion Workbook (and DVD product), by José Eladio Amat and Curtis Lanoue

Bata Drumming, by Don Skoog, www.contemporarymusicproject.com

Cantos afrocubanos, by Luca Brandoli, www.cdbabyn.com

Trips to Cuba:

Chuck Silverman – www.chucksilverman.com

PlazaCUBA – www.plazacuba.com

Suggested Listening

** indicates album download (w/full booklet) is available on www.latinpulsemusic.com as of 2012.
This list is chosen for both overall musical quality and relevance to other volumes of the "Beyond Salsa" series.

GROUP	ALBUM	DRUMMER/TIMBALERO	LABEL
Paulito FG y su Élite	*Con la conciencia tranquila*	Yoel Páez	Nueva Fania **
	Paulito FG (El bueno soy yo)	Yoel Páez	Nueva Fania **
Bamboleo	*Yo no me parezco a nadie*	Ludwig Núñez	Ahí Namá **
	Ya no hace falta	Ludwig Núñez/Herlan Sarior	Ahí Namá **
	Ñññño!	Ludwig Núñez/Herlan Sarior	Ahí Namá
Charanga Habanera	*Hey You Loca*	Eduardo Lazaga	Magic Music **
	Pa' que se entere La Habana	Eduardo Lazaga	Magic Music **
	Tremendo delirio	Eduardo Lazaga	Magic Music **
	Charanguero mayor	Yulién Oviedo	Ciocan Music **
	Live in the USA	Yulién Oviedo	Ciocan Music **
	Chan Chan Charanga	Yulién Oviedo/Pavel Rodríguez	Ciocan Music **
Danny Lozada	*Tanto le pedí*	Raúl Hernández/Pepe Espinosa	Caribe**
Issac Delgado	*Rarities (Exclusivo para Cuba)*	Georvis Pico/Andrés Cuayo	Ciocan Music **
	Con ganas	Giraldo Piloto/Yonder Peña	QBADisc
	El año que viene	Jimmy Branly/José Miguel	RMM
	Otra idea	Luis Quintero	RMM
	La primera noche	Georvis Pico/Yuri Noguiera	RMM, ARTEX**
	La fórmula	Oscar Valdés/Pepe Espinosa	Ahí Namá **
	Prohibido	Luis Quintero	Pimienta Records
	En primera plana	Luis Quintero	Univision La Calle
	Supercubano	Luis Quintero	Planet Records
Manolín	*Para mi gente*	Alexis and Ángel Arce	Ahí Namá **
	De buena fe	Alexis and Ángel Arce	Blue Metro
	Jaque mate	Alexis and Ángel Arce	Caribe
	El puente	Reinier Guerra	Ciocan Music **
Los Van Van	*Disco Azúcar*	Changuito	ARTEX **
	Lo último en vivo	Samuel Formell	QBADisc
	Ay Diós, ampárame	Samuel Formell	Caribe Records**
	Esto te pone la cabeza mala	Samuel Formell	Caribe Records **
	Llegó Van Van	Samuel Formell	Pimienta Records **

GROUP	ALBUM	DRUMMER/TIMBALERO	LABEL
	Chapeando	Samuel Formell	Unicornio Records **
NG La Banda	*En la calle*	Giraldo Piloto	QBADisc
	Simplemente lo mejor de NG	Calixto Oviedo	ARTEX (BIS) **
Klímax	*Mira si te gusta*	Giraldo Piloto/Yonder Peña	Eurotropical
	Juego de manos	Giraldo Piloto/Yonder Peña	Eurotropical
	Oye como va	Giraldo Piloto/Yonder Peña	Eurotropical
Klímax and Manolito	*Concierto Eurotropical I*	Yuri Noguiera	Eurotropical
Manolito y su Trabuco	*Directo al corazón*	Carlos Rodríguez	Bembe Records
	Contra todos los prognósticos	Carlos Rodríguez	Eurotropical
	Marcando la distancia	Yuri Noguiera	Eurotropical
	Para que baile Cuba	Roicel Riverón	Eurotropical
	Se rompieron los termómetros	Roicel Riverón	Eurotropical
	Hablando en serio	"Roicel Riverón	EGREM
Los Que Son Son	*Qué cosas tiene la vida*	Bombón Reyes/René Suárez	EGREM
	La buenagente	Bombón Reyes/René Suárez	Pimienta Records
	Mi timba cerrá	Bombón Reyes/René Suárez	EGREM
	Tranquilo que yo controlo	Bombón Reyes/Miguelito Escurriola	EGREM
	Siempre Pupy	Bombón Reyes/Miguelito Escurriola	EGREM
Revé y su Charangón	*45 años*	Carlos Rodríguez	Tumi Records
	Se sigue comentando	Jorge Bravo	BIS**
	Fresquecito	Andy Fornet	BIS**
	De qué estamos Hablando	Andy Fornet	BIS
Azúcar Negra	*Azúcar Negra*	Pavel Rodríguez/Pepe Espinosa	mp3.com
	Andar andando	Maikel Zamora	BIS**
Michel Maza	*Fieeesta*	Karel Páez	Envidia**
	Que hablen los habladores	Karel Páez	Envidia**
Angel Bonne	*Circunstancias*	Javier Ochoa	EGREM
	Bonne & Bonne Co.	Carlos Leal	EGREM
Havana d'Primera	*Haciendo historia*	Rodney Barreto/Güillermo del Toro	EGREM
	Pasaporte	Rodney Barreto/Güillermo del Toro	EGREM
Various	*Gracias Formell*	Georvis Pico/Andrés Cuayo Yoel Páez	Ciocan**

For suggested listening within the 1960-1989 time period, please see the Discography and Online Book sections of the Timbapedia section of www.timba.com. For pre-revolution discographical information, please see Cristóbal Díaz-Ayala's exhaustive online discography at www.fiu.edu.

Acknowledgments

Photoshop Gurus: Kris Förster, Tom Krabbe
Finale Guru: Peter Thomsen

Photography:

Tom Ehrlich, Peter Maiden, Richard Robinson, Patrick Hickey, Bob Kraft, Bohdan Kiszczuk, Tom Bauer, Gabriel García, Mary Brassell, Patrick Bonnard, Michelle White, Brett Gollin, Michael Cába, Will Douglas, Chuck Silverman, Robert Fernández, Sue Taylor.

Editing and Conceptual Guidance:

Orlando Fiol, Robert Fernández, Sue Taylor, Kris Förster, David Peñalosa, Osvaldo Martínez, Javier Muñiz, Dave Dreyfus, Richard Robinson, Tom Ehrlich, Jiovanni Cofiño, Paul de Castro, Tomás Cruz, Walfredo de los Reyes, Sr., Emiliano Echeverría, Andrés Espinoza, Rebeca Mauleón, Jérôme Vaccari, Carlos Caro, Chuck Silverman, Michelle White, Gabriel Wilder, Ryan Mead, Sidney Weaverling, Edgar Hernández, Olavo Alén, Gabriel García, Curtis Lanoue, Mike Racette, Victor Barrientos, Vašík Greif, Bill Tilford, Michael Spiro, José Reyes, Abel Robaina, Majela Serrano, Mike Lazarus and Wendy Black.

About the Author

Melón Lewis, Kevin Moore – Los Angeles – 2009 – photo by Tom Ehrlich

Kevin Moore (kevin@timba.com) is the co-founder and music editor for the world's largest Cuban music website, www.timba.com, to which he has contributed the free online multimedia book series, **The Roots of Timba,** dozens of extensive articles, discographies, record analyses, interviews and the Cuban music blog **La última,** now in publication for over 10 years.

In the early 2000s, Kevin co-wrote **The Tomás Cruz Conga Method, Volumes 1-3,** a critically acclaimed method book series used as a text at various educational institutions. More books on Tomás Cruz (including the long-promised volume on the adaptation of folkloric rhythms to timba conga marchas), may be in the works as part of the *Beyond Salsa Congas* series.

Various other important congueros will also be featured in that series.

The Tomás Cruz Conga Method – Volumes 1, 2, & 3

Published by Mel Bay Publications, Inc.

As musical director, composer, arranger and violinist of the California-based salsa band Orquesta Gitano, Kevin co-produced the 1998 CD *Salsa Gitana,* songs from which have been used in various films and television shows. In addition to the audio tracks, full salsa band charts for this album can be purchased at Latin Pulse Music [www.latinpulsemusic.com/albums/show/2]

Available for purchase and download at www.latinpulsemusic.com/albums/show/2

The *Beyond Salsa* Catalog – 2012

www.createspace.com/4035244
www.latinpulsemusic.com/albums/show/433

Beyond Salsa for Beginners alternates between singing, dancing and clapping exercises and listening tours covering the full history of Latin music. It also contains an extensive glossary, and a long section on the special challenges of Afro-Cuban folkloric music.

This book shares several chapters with *Beyond Salsa for Percussion, Vol. 1*. The latter contains many more advanced rhythms, but not the listening tours. The two books can be purchased together for a reduced rate by contacting the author directly. Each book has both a free audio download and a $10 audio download.

www.createspace.com/1000252022
www.latinpulsemusic.com/albums/show/353

Beyond Salsa Piano, Volume 1 begins around 1900 and covers the origins of the tumbao concept using exercises adapted from genres – such as *changüí, danzón,* and *son* – that pre-date the use of piano as the primary instrument for tumbaos in Cuban music. This material is designed to be playable by near-beginners, musicians who play other instruments, and arrangers seeking to acquire a basic facility on piano.

Among the artists covered are Grupo Changüí de Guantánamo, Sexteto Habanero, Sexteto Boloña and Arsenio Rodríguez.

www.createspace.com/3419799
www.latinpulsemusic.com/albums/show/359

Beyond Salsa Piano, Volume 2 covers the period from 1940-1959, during which the piano became a constant and dominant presence in nearly every Latin rhythm section, and during which Cuban music had a profound global influence on all forms of popular music. The difficulty level ranges from beginning to intermediate.

Artists covered include: Arcaño y sus Maravillas, Orquesta Aragón, Chappottín y sus Estrellas, Celia Cruz y Sonora Matancera, Beny Moré, Pérez Prado, Orquesta Sensación, José Fajardo y sus Estrellas, and Conjunto Modelo.

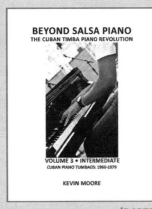

www.createspace.com/3427343
www.latinpulsemusic.com/albums/show/361

Beyond Salsa Piano, Volume 3 begins our coverage of the eclectic period between the Cuban Revolution and the Fall of the Berlin Wall – from 1959 to 1989.

Volume 3 covers *mozambique, pilón, changüí-68, songo,* and artists such as Irakere, Ritmo Oriental, Los Van Van, Pacho Alonso, Orquesta Aragón, Opus 13, Orquesta 440, and AfroCuba.

Volume 3 also contains an extensive section on Afro-Cuban folkloric rhythms and their application to popular music piano-playing.

www.createspace.com/3427345
www.latinpulsemusic.com/albums/show/363

Beyond Salsa Piano, Volume 4 continues our survey of post-revolution, pre-timba Cuban piano styles.

Styles covered include those of Elio Revé y su Charangón, Rumbavana, Son 14, Adalberto Álvarez y su Son, Orquesta Original de Manzanillo, Maravillas de Florida, Orquesta Aliamén, and Los Karachi.

We also introduce the concept of "controlled improvisation", which runs through the entire series.

www.createspace.com/3427349
www.latinpulsemusic.com/albums/show/363

Beyond Salsa Piano, Volume 5 introduces the *timba* genre that began in the 1990s. Volume includes:

- a history and discography of the timba era

- a detailed description of rhythm section "gears"

- a list and analysis of the 10 most important piano innovations of the 1990s

- 32 instructional tumbaos on the same chord progression, demonstrating these innovations

- a Harmony Appendix with hundreds of timba tumbao chord progressions in Roman numerals

www.createspace.com/3427351
www.latinpulsemusic.com/albums/show/364

Beginning with **Volume 6**, each book concentrates on the style of one Cuban pianist, with note-for-note transcriptions, based in most cases on MIDI files performed by the volume's featured pianist.

Volumes 6 through 9 are on Iván "Melón" Lewis, the phenomenally innovative pianist who played with The Issac Delgado group from 1995 to 1998.

Volume 6 begins with Melón's biography and discography and continues to in-depth studies of his piano style on the extended live concert versions of *No me mires a los ojos* and *La vida sin esperanza*.

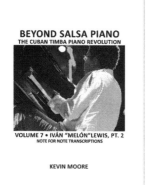

www.createspace.com/3427354
www.latinpulsemusic.com/albums/show/365

Beyond Salsa Piano, Volume 7 moves on to Melón's approach to two more live classics of the Issac Delgado group: *Luz viajera* (arranged by Melón) and *Por qué paró.*

In the process of detailing the many types of tumbaos Melón uses in these extended live arrangements we cover the timba gears of marcha, muela, bomba and presión and delve even more deeply into Melón's approach to "controlled improvisation".

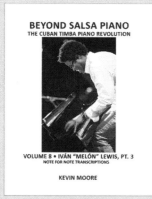

www.createspace.com/3427355
www.latinpulsemusic.com/albums/show/366

Beyond Salsa Piano, Volume 8 continues our chronological survey of Melón's unique tumbaos and improvisational live style with *Deja que Roberto te toque* and the extremely polyrhythmic *Brindando con el alma.*

La chica del sol is then used as a vehicle to present exercises to understand how timba relates to salsa and Latin jazz.

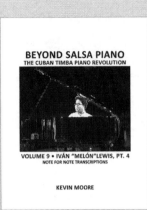

BEYOND SALSA PIANO
THE CUBAN TIMBA PIANO REVOLUTION

VOLUME 9 • IVÁN "MELÓN"LEWIS, PT. 4
NOTE FOR NOTE TRANSCRIPTIONS

KEVIN MOORE

www.createspace.com/3427357
www.latinpulsemusic.com/albums/show/367

Beyond Salsa Piano, Volume 9, our final volume on Iván "Melón" Lewis, is the longest of the series and includes his unusually sophisticated approach to cuerpos as well as tumbaos. It begins with Melón's approach to the I-IV-V-IV progression, using his arrangement of *Catalina* as a jumping-off point. We then cover the remaining important live staples of the Delgado repertoire during Melón's tenure: *Con la punta del pie, Por la naturaleza, Se te fue la mano, Pa' que te salves,* and *La competencia ("Hit Parade").*

Finally, we cover the tumbao from *Movimiento,* from Melón's latest Latin jazz album, and a tumbao from his recent work with Manolín, el Médico de la Salsa.

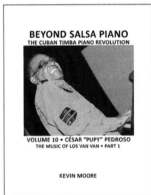

BEYOND SALSA PIANO
THE CUBAN TIMBA PIANO REVOLUTION

VOLUME 10 • CÉSAR "PUPY" PEDROSO
THE MUSIC OF LOS VAN VAN • PART 1

KEVIN MOORE

www.createspace.com/3573344
www.latinpulsemusic.com/albums/show/406

Beyond Salsa Piano, Volume 10 begins our study of César "Pupy" Pedroso of Los Van Van and Los Que Son Son.

Volume 10 begins with extensive biography and discography chapters and covers piano tumbaos for songs first released between 1979 (when Pupy began to compose for Los Van Van) and 1983, including *El bate de aluminio, Fallaste a sacar tu cuenta, Después que te casaste* and many others. On the classic *Hoy se cumplen seis semanas,* we present a full chart of Pupy's new arrangement with his current group, Los Que Son Son.

BEYOND SALSA PIANO
THE CUBAN TIMBA PIANO REVOLUTION

VOLUME 11 • CÉSAR "PUPY" PEDROSO
THE MUSIC OF LOS VAN VAN • PART 2

KEVIN MOORE

www.createspace.com/3573347
www.latinpulsemusic.com/albums/show/407

Beyond Salsa Piano, Volume 11 covers the next phase of Pupy's career, 1984-1988 with Los Van Van, including songs such as *Si quieres que te llegue pronto, Ya tu campana no suena, and Será que se acabó.*

Also included are complete piano and bass charts for *El buenagente* and *Calla calla,* based on the modern Los Que Son Son versions.

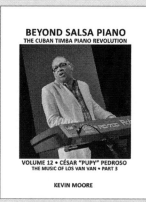

Beyond Salsa Piano, Volume 12 is scheduled for release in 2013 and will cover the remainder of Pupy's career with Los Van Van (1989-2001).

Beyond Salsa Piano, Volume 13, scheduled for release in 2013, is our final volume on Pupy Pedroso, will cover his work with his own group, Los Que Son Son, founded in 2001 and one of Cuba's top groups today.

Beyond Salsa Percussion, Volume 1 is for people who are considering taking drum or timbales lessons and want to learn to clap and sing the basic rhythms to prepare themselves.

This book shares several chapters with *Beyond Salsa for Beginners* before moving on to add more advanced rhythms. The two books can be purchased together for a reduced rate by contacting the author directly.

www.createspace.com/3500639
www.latinpulsemusic.com/albums/show/397

Beyond Salsa Percussion, Volume 2: Basic Rhythms is the first of two books on legendary timbalero/drummer Calixto Oviedo, who played with Pacho Alonso, Adalberto Álvarez and the first timba band, NG La Banda. The book begins with a long biography and discography section and presents Calixto's approaches to six classic Cuban rhythms, ranging from traditional timbales to various combinations of timbales and drumset. The rhythms covered are: ***danzón, chachachá, mozambique, pilón, simalé*** and ***upa-upa***.

www.createspace.com/3500640
www.latinpulsemusic.com/albums/show/399

Beyond Salsa Percussion, Volume 3: Timba Gears is one of our longest and most adventurous books, explaining what gears are and demonstrating the almost endless ways that each can be orchestrated on timbales and drumset.

In addition to exhaustively detailing Calixto's styles, the book explains how the various top Cuban bands produce their signature rhythm section *sellos* by dividing the rhythmic responsibilities creatively between the percussionists. The gears covered are: ***marcha abajo, marcha arriba, marcha de mambo, muela, presión*** and ***bomba***.

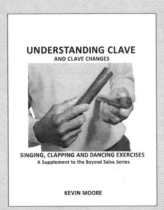

www.createspace.com/3711464
www.latinpulsemusic.com/albums/show/414

Understanding Clave and Clave Changes is a special supplement to the *Beyond Salsa* series. It's divided into four sections, and uses hands-on singing, clapping and dancing exercises to become intimate with clave and avoid the excruciating intellectual confusion that results from trying to learn it with one's left-brain!

Part 1: For Beginners – What is Clave?
Part 2: Demystifying Clave Terminology
Part 3: Intermediate –Clave Direction
Part 4: Advanced –Clave Changes

Unlike the other books, the clave course absolutely requires both the audio files and book, so the audio files are provided as a free download to anyone who buys the hard-copy book or the eBook.

BEYOND SALSA FOR ENSEMBLE
A GUIDE TO THE MODERN CUBAN RHYTHM SECTION

PIANO • BASS • CONGAS • BONGÓ • TIMBALES • DRUMS
VOLUME 1 • EFECTOS

KEVIN MOORE

www.createspace.com/37164505
www.latinpulsemusic.com/albums/show/419

Beyond Salsa for Ensemble Vol. 1, at 368 pages, with 464 audio files, is our most adventurous project to date.

Part 1: The Point of Departure: The Home Gear – Explains the differences between salsa and timba and teaches the most common timba groove, from which all other exercises begin.

Part 2: Efectos – 36 rhythm section breaks, or *efectos,* completely notated, in 2-3 and 3-2 clave/

Part 3: Complete Performance Chart – A meticulous note-for-note transcription of all instruments for *El buenagente* by Pupy Pedroso y Los Que Son Son.

BEYOND SALSA BASS
THE CUBAN TIMBA REVOLUTION

VOLUME 6 • ALAIN PÉREZ, PART 1
COMPANION TO BEYOND SALSA PIANO, VOL. 6

KEVIN MOORE

www.createspace.com/3810546
www.latinpulsemusic.com/albums/show/421

Beyond Salsa Bass , Volume 6 – will closely mirror *Beyond Salsa Piano,* with introductory volumes covering the history of Cuban bass, starting at the beginning level, and continuing with books about specific bassists. The introductory volumes will be released in late 2012 and early 2013. Volume 6, pictured here, was released in March 2012.

BEYOND SALSA BASS
THE CUBAN TIMBA REVOLUTION

VOLUME 7 • ALAIN PÉREZ, PART 2
COMPANION TO BEYOND SALSA PIANO, VOL. 7

KEVIN MOORE

www.createspace.com/3810550
www.latinpulsemusic.com/albums/show/TBD

Beyond Salsa Bass , Volume 7 – The second of four volumes on Alain Pérez, Volume 7 is the bass companion to Volume 7 of the piano series and will be released in mid-2012.

Volumes 8 and 9 will be released in late 2012 and early 2013.

COMING IN 2012	***Beyond Salsa Bongó*** will feature Carlos Caro, winner of timba.com's Readers' Poll for Best Timba Bongosero. These books will begin with instruction in technique, starting from a beginning level and then work their way from the early son styles of bongó-playing to Caro's timba style with Opus 13, Paulito FG and Jacqueline Castellanos.
COMING IN 2013	***Beyond Salsa Congas*** is in the development stages. It will hopefully include volumes on Tomás Cruz as well as other top congueros.

PRICE LIST

TITLE	Physical Book	eBook (PC only)	Audio Download	Video Download	DVD
Beyond Salsa for Beginners • Introduction to Latin Music for Dancers & Listeners	$30	$15	free/$10*		
Beyond Salsa Piano, Vol. 1 • Beginning • The Roots of the Piano Tumbao	$20	$10	$10		
Beyond Salsa Piano, Vol. 2 • Intermediate • Early Cuban Piano Tumbaos • 1940-59	$20	$10	$10		
Beyond Salsa Piano, Vol. 3 • Intermediate • Cuban Piano Tumbaos • 1960-79	$20	$10	$10		
Beyond Salsa Piano, Vol. 4 • Intermediate • Cuban Piano Tumbaos • 1979-89	$20	$10	$10		
Beyond Salsa Piano, Vol. 5 • Advanced • Introduction to Timba	$20	$10	$10		
Beyond Salsa Piano, Vol. 6 • Iván "Melón" Lewis • Part 1	$20	$10	$10	$10	
Beyond Salsa Piano, Vol. 7 • Iván "Melón" Lewis • Part 2	$20	$10	$10	$10	
Beyond Salsa Piano, Vol. 8 • Iván "Melón" Lewis • Part 3	$20	$10	$10		
Beyond Salsa Piano, Vol. 9 • Iván "Melón" Lewis • Part 4	$30	$15	$10		
Beyond Salsa Piano, Vol. 10 • César "Pupy" Pedroso • Part 1	$25	$15	$10		
Beyond Salsa Piano, Vol. 11 • César "Pupy" Pedroso • Part 2	$25	$15	$10		
Beyond Salsa Percussion, Vol. 1 • Introduction to the Cuban Rhythm Section	$30	$15	free/$10*		
Beyond Salsa Percussion, Vol. 2 • Calixto Oviedo – Basic Rhythms	$30	$15	$10	$10	*
Beyond Salsa Percussion, Vol. 3 • Calixto Oviedo – Timba Gears *DVD includes both Vol. 2 and Vol. 3 footage	$30	$15	$10	$10	$25*
Understanding Clave and Clave Changes	$15	$10	FREE		
Beyond Salsa for Ensemble, Vol. 1 • Efectos	$40	$25	$10		
Beyond Salsa Bass, Vol. 6 • Alain Pérez • Part 1	$30	$15	$10	$10	
Beyond Salsa Bass, Vol. 7 • Alain Pérez • Part 2	$30	$15	$10	$10	
Beyond Salsa Bongó, Vol. 1	TBD	TBD	TBD	TBD	
Beyond Salsa Congas, Vol. 1	TBD	TBD	TBD	TBD	

*free/$10 = free files downloadable at timba.com/audio – additional files available for $10

this page left intentionally blank

For completely updated lists of all *Beyond Salsa* products,
sample videos and other free downloads:

clave.latinpulsemusic.com
www.timba.com/audio
www.timba.com/bass
www.timba.com/bongo
www.timba.com/clave
www.timba.com/ensemble
www.timba.com/percussion
www.timba.com/piano

comments, questions, suggestions, requests:

kevin@timba.com

Printed in Poland
by Amazon Fulfillment
Poland Sp. z o.o., Wrocław

25663829R00141